Motherhood

A WOMAN'S JOURNEY

Deferred

Motherhood

A WOMAN'S JOURNEY

Deferred

ANNE TAYLOR FLEMING

FAWCETT COLUMBINE • NEW YORK

A Fawcett Columbine Book
Published by Ballantine Books

Copyright © 1994 by Anne Taylor Fleming

This edition published by arrangement with Putnam Berkeley Group, Inc.

Library of Congress Catalog Card Number: 94-90794

ISBN: 0-449-98364-1

Cover design by Kathleen Lynch
Cover painting courtesy of the San Francisco Museum of Modern Art,
bequest of Howard E. Johnson

Manufactured in the United States of America
First Ballantine Books Edition: June 1995
10 9 8 7 6 5 4 3 2 1

ACKNOWLEDGMENTS

It was a long road to this first book, and there are many to acknowledge. First off, the women who talked anonymously to me and goaded my memories with their own. They know who they are, and I thank them all, especially those whose stories are included here. Thanks, too, to all the women writers whose books and articles I cite, and who in many ways made my own writing life possible.

I was blessed with a patient publisher who also became a friend, Phyllis Grann, and a very enthusiastic and sensitive editor, Stacy Creamer, who knew just what to take out. A thank you also to the others at Putnam, some known to me, others not, who in some way touched the book.

Thanks, of course, to my longtime, first-rate agent, Lynn Nesbit, also a friend.

And to the people at *The MacNeil/Lehrer NewsHour*—Robin MacNeil, Jim Lehrer, Lester Crystal and my producer/friend Michael Saltz—thanks for a chance to explore some of the ideas in this book out loud.

On the personal side, I acknowledge my mother for her boundless warmth and maternal pride, and my father for his constant encouragement and commiseration during this protracted project. I am grateful for the friendship and daily goodwill of Judith Pinero Kieffer and George Kieffer, and the support of Tony Cook, Ciji Ware, Kathleen Brown and Van Gordon Sauter.

I offer special thanks to three friends of long standing, Judy Kessler, Meg Zweiback and Victoria Brown, for their early excitement over the manuscript, and to my sister, Avery Taylor Moore, for her lifelong companionship and sharp-eyed suggestions.

I owe a very special debt to A. J. Langguth for his ongoing example and for his active involvement in the conception of this book.

My final acknowledgment is for Karl Fleming, whose loyalty as husband and editor are unmatched, and who, at any hour of the day or night over our quarter of a century together, has been willing to look at my prose with a discerning eye and a sharp pencil, and has always encouraged me to listen to my own voice, however faint it sometimes seemed.

For Karl, for all of it

CONTENTS

1

REVENGE OF THE WOMBS

On a beautiful spring day of 1988 I am driving down the Santa Monica freeway with a jar of my sixty-year-old husband's sperm in my purse en route to The Institute for Reproductive Research at the Hospital of the Good Samaritan in downtown Los Angeles. He is home sleeping after having yielded up this specimen, and I am gingerly maneuvering through the heavy morning traffic with my secreted stash, careful not to swerve or speed lest I upset my cargo or get stopped by a cop—images of his big face peering in my car window while I fumble for my license. This is what I have come to, what we have come to, after sixteen years of marriage: this detached, this clinical breeding. Oh my, how did I get here? I ask myself over and over as I park the car, surrender the sperm to the lab tech and take my place in the waiting room. What quirk of fate, of timing, of biology has brought me to this infertile point and this clinic, presided over by Dr. Richard Marrs, one of the new breed of high-profile infertility experts who have cropped up to do the procreative bidding of those of us who cannot do it on our own? A soft-spoken forty-year-old Texan with a specialty in reproductive endocrinology, Dr. Marrs spouts acronyms for all the out-of-body pregnancy procedures—IVF, GIFT, ZIFT, IUI, ITI—with optimism and assurance, and his waiting room is usually full of anxious women from all over the country, from all over the world, for that matter, who have come here to avail themselves of these procedures.

I am now one of them, this sisterhood of the infertile.

There is low-decibel chatter, and on a wall-mounted TV one of the morning news shows is babbling in the background, though in our nervousness most of us aren't really listening. At age thirty-eight, I have entered the high-tech world of post-sexual procreation where things are done in dishes and through catheters, not in bed.

I still can't quite believe I am here. I am giddy, hopeful, lonesome, a babyless baby boomer now completely consumed by the longing for a baby, a feeling akin to heartbreak when you can't breathe but for the sensation of loss. My pulse is racing. I am about to have some kind of sexual encounter, but of this weird new kind: not with a person, but with a syringe of sperm.

As I look around at the other women, some in blue jeans like me, some in suits en route to work just stopping by to get a shot of sperm before heading out to do battle in corporate America, I smile a small repressed smile at them and for them. We have sailed together into a strange, surreal country, the Land of the Disembodied Procreators, mutually dedicated to practicing biological warfare against our very own bodies in the hope of reversing time, cheating fate and getting our hands on an embryo, a baby, a life. We're hard-core, those of us here. Last-ditchers. And there's a kind of stubborn, exhilarating pride radiating from us. No wimps we. Toting around small white paper bags of hypodermic needles and hundreds of dollars' worth of fertility drugs, we shoot up once or twice daily with the expertise of junkies, our hips tight and swollen like cheeks with wads of tobacco in them. We are fearless, Amazonian in our baby-hunger, bereft. The small waiting room vibrates with our hope.

"Anne."

I go into an examining room, strip from the waist down and take my place in the stirrups. The doctor appears. Boyish and solicitous, his hair beginning to gray like that of many of his patients, he is perfectly cast for his role as procreative assistant to a bunch of desperate women. Gently he inserts the dildo-like scanner inside me and voilà, my ovaries appear as if by magic on the grainy black-and-white ultrasound screen next to me. I stare at it, trying to pick out the eggs that have ripened on each ovary over the past fourteen days under the onslaught of the fertility drugs. My ovaries ache with their unaccustomed burden as the doctor expertly rotates the scanner inside me. We count together: one, two, three on the left side; one, two on the right. He smiles. "You have the ovaries of a twenty-five-year-old," he says, reaching for the syringe of my husband's sperm—now washed and sorted and counted—that lies beside me on a tray. And with one deft whoosh through a thin catheter inserted up through my vagina and cervix, the sperm are sent spinning into my uterus. I feel nothing, no pain, but strangely enough, tears hover. There is something in the matter-of-fact gentleness with which the doctor folds my legs back up off the stirrups that affects me, a reminder of touch, flesh, normal procreation instead of this cold, solo breeding. I hold them until the doctor leaves. In my supine position, which I must maintain for fifteen minutes, I imagine the sperm settling in, looking around after their frantic, accelerated journey. I implore my eggs to make their move, to come down my fallopian tubes into the sperm's frenzied midst, there to be pursued and penetrated. I drift off into a reverie, remembering being pursued and won and indeed penetrated myself as a young college girl in northern California in the late 1960s. Mostly, in this bland, antiseptic room I remember the wonderfully sticky smells that hung over those years, an erotic brew of sweat and incense and marijuana. I remember the aromatic afternoons in bed in my small dorm room, the sun filtering in through the redwoods outside the window, the light filigreed across our skin and the spines of my books—Rousseau and Thoreau and Marx and Marcuse—while from a record player down the hall Janis Joplin wailed about freedom. A cocoon of passion and politics, of pine trees and patchouli oil. I sometimes go into one of those New Age bookstores just to smell again the incense, that peppery perfumed air. It carries me right back to that room, to those days when everything seemed so possible, so hopeful. The world was coming deliciously unglued and I was part and parcel of it there on my wooded campus. Armed with my contraceptives and my fledgling feminism, I was on the cusp of a fabulous journey. My sisters and I were. The best and the brightest. The luckiest young women on earth. Everything was before us. With our birth control pills and the exhortations of the feminist foremothers to urge us on, what could stop us? Who could? We were the golden girls of the brave new world, ready, willing and able to lay our contraceptively endowed bodies across the chasm between the feminine mystique and the world the feminists envisioned. Strong, smart, educated, we were the beneficiaries of unique historical timing when the doors were opening, the old male-female roles were falling and the world was ours to conquer, to be part of, to matter in, the world of men, of lawyers and doctors, astronauts and poets. I wanted in that world. I wanted to matter. I wanted to be somebody. I wanted to send dazzling words out into that world. Babies didn't cross my mind, there in my sweaty aerie among the redwoods. And not for a long, long time after. I took contraception for granted: birth control pills for a brief time in my late teens and then a diaphragm, which became not only a fixed part of my body, but a fixed part of my mind, entrenched, dogmatic, reflexive, the ticket to my female freedom, to everything I wanted to be. Not for me an unexpected pregnancy, the fate of women throughout the millennia. No, not for me. Later when my new husband whispered above me about wanting to have a baby, I shrank from his ardor. I couldn't imagine it; I didn't even feel the connection between lovemaking and baby-making, so methodically had I put contraception—and ambition—between my womb and pregnancy. I had been adamant, powerful in my rebuff of the sperm ejaculated into my body, the sperm I am now importuning to do their fertilizing dance.

So after all those years of sex without procreation, here I lie, engaged in this procreation without sex. It is a stunning reversal, a cosmic joke. It contains my history, that arc—all that sex to no sex, a lifetime of trying to be somebody, my whole own woman in the latter half of twentieth-century America, a lifetime of holding motherhood at bay. From its little blue plastic clam shell in the bathroom drawer, I can hear my diaphragm mocking me in the night: "Ha, ha," it seems to say, "you probably never needed me in the first place." Indeed.

The nurse gently knocks and I am released to go. Now I am back on the freeway heading home, already beginning the fourteen-day count-down to the pregnancy test: am I, aren't I, am I, aren't I, a moment-by-moment monitoring, an imaginary ear to the womb intent on picking up any uterine sigh of life. I am listening to the oldies-but-goodies station on the radio, humming along with Simon and Garfunkel. "Kicking down the cobblestones, looking for fun and feelin' groovy." In my hope and in my angst I am tempted to roll down the window and shout out into the smoggy Los Angeles air: "Hey, hey, Gloria! Germaine! Kate! Tell us, how does it feel to have ended up without babies, children, flesh of your flesh? Did you mean it to happen that way? Did you really mean to thumb your noses at motherhood or is that what we heard or intuited for our own needs? Tell us, please, your eager, aging novitiates. Do you wish it had been otherwise so that now you'd be surrounded by children and even bouncy, healthy grandchildren—firebrand feminists subsumed at last into a Norman Rockwell tableau? Tell me: Do you wake in the night and bemoan the unused magic of your aging bodies? Tell me: What does it feel like to face the grave with none of your own DNA to leave behind? Do you tote up your accomplishments and throw them at the void? Simone, Simone de Beauvoir and Virginia Woolf, can you wade in here too, please, share any regrets, my barren heroines from the great beyond? Tell me: Was your art worth the empty womb, predicated on it, in fact, no children to divert attention, to splinter the focus? Can you tell me, any of you: Am I going to get over this?"

The clouds do not part; no feminist goddess peers down with a benediction on my emptiness. I am on my own here. I pat my swollen lower abdomen, with its intimation of pregnancy, and listen again to my womb, an agnostic mid-life feminist sending up silent prayers to the fertility gods on high. Please let it work, please let me be pregnant, please hear my plea. I also send up apologies to the mothers of yore, the station-wagon moms with their postpartum pounds who felt denigrated in the liberationist heyday by the young, lean, ambitious women like me who were so intent on making our way. Sorry. Sorry. Sorry. Is this the infertile payoff for my former bravado? In my most aggrieved moments I think that—infertility as a metaphor, as comeuppance for having so fervently and so long delayed motherhood. The data on this score are irrefutable: Fertility declines with age, pure and simple, especially after thirty-five, and I am three years past that now. A thousand whys dance through my brain, a thousand questions, threads that wind around each other containing the secret to my babylessness. How could something so primal as this longing to procreate have been so long repressed, so long buried? Out of what need, what fear, what history? Not only am I infertile, but worse, a cliché, a humbled renegade haunting the national imagination, held up as some sort of dupe of feminism, rather a double dupe of the sexual revolution and the women's revolution. Is that what I am? Did I get it wrong, or rather, too right? Certainly we did take them hard, those movements, my contemporaries and I, and now I can't remember the exhilaration of those days for the increasing discomfort of these. Had I been led astray, had we, by bruised and bitter women who had warned us away from something magic, important, noble even? Had we, in the name of liberation, simply ended up aping the cultural dismissal of women, femaleness, motherhood, our mothers? Or was there something else, something earlier that had skewed me away from having children, something in my own childhood or adolescence? What, what combination of things led me here and where oh where do I go to trade a byline for a baby?

The questions continue to swirl through my hormonally wired brain as I finally pull into my street. I am not alone, of course. The culture is awash in baby talk as my late-breeding thirty- and forty-something contemporaries try to get pregnant or exult in maternity. All around me I hear it: the collective oohs and ahs of the new mothers or the laments of the infertile. This maternal celebration is not just a media canard, as some have suggested, the plot of the traditionalists angling to get women back in their old places. No, the fertility statistics are actually climbing back up toward the levels of the 1950s, and I hear paeans to motherhood from women I know and women I don't, from friends and strangers. Who would have thought it, who would have anticipated this reembrace of maternity after our determined and protracted journey away from it, our adamant sexual and professional ambitions? I am amused by it, driven by it, in thrall to a tactile hunger that makes my fingers tingle around babies, eager to stroke their soft flesh, my breasts yearning toward their newborn mouths, longing to give sustenance, hungry for their hunger. I will persevere in this pregnancy quest. That I know. I know that about myself. And as I turn into the driveway I breathe a pride-filled sigh. I've done it again, I'm OK, I can manage this, I can hang in until my reward comes. If it doesn't work this time, I will try again next month and the next and the next. I will be tenacious, optimistic, as dogged in my pursuit of motherhood as I have been about everything else, Our Lady of the Stirrups shooting up and running up and down the smoggy LA freeways with containers of sperm if need be. I will go the distance as I have in every other part of my life, in work, in love. If the insemination doesn't work this time, there is always the next and the next, and out beyond that, those amazing high-tech procedures: GIFTs and ZIFTs and IVFs. I know myself well enough. I will keep going. I am hooked, a true junkie hungry for the next fix, ready to conjure up a baby with the help of these cutting-edge fertility wizards who, in procedures both lonesome and stunning, can play God. I am now at the mercy of their invasive magic. And of my memory. I am on a journey. When I return, the self I return to will be different. Baby or no. One way or the other. I will be different. This is that kind of journey. I am already different, raw, humbled, manhandled, invaded. On the cusp of a fine loneliness. I am being redefined by my infertility. I know that. I cannot stop the redefinition, and for a blessed baby boomer, someone who has always sought to control the vagaries of life, to dictate the contours of my ambition, this is maddening. On top of which this is not a very sexy malady nor in some ways a very sympathetic one. We infertiles won't die for want of a baby. We are not growing pale and thin with disease. We do not, for example, have AIDS, though many of us have come by our infirmity through the same avenue, through sex, or more specifically some sexually transmitted disease, some STD or PID (pelvic inflammatory disease), to add to the acronyms, which has scarred our reproductive parts and left us, like those with AIDS no doubt, scanning back through our histories to remember the precise encounter, the exact, the fatal fuck, if you will, that delivered this infectious blow, that made life-giving difficult if not impossible. Was it special, was it lovely, was it necessary, can it be undone? Can I take it back, not have done it, not have been there, in that particular bed on that particular night, not have moaned out with unsuspecting pleasure? Can I, can we, be unfucked, just this one time, just that one time—please, oh please? I would wish it for all of us, ever mindful that indeed I am not dying, though on some days it feels as if something in me is or has. But no, I will go on scrounging around for the latest therapy, the latest antidote for my nonpregnancy, overtly healthy all the while, save perhaps for a giddy hunger that makes us infertiles seem a little wacky and unstable at times, prone to both huge hope and rabid despair—a state certainly exaggerated by the drugs. In the de-eroticized world of high-tech breeding, the longing itself carries a kind of erotic sting, causing one's eyes to tear up at the mere prospect of seeing at long last the elusive loved one. A baby, my baby, my own.

As I walk toward the same small white house I have lived in for all those sixteen married years, I finally notice the day, sunny and soft. Our yard looks green, fertile, fecund, and I, achy and hopeful, long to join the life-giving cycle, to be part of a birth, to give birth, to be green and lifeful. Fecund, suckle—those hard sensual words. I want them. I want to be them, to do them, to feel them. I want to crawl back into my female sex. I want to start over. I want to unwind the reel.

2

REWINDING THE REEL

And so it began, my journey into the hard-core, high-tech world of out-of-body breeding, my late-in-life search for a baby. But it was really two journeys I had begun lying there on my back, not just the baby quest, but also a backward journey down into my past. It was inescapable. You couldn't take one journey without the other. You couldn't just run up and down that freeway with a jar of sperm in your purse or lie in those stirrups day after day and not sort through memories. They came together, a compound package: baby-making and soul-searching. Like any major life crisis—a loss, a failure, a divorce, a death—the baby quest was so intense and personal and raw that it put you up against everything you had been before and who you would be after. It certainly did me, no matter how I tried to fight it, no matter how much of my feminism I threw against it. This obsession is nonsense, said I, the rational, functioning-in-the-world I. You are just caving in to all those old notions of biological destiny, you mommy manqué. Get on with it. Get a life. Get back to your life. But I berated myself to no avail. Another part of me would have none of that rationality. I was engaged instead in a constant soul search. What was I and what would I be if my quest failed: a non-mother, a half-woman? What did it mean to me to be a woman anyway; what had it ever meant? It seemed to me that I had fought it so hard, always divided against myself. I had never been wholly happy in my female skin, always pushing against its implied limitations. And who—what women, what men, what pieces of the culture—had fostered those feelings and helped push me so emphatically away from motherhood for so long? That was the question, the one I would constantly toss up and down as I lay there on the table in the doctor's office, my lower half draped in paper, my pelvis pointed skyward in that humiliatingly optimistic posture.

Arriving home that spring day, high on hope and desperate for clues, I immediately went into my small, book-crammed office and started riffling through the shelves, looking above all for the old women's lib manifestos, looking for the reasons for my long resistance to motherhood. Surely they would yield something up. And there they all were, tucked in the shelves, magazines with articles I had practically memorized at the time and books with densely underlined passages. They had been there for twenty years, virtually unopened except for the occasional stroll down memory lane, and now as I turned the pages, it was like releasing into the air again the old haranguing chorus that had warned us off domesticity and the trap of the traditional female roles. Here were Friedan and Greer, the radical feminists and debunkers of the vaginal orgasm, all the impassioned ideologues of yore and, of course, the matriarch of them all, Simone de Beauvoir, whose seminal *The Second Sex* had set the liberationist ball rolling back in the early fifties. Their words seemed to leap from the pages and my memory at the same time, and I could remember, looking at them now through the mid-life lens of my infertility, the impressionable and eager young woman I had been when I first read them all. I could see her, that young woman, circa 1970, in blue jeans, blond hair to the waist, slender, intense, ambitious, devouring all those books, starting with de Beauvoir's firm-eyed, well-reasoned rant against patriarchy and biological destiny. As I flipped through it, I found whole pages underlined and starred by my emphatic twenty-year-old hand, like the one that began:

Since the oppression of woman has its cause in the will to perpetuate the family and to keep patrimony intact, woman escapes complete dependency to the degree in which she escapes from the family.

That about summed it all up—a perfect sound bite of hard-core feminism. To be independent you had to forswear family bonds, not fall for the lure of hearth and home. It was that simple and that stark. The sections on puberty and menstruation and pregnancy were equally crisp and unsentimental, talking about the messy bodily rhythms the emphatically childless de Beauvoir clearly wanted none of, finding them both demeaning and alienating and, one gathered, somehow embarrassing.

Woman experiences a more profound alienation when fertilization has occurred and the dividing egg passes down into the uterus and proceeds to develop there. True enough, pregnancy is a normal process, which, if it takes place under normal conditions of health and nutrition, is not harmful to the mother; certain interactions between her and the fetus become established which are even beneficial to her. In spite of an optimistic view having all too obvious social utility, however, gestation is a fatiguing task of no individual benefit to the woman but on the contrary demanding heavy sacrifices.

That was quintessential de Beauvoir, clear-eyed and unsentimental as she could be, and who, reading that, wanted to be pregnant? She made it sound about as appetizing as having the flu. No, not for her, this lofty think-mate of Jean-Paul Sartre, not for her the trap of marriage or motherhood or some idyllic, round-bellied pregnancy, not when she had such serious work to do.

I smiled as I turned the pages, remembering the thrill of reading those words two decades earlier, remembering how they resonated then, how they hit a mark deep within my young soul. I wanted to follow her into the sunset, mimic her brave, high-minded example, live in a high-voltage duo without benefit of legal bindings or the trap of maternity. What could be more liberating, more exciting, more intellectually erotic?

Appropriately enough, Betty Friedan's *The Feminine Mystique* was next to de Beauvoir on the shelf. Published ten years after *The Second Sex,* hers was the first shot over the American barricades, but I read her along with de Beauvoir when the women's movement really took off for me and my friends in the early seventies. Prescient, Friedan was, and in her own American way, fierce, optimistic. I opened the book and read again:

The feminine mystique has succeeded in burying millions of American women alive. There is no way for these women to break out of their comfortable concentration camps except by finally putting forth an effort—that human effort which reaches beyond biology, beyond the narrow walls of home, to help shape the future.

That's where my friends and I were adamantly heading—beyond biology, away from the home, that comfortable concentration camp, away from motherhood and dishes and diapers, away from the feminine mystique. Not for us the traditional wifely role. No way were we going to be buried alive. We would sign on and help shape the future with our now licensed ambitions.

Right next to Friedan on the shelf was the more irreverent literary swagger of Germaine Greer's *Female Eunuch* from 1970, again whole pages of which had been marked up, the margins jammed with my comments.

What happens to the Jewish boy who never manages to escape the tyranny of his mother is exactly what happens to every girl whose upbringing is "normal." She is a female faggot. Like the male faggots she lives her life in a pet about guest lists and sauce béarnaise, except when she is exercising by divine maternal right the same process that destroyed her lusts and desires upon the lusts and desires of her children.

Cultural stereotypes be damned. Jewish mothers, female faggots—in her emphatic anti-maternalism, Greer was ever eager to offend. A little farther along there was this passage, beside which I had scrawled "battle cry":

If marriage and family depend upon the castration of women let them disappear. The alternative is not a brothel, for brothels depend upon marriage and family for their existence. If we are to escape from the treadmill of sexual fantasy, voracious need of love, and obsessiveness in all its forms we will have to reinstate our libido in its rightful function. Only then will women be capable of loving. Eternal Eros is imprisoned now in the toils of sadomasochistic symbiosis, and if we are to rescue him and save the world we must break the chain.

That's what we would do: We would break that chain. We would not be castrated. We were the golden girls of the brave new order. We would do it differently, redefine the gender, fly free of our very own sex. That was the message we were getting then in our vulnerable early twenties as we prepared to step out in the world, and it resonated through our collective souls and psyches, singing, stinging days of feeling lit up with rhetoric and moxie. We were the eager tools of history, of progress, of liberation, and it was thrilling, hopeful, exhilarating. I reached next for that vibrantly vitriolic anthology of the movement from 1970, *Sisterhood Is Powerful,* with its evocatively sloganeering table of contents: "Know Your Enemy: A Sampling of Sexist Quotes"; "Media Images 1: Madison Avenue Brainwashing"; "Media Images 2: Body Odor and Social Order";

"The Politics of Orgasm"; "Notes of a Radical Lesbian"; "Must I Marry."
It all seemed long ago and far away in its vehemence, even humorous, all
that talk of brainwashing and body odor! But it was dazzlingly potent stuff
back when, exciting, daring, conscripting—if you were young and female
and well placed, by dint of economics and education, to take advantage
of all these feminist exhortations. Again, marked passages littered the
pages, like this from Beverly Jones' fierce treatise on "The Dynamics of
Marriage and Motherhood."

> Is it any wonder that [a woman] is tempted to scream when at the
> very moment she has gotten rid of the company, plowed through some
> of the mess, and is standing in a tiny kitchen over a hot stove her
> husband begins to make sexual advances? He naively expects that these
> advances will fill her with passion, melting all anger, and result not only
> in her forgetting and forgiving, but in gratitude and renewed love. Ever
> heard the expression, "A woman loves the man who satisfies her"?
> Some men find that delusion very comforting. A couple of screws and
> the slate is wiped clean. Who needs to pay for servants or buy his wife
> a washing machine when he has a cock?

Pretty fierce stuff it was, all that talk of dirty dishes and obligatory
"screws." If that was marriage—who wanted it? But even that piece had
seemed tame compared to Mary Jane Sherfey's eye-opening "A Theory
on Female Sexuality" in the same volume, a corroboration of what a lot
of birth control pill–popping women were learning firsthand back then,
i.e., that a woman had fairly unlimited sexual capacity, that she could, in
fact, have a multitude of orgasms to a man's one. (Did our mothers know
that, our grandmothers, our grandmothers' grandmothers' grandmothers
and so forth? If so, the knowledge certainly hadn't been passed on.) The
entire thrust of civilization—the emphasis and insistence on monogamy
and motherhood—had been aimed therefore at circumscribing female
lust, what Sherfey called "the fluctuating extremes of an impelling, aggressive eroticism." Down with Freud. Down with penis envy. Down with
the vaginal orgasm, which was debunked in Anne Koedt's equally eye-
opening piece in the 1973 collection *Radical Feminism*. I reached for that
and again found underlined sentences, like: "It seems clear to me that
men in fact fear the clitoris as a threat to masculinity"; and, "The estab-

lishment of clitoral orgasm as fact would threaten the heterosexual institution."

That's what they were all telling us young women, these feminist theoreticians, these militant clitorists, that we were the true sexual beings, history's sensate live wires capable of random couplings—with men or more threateningly, with women, for that matter—when everything we had been told growing up was the opposite: that women were the passive receptacles, the often frigid on-your-back brigade for whom sexual pleasure was iffy at best while marriage and motherhood and making the perfect béarnaise sauce were the height of fulfillment. Not for us, not anymore, no way. We had our resolve and we had our own sexuality in hand, literally and figuratively. We were going to lead our own lives. We were going to matter, if we kept our heads down and didn't get tangled up in old notions of correct feminine behavior, didn't get tangled up in marriage and motherhood—that's what they were all warning us against, the Friedans and Greers and Steinems. I started rummaging through my stacks of old *Ms.* magazines and piles of xeroxed articles, and came upon the much-talked-about 1971 piece by Matina Horner, then president of Radcliffe, on why women not only fear failure but also fear success, the following paragraph circled and annotated in my slanty left-handed script:

> A bright woman is caught in a double bind. In testing and other achievement-oriented situations she worries not only about failure, but also about success. If she fails, she is not living up to her own standard of performance; if she succeeds she is not living up to societal expectations about the female role. . . . If a woman sets out to do well, however, she bumps into a number of obstacles. She learns that it really isn't ladylike to be too intellectual. She is warned that men will treat her with distrustful tolerance at best, and outright prejudice at worst, if she pursues a career. She learns the truth of Samuel Johnson's comment, "A man, is in general pleased when he has a good dinner upon his table than when his wife talks Greek." So she doesn't learn Greek, and the motive to avoid success is born.

How those words had burrowed into my resolve. I remembered where I first read them, on my girlfriend's bed, a sweaty summer afternoon filled with heat and sweet ambition. I had graduated from college by that point and was thinking that I myself might be a writer, add my own voice to the revolutionary din. Of all the writers back then, all the voices, none had so startled me with its crisp pain and so lingered in memory as that of Sally Kempton, columnist Murray Kempton's daughter, in an article that appeared in *Esquire* in the summer of 1970. I finally located it under stacks of other old magazines, not the original but a reprint in the 1983 Fiftieth Anniversary Collector's Issue. "Cutting Loose," it was called, a searing indictment of male-female relations—father-daughter, husband-wife— one line of which had in effect needlepointed itself across my memory:

> I used to lie in bed beside my husband after those fights and wish I had the courage to bash his head in with a frying pan.

There it was again in black and white, just as I had remembered it, as unapologetically angry a sentence as I had ever read by a woman. The passage continued in the same tone of vibrantly restrained rage:

> I would do it while he slept, since awake he would overpower me, disarm me. If only I dared, I would mutter to myself through clenched teeth, pushing back the realization that I didn't dare not because I was afraid of seriously hurting him—I would have loved to do that—but because even in the extremity of my anger I was afraid that if I cracked his head with a frying pan he would leave me. God, how absurd it was that my whole life's effort had been directed toward keeping men from leaving me, toward placating them, submitting to them, demanding love from them in return for living in their style, and it all ended with my lying awake in the dark hating my husband, hating my father, hating all the men I had ever known. What I couldn't figure out was whether I hated them because I was afraid they would leave me or whether I was afraid they would leave me because I hated them.

No other passage from all the lib lit had so haunted me. I had carried it with me, losing a line here or there, but never forgetting the tenor of it, the elegant fury. Her father, she said, had informed her when she was fifteen that she would never be a writer because she wasn't hungry enough, because there would always be a man to look after her. And indeed, the year after her *Esquire* piece appeared, Sally Kempton and her husband divorced and she later became a seeker, a swami, a teacher of meditation. Was that the morality lesson: that anger like hers wasn't finally supportable, that it imploded leaving an inner space of calm and bliss? Or was she simply the cautionary living proof of Matina Horner's contention: that smart women would opt out? That's what they were all warning us against, all of these women, warning us not to opt out, not to get stuck, not to accept marriage and motherhood and male-defined sexuality as our true and only lot, and it occurred to me sitting there, reading all of them again after twenty years, that never had men and women been more alike, sounded more alike in their sexual swagger and rage at marriage than at that angry moment when the gap between the sexes seemed to be at its widest. After all, weren't Norman Mailer, the self-described "Prisoner of Sex" with his "great bitches reeking of rot and musk," and Germaine Greer with her "female faggots" really soul brother and sister when you came down to it?

It also occurred to me, sitting there on my aching hips on the hard wooden swivel chair I had used since I'd started writing twenty years earlier, that I had started late in my detective story, which is what this search was beginning to feel like: a historical detective story, a backward counterpoint to my ongoing pregnancy quest, which was a different kind of detective story, a medical one. The journeys were inseparable. I had to take both at the same time. Backward and forward, forward and back- ward. I had to know what had brought me—what decisions, what history, what manifestos, what courage or lack thereof, had brought me to this infertile point. I could not let it be. I resented the fact that I had turned into a cliché, one of those achievement-oriented, liberation-intoxicated, narcissistic baby boomers who forgot to have babies until it was too late, part of a "tiny blip in modern Western history, when, given the perceived importance of what used to be a job and now became a 'career' to women, liberal attitudes about sex, and the widespread use of contracep- tives, some women experimented with the radical idea of remaining childless." Zing! There we were, laid bare, we late breeders, by the authors of the 1988 book *The Baby Makers*. Theirs was the media-typical explana- tion, and yes, in my wounded or glib moments I acceded to the cliché. Oh yes, my work was all-important, I was a driven, fame-and-lust-crazed baby boomer who'd simply had too much to do back then, I would cheekily respond to people who queried me about my childlessness. But

I knew that was a deflection, knew it was only the tip of the truth. I was indeed ambitious and intent on making my way under the fierce tutelage of the feminist thinkers. But the real question, as I sat there in my office, my heart in my womb, my eyes wandering over the spill of heavily underlined books and articles now heaped around me, was: Why, why had we, why had I, so resonated to all that female rage, been so thirsty for it, so lit up by it? Where had we come from to be so exhilarated by it? What need of ours, what fear, what hope, what dreams made us such responsive novitiates of the feminist foremothers, responsive enough to ignore or dampen or suppress the procreative urge—no small urge, as I was certainly in the process of finding out—until the clocks ticked down. No, no, not our biological clocks; that was just more of the cliché. What we heard was the mortality clock.

I heard it again as I started to clean up my small office, close all the books and put the magazines back. Bye-bye, sisters, back on the shelves, you ferocious, marriage-hating motherhood debunkers. With their voices stilled, the ticking picked up again, a drone in my ear, the palpable womb-cry of hunger that reasserted itself in their absence. Tick-tock tick-tock tick-tock. But could I in good conscience blame feminism for my long abstention from motherhood? Could I blame Simone de Beauvoir and Germaine Greer and Gloria Steinem and Sally Kempton and Kate Millett, all childless themselves? (Of the high-profile ideologues, the really big guns, only Betty Friedan had children.) How convenient it would be; how easy. How devoutly I wanted to do that—find an easy scapegoat. Many were doing it and had been doing it for years: scapegoating feminism. It was a national sport, indulged in by disappointed women and retro-chauvinists—even many a commentator with a liberal patina—and anyone and everyone in between. But I knew it was more complicated than that, much more, and I knew that the point of my journey into the past was to take responsibility for what had befallen me, for the choices I had made along the way and for whatever long-ago grapple or grapples that had marred my innards. My determination to do so would not keep me, some days down the road, from railing at my heroines there on the shelves, those angry, childless and unmarried ideologues of yore who had played their part in my long resistance to motherhood, intensifying my love-hate relationship with my own sex at a crucial moment when I was young and barely formed and eager to be filled with their fervor.

"How could you have done this to me?" I would groan at them. "How could you have been so positive, so adamant in your anti-maternalisms?"

But there was gratefulness underneath the groans. I knew in my heart of hearts that they had also given me a life, washing me out into the world on the tidal wave of their rage. And I also knew that the roots of my personal journey away from motherhood—and that of my contemporaries—had begun much earlier, in our own childhood homes, not in the 1960s and seventies. You couldn't pick up the narrative midstream, which is what I had inadvertently done by rummaging around in those manifestos. That was obvious now. I had jumped the gun, gotten ahead of myself. Now I had to go back down into the preceding decades and see why I for one was so predisposed to hop on the anti-motherhood bandwagon in the first place. What had I, what had we, picked up back then that so inclined us toward the women's movement and for such a long time emphatically away from motherhood?

That was the key, and so as I went forward into the maw of assisted reproduction, as they called it, I would also go backward. I had no choice. My contemporaries and I had had an incredible journey, a journey into rage and out again (and in and out and in and out and in—it was never done, that particular part of the journey, as we continued to bump our heads against male instransigence), a journey away from motherhood and then back to it. In many ways we were the story of the women's movement, of how it had played itself out, not in some abstract, theoretical way, not just on paper, but up close, in daily life, at home, at the office, in bed. We were a kind of Sacrificial Generation of Women, a phrase I had used in one of my very first magazine articles about the daunting array of choices we then saucy young women faced in the early 1970s as the world order, the gender order anyway, was changing.

I was talking about women born roughly between 1943 and 1955 (women who graduated from high school, say, after 1960 and before 1972). By my reckoning and interviewing, women born earlier were often already in the suburbs with the kids when everything began to change; women born later inherited an already reconfigured world in many ways. We were the in-betweeners, the Girls of the Chasm, raised in the old world, expected to flourish in the new. That's where we got caught, in that straddle. It wasn't about feminism per se, or certainly not about feminism in isolation, but rather about the historical combination of events, the one-two punch of the sexual revolution and then the women's revolution slapped on top of our good-girl fifties childhoods. All the rules had changed at a key moment just as were about to step out into life. It was a lot to assimilate, to adjust to, and the combination had left many of us with a kind of gender whiplash as we went around trying to satisfy the old notions of correct feminine behavior we had been raised with while also trying to satisfy the dictates of every ensuing decade—the liberationist sixties and seventies, the materialistic Reagan eighties and now the nineties. And every one of those decades also came with its own requisite body shape, from the late sixties tomboys to the zaftig Barbie dolls of the late eighties and the suitable fashions for the given figure. There was always something we were supposed to be as women, something we were supposed to do, some way we were supposed to look, and it occurred to me, not for the first time certainly, but with clarity sitting there awash in memories of the heyday of liberation, that I had not been a full-fledged feminist revolutionary after all.

Like so many of the women I knew or had interviewed over those twenty years of writing, I had always been a kind of mixed breed, a feminine-feminist compote gyrating through those decades, alternately adoring and angry, alternately full of ambition and full of caretaking fervor, alternately exhilarated and depressed, fiercely independent one minute and wobbly of will the next, aroused by pornography and angered by it all at the same time. I was a mixed metaphor of an American woman, an American wife, buffeted about by all the cultural signals, all the pushes and pulls, the go-for-it signals weighted down with old notions of correct feminine behavior and feminine beauty, all the while groping toward liberation, toward some sense of an authentic, integrated life, toward some sense of reconciliation with my own femaleness. There were so many crosscurrents, so much old conditioning and so many new expectations. And like so many women who had been caught in the crosscurrents, I had not imagined myself fully. I did not sit down and say to myself: What do you want? How do you see your life? Do you want children? I began to see that now, began to see that life was finally nothing more than an act of the imagination, of self-envisioning, which was much harder for women than for men, given the way we were raised to look after everyone else (still), given all the mixed messages that continued to be heaped on us (still) and certainly given those men themselves, especially the ones we lived with and loved.

They too, of course, played an inescapable part in our journey away from motherhood. Those men, those men, those men, those fathers and father figures with their prerogatives and privileges and penises and their seemingly primal fear of strong women. We all ran up against it. All along the way it had been there, bubbling along under the liberationist wave, that dark phallic undertow of male fear trying to countermand our efforts to be free and whole and liberated. The manifestations of that fear were everywhere—in our kitchens and bedrooms and workplaces and in the culture that increasingly pornographized women as a way of reappropriating our freed-up sexuality. Skillfully, manfully, they turned liberation against us in many instances, turning us into postliberation pinups, self-supporting nouvelle sex objects in garter belts and gabardine.

Some days, rolling up and down the freeway to the clinic, I made myself listen to the misogynistic grunts and groans of the rappers, their rhyming couplets full of "bitches" and "ho's," and I would grieve with rage for my sex, realizing as I drove that like so many women I had spent so much time fighting against that phallic undertow, learning along the way to identify with the aggressor, as they term it, learning to identify with the men, the fathers, the husbands, the bosses, so that the impulse to mother got further away from me as I got older, instead of getting closer. I was always shadowboxing with the patriarchs, courting their kindness, deflecting their resentment, ducking their anger or matching it with my own. In time, like many women I knew, I got harder, sharper, more competent, more brittle, less maternal. In fact, we late mothers, or would-be mothers, were, I was beginning to think, a real clue to the history of the past forty years and to the world in which women now found themselves. We were not the caricatured career-obsessed men- and baby-haters, not at all, but often the opposite: the most reactive and love-damaged of the lot, women holding on to work and ambition for fear of being dismissed, diminished, sidelined, the fear that Sally Kempton had so eloquently spoken to way back when. That was always my fear, of somehow losing my voice, or of never having one at all. And when I was ready, finally, finally ready to be a mother, finally feeling secure enough and certainly old enough, whammo—here came the big surprise as it had come to many a contemporary of mine. Infertility. Around 8.4 percent of all women between the ages of fifteen and forty-four (that's one out of twelve couples) are affected by infertility, but the numbers go up with age so that 20 percent of women and 36 percent of childless couples between thirty-five and forty-four have fertility problems. (That's one out of every six couples, up from one out of seven just since 1982.) And interviews with successful women of my generation show that many postponed marriage and/or childbearing for their success until it was too late, until they—like me—hit the brick wall of infertility.

In some ways maybe that infertility is a dark and distorted lens through which to look back; but maybe in its own way it is as clear a lens as any, one that forces uncharacteristic honesty on those of us with the Scarlet "I" writ, if not across our foreheads, certainly across our hearts, we modern-day Hester Prynnes, transgressors who had, as the cliché went, put work ahead of motherhood.

I couldn't stand being a cliché any longer, a baby-hungry object of embarrassment to the feminists, an object lesson for the counter-feminists. Not being able to conceive was bad enough. Being reduced to a cliché—one more whiny boomer who forgot to have a baby—was a further indignity. No, the story was more convoluted than that, more maddening and finally more revolutionary, slowly, painstakingly revolutionary, as we sought to be part of the redefinition of our sex. And where it began, where we began, we of the Sacrificial Generation, was not in the late sixties–early seventies, not with the feminist heyday—we had not been sprung, as some would have it, from the heads of those fire-breathing, militant clitorists—but in the 1950s, the decade that continued to haunt the national imagination and whose dictums about femininity and caretaking we had trailed after us like a child's blanket. We were the daughters of the post–World War II American dream, the daughters of those idealized fifties sitcom families in which father knew best and mother knew her place and a kind of disappointment, and tense, unspoken sexuality rattled around like the ice cubes in their nightly cocktails. That is where we had come from. That's really where American feminism was reborn at mid-century, not in the 1970s. That's where the later explosion took seed. And that's where I would pick up my journey into the past. Call it the memoir of an infertile feminist. Call it a generational reckoning. Call it, for me, an exercise in healing, personal and philosophic. I was looking for redemption, for reconciliation—with myself, my sex, my faith, which in many ways had been feminism itself.

Coming of age when I did, pen in hand, ambition on sleeve, it was inescapable that writing about women's lives would be my lot, and I had armwrestled with feminism all along the way, trying to make it my own, make it fit. Feminism definitely needed a more embracive spin, one that took into account the elegant if subtle differences between the sexes, the joyous differences (we were the birth-givers after all), the sexual differences (we took them into our bodies and not vice versa and were therefore vulnerable in ways they were not), the way-of-relating differences (our easier intimacy with one another) before we handed it on to younger women as they tried to put their own lives together, and decide when and whether to have children and how to fit them into their lives and, above all, how to imagine themselves fully. To suggest that there were no differences between men and women was, to me as I got older, as ludicrous as suggesting that those differences should dictate the contours or limitations of a life.

All through my writing life I had found myself in some irreverent middleland, always wanting both, wanting to insist on our overall symmetry with men—the skin, the bones, the dreams, the same conflictedly hopeful posture toward marriage and monogamy—and on our uniqueness and vulnerability as women at the same time, a tightrope walk that had often put me at odds with some of the more fervent feminists, just as my baby quest now put me at odds with some of them, those who judged high-tech baby-making to be invasive, inorganic, patriarchal, antifemale, even, in a perverse twist, anti-motherhood. Grief, like love, I had learned, was not necessarily politically correct.

Incorrect or not, my hand was being forced by it. I could not let go. I had to know how I got here, I had to know in order to heal. I had to know so I could get some surcease from the sorrow I was now carrying around with me along with those little plastic containers of sperm. Backward and forward, forward and backward. I had set sail. I was now off on my two-pronged journey.

Leaving my office that day, after my mad dash through the lib lit and my beginning reckonings, I felt a slight whisper of a cramp through my lower abdomen, the aftershock of the insemination. Could it possibly be? Could I possibly be that lucky? In two weeks I would know, two interminable weeks until the pregnancy test. Damn you. I smiled at all the now once again silenced ideologues as I left the room and closed the door behind me. Damn you, my saviors. Damn you.

3

THE CASE OF THE
RELUCTANT EGGS

Of course it was not to be, not that time, nor the next three or four times after that. Now I am beginning to lose count, they are blurring together, but I continue, here on the brink of insemination number five—or is it six?—to be quite cheerful and am astonished, with what little distance I have left on this baby-making process, at how quickly I have completely adapted my life to it, how quickly it seems to have become my life.

Once again in a bright, hopeful morning I am here in the waiting room anticipating my dose of sperm, pawing nervously through a magazine and peeking around at my co-breeders, my kempt, my distracted co-breeders clutching their discreet little white paper bags full of needles and drugs. We don't leave home without them. But this is our home now, our second home, our home away from home. We are spending hours here each month, a lot of us, having blood tests and sonograms and inseminations, and within these walls we sometimes strike up intense, temporary friendships, born of a shared plight, spilling out our gynecological histories for each other with the accuracy of scientists. How many previous inseminations, previous pregnancies or abortions or infections, how many previous surgeries or high-tech attempts? We can discuss these procedures with detailed, clinical accuracy. I meet women from Europe and Latin America who are temporarily holed up in motels nearby, whose husbands fly in to make the all-important sperm donation at the appointed time. I meet women married to younger men who are worried about losing them should they not be able to conceive. I meet mid-life women who had abortions way back when and now rue them with a tinge of bitterness. And women who in earlier days gave up babies for adoption and now want families of their own. An adoption here, an abortion there. We are a collage of secrets, of intimate details, of loss, of longing. Nursing our endless cups of instant coffee, we talk intimately, as women will do, not just about our pasts but also about our bodies, comparing our hormone levels, the state of our uterine linings, our insurance—or lack thereof—our mood swings. Some say they feel nothing from the fertility drugs we are all taking, some can't bear them, feeling flushed and crazy. I tend to feel a little dark-hearted, often without realizing it, though you can't tell where the drugs leave off and despair begins. They are an overlapping duo.

We talk about our marriages fraying at the edges and of our sometimes supportive, sometimes exasperated mates who must watch us gyrate and then, once a month, ejaculate into a cup in hopes of assuaging our longings. Sex we don't talk about; it is a dead issue, nonexistent, something in a forgotten country where we used to live. We have moved on into this Land of the Disembodied Procreators where the talk is not about bodies but body parts: ovaries and eggs and sperm. We do talk about that, about sperm and sperm counts, but with tenderness and faint amusement. This is, after all, the ultimate male stuff we are toting around here, the stuff of patriarchy. This is it, the building block of fatherhood and father-rule. With this sperm I thee wed and you shall bear my legitimate heirs and they shall bear my name. That is the refrain I sometimes hear emanating out of my little plastic cup—the unnerving voice of male authority telling me what to do.

More often, though, I feel tender toward the swirl of milky liquid as I hand it over to the lab tech. After all, the sperm belong inside me, hidden, swimming along on their gallant journey, instead of this, being handled and peered at and counted. But I cannot protect them, harbor them from scrutiny. I am a failure somehow, less than female—too taut, too unyielding, too damaged.

My initial hope and enthusiasm are being toyed with as these inseminations add up with no results. This is the standard beginning down the slippery slope of infertility—these inseminations are nothing more than retrieving the sperm, examining them, washing them and then injecting them up into the uterus through the cervical opening in order to bypass the sometimes "hostile" cervical mucus that might impede the sperm's progress and/or literally kill some or all of them off. From there they should make their way up into the fallopian tubes to find an egg, a long, bruising journey that few of the millions will survive. (One healthy, normal ejaculation, they tell me, contains on the order of 20–150 million sperm.) Those tubes are all-crucial, the conduits between ovary and uterus and the locale of fertilization, the place where sperm and egg do their thing and down which the resulting embryo will make its way into the womb. This is elegant, precarious stuff—even the young and fertile have only a 30 percent chance of getting pregnant per menstrual cycle.

I cannot imagine what my odds are—not too good, clearly. And this in spite of the fact that my husband's much-handled sperm are indeed pretty good. They have been punishingly tested and is plentiful enough and motile enough (meaning they swim well) and has passed the amusingly named hamster penetration test, during which said sperm were unleashed on a hamster egg, fertilization achieved. Good news, the nurse said when she called: The hamster penetration test was OK, causing me, not for the first and certainly not for the last time, to shake my head over the surreal world into which my husband and I had ventured. Hamster eggs, my husband's sperm. Who or what could possibly result from that marriage? How silly, how sad, how hopeful.

Not that I have been much in doubt these years as to his fertility. After all, he is a man with a history of procreative success. He has four sons, big, healthy adult sons from his previous marriage. It is I who cannot bear. In 30 percent of infertility cases, the woman has the problem; in another 30 percent, men are the cause, and in the remaining 40 percent it is a joint problem. In our case, though my husband's age is a factor, the problem is pretty clearly mine, and somehow these inseminations aren't doing the trick. Why not? I do ovulate; that we know. I make the right hormones at the right time of the cycle. That we also know from a series of blood tests. (If you had told me as a needle-phobic child that I would one day sit still for three and four shots a day, I would have grimaced in disbelief.)

During the first part of our menstrual cycles, we women make follicle-stimulating hormone, or FSH (I'm beginning to speak and think and dream in acronyms), which causes the egg-bearing follicles to ripen near the surface of the ovary; it is actually those I see on the sonogram screen each time, not the actual eggs themselves. In a normal, unstimulated cycle, only one of the eggs will continue to full maturity and then the brain will zap it with luteinizing hormone (LH) and it will burst out of the follicle to be picked up by one of the tubes, providing, of course, that they work properly. I have been repeatedly assured that mine do. Three years ago I had major surgery to remove some scar tissue from around the outside of my tubes and ovaries—scar tissue from some long-ago undiagnosed STD—and was assured at that point that the tubes themselves were fine inside. Just recently I have had a follow-up X ray, a so-called hysterosalpingogram, and the dye flowed through both tubes without hindrance or much pain, just a fleeting twitch. This does not, however, automatically mean that the little cilia within undulate appropriately to nudge eggs and embryos on their respective ways. And indeed, all the doctors' assurances to the contrary, I grow doubtful about the worthiness of these tubes as the inseminations progress and everything else seems to be going fine: sperm good, plenty of eggs, hormone levels high.

But now, this time, I have a new twist. This time my hyped-up ovaries will not release their cargo of eggs. The follicles will not rupture and let them go. In fact, I am now two days past the day I should have ovulated, and when I get my turn and lie on the table, legs akimbo, scanner in place, I see that what my heavy gut tells me is indeed the case: They are all still there, three reluctant follicles, dark and adherent, like barnacles on a ship. They will not pop and release those eggs. The doctor adds a possible new diagnosis: I am suffering from polycystic ovarian disease (PCOD), which causes my system to be hyperactive, producing a lot of immature follicles that won't burst—the unruptured-follicle syndrome (UFS). Just what I needed, a couple of new acronyms. So the whole process this time has been for naught, all the drugs, all the shots, ten days of Pergonal to be exact, the big mama of the fertility drugs, a combination of FSH and LH gathered from the urine of postmenopausal women. It costs $50 a shot and causes multiple follicles to ripen per cycle. So I've been spending $100 a day, uninsured, not to mention the $50 per sonogram. Two days ago I was given the final shot, this one of hCG (human chorionic gonadotropin), which is supposed to bring the eggs to final maturity and urge them to let go some thirty-eight to forty-two hours hence. But here they still are, glaring back at me. I am a little ragged from the drugs, a little hyper—they are stimulants, after all. I reach out to touch the screen, as if I could somehow dislodge the eggs by doing so. I am just beginning to learn, to be humbled, to wonder how in the world anyone so easily gets pregnant and how inept we are at trying to duplicate the elegant choreography of nature. I am beginning to see how little the doctors know for all they do know. Their knowledge is vast, dazzling, and then it stops before something like this, some hitch, some unforeseeable biological quirk, like these recalcitrant follicles. In many ways this is a science in its infancy (after all, the first test-tube baby, Louise Brown, was conjured up in 1978) and quirks like mine are still not well understood. I look at the follicles there on the screen, the doctor shaking his practiced head in commiseration, and I curse this entire process. This is not going to do. Can't they somehow be dislodged? I ask. What if I jump or dance or, dare I say it in this extra-corporeal world, have sex? How about that? Isn't that what nature intended: a hearty shake of the ovaries, a penetrating lunge from a partner? The doctor laughs gently at my rough-hewn poetry. It's too late for any of that, he says calmly. There has been some hormonal maladjustment. The message to my ovaries from my brain has not come or has come too early (in their parlance: I have had a premature LH surge) before the eggs were ready to leap into the void. Possibly that's been part of my problem all along, a premature LH surge problem. Or possibly it's a result of the fertility drugs themselves, which have caused my cycle to rev up too fast. Isn't that a laugh? The process defeats itself. Now these follicles will bloom awhile longer, turn into cysts perhaps, and I am doomed to tote some of them around until I bleed again in two weeks, little fists in my lower belly. The cycle is a total waste, the endless drugs, the endless sonograms, the endless clinic visits, the endless rides up and down the freeway. I have my first real inkling of despair. It seems I am getting farther from my goal instead of closer. Isn't that the way? I am now a guinea pig of medical science. And the truth is that like so many of the other women going through this, I have only about a 20 percent chance of leaving this clinic with a baby, about a 10 percent chance as I pass age forty. Translation—between 80 and 90 percent of us will not get babies. I know the odds. Despite his contagious, manly optimism, the doctor has been honest. And yet with the instinct of a gambler, I hang in, waiting for the next draw, hoping against hope that I will be the next lucky one, alternately grateful to the wizards who make this possible at all and bitter at the whole process.

I glance at the big, dark follicles on the screen one last time as the doctor withdraws the scanner. Over time, over the months I have become familiar with this screen, my eyes vigilant and practiced, and there is not an egg I have not cooed to under my breath, imagining it as the beginning of a life. Not a one of these black polka dots has escaped my scrutiny or the anticipatory reach of my maternal love. I think of all my eggs, the roughly 200,000 of them still stored in my ovaries (we don't make them as we go along, the way men manufacture sperm, veritable factories manufacturing some 50,000 new sperm every minute of every day till they're well into their seventies, the lucky old procreators), and I curse and mourn the lot, the used and unused ones, my genetic destiny unrealized. How can this be? So many to end up with nothing. I bid a last grim farewell to my three big juicy unruptured follicles. My triplets, my lovely, luminous triplets. A whole Volvo station wagon full of children.

The doctor decides we should go ahead with the insemination as planned. There is a chance, he says consolingly, that an egg has escaped from one of these seemingly unruptured follicles and the sperm will find it. I submit, as I always do, even as I wish to race out into the sunlight and nurture my irritation. Instead, I lie there dutifully, feeling again the cold metal speculum that pries me open, then the catheter being threaded up through the cervix and into my uterus and the slight cramping as the sperm is injected. For nothing, I feel sure. At least I will be spared the anxious two weeks. Now, a little numb and heavy-gutted, I will lumber toward the inevitable period, knowing it will be fierce. The drugs do that, thicken the uterine lining so there is more to slough off each month. It's one of the little added dividends of going through all this. And beyond that shedding, I know what lies ahead. We have agreed. If I did not conceive after a half dozen inseminations, it was time to move on to something more dramatic given my age, one of the new fancy and definitely more invasive surgical procedures in which the eggs will be forcibly removed from my stubborn ovaries and then joined with the sperm, either in my tubes (as in GIFT—gamete intrafallopian transfer) or in a dish (in IVF, in vitro fertilization, that which begat Louise Brown). At least there will be no unruptured follicles to contend with. At least that problem will be gotten around. But no doubt more will arise. That's what I'm beginning to understand here. This isn't a straight road at all. It doubles back on itself. The solution to old problems gives rise to new ones. Should I resist then, back out? Is that what I am being told? Is all this medical intervention ultimately doing more harm than good? Isn't that the object lesson here? To knock it off, get off the procreative treadmill and get a baby somewhere else, somehow else, someone else's baby? That's what it would be, of course—what he or she would be. I cannot do that yet. I am not done here.

I drift to thoughts of my own mother, my glamorous fifties mom with her hourglass figure and her own difficulty conceiving children. She had had one ovary and one tube removed and two miscarriages before getting pregnant with my older sister, a difficult pregnancy for which, as was standard practice then, she was given DES (diethylstilbestrol), a synthetic form of estrogen that supposedly prevented miscarriages and was given to some six million women between the late 1930s and early 1970s. DES has been widely implicated in the infertility of the next generation, in miscarriages and non-carriages and a rare form of vaginal cancer. Worst of all, it turned out not to be effective. Women who took it, like my mother, were also routinely told to take to bed, and that apparently was the trick for holding on to the pregnancy. Everywhere I turn, medical science is itself the culprit. Indeed, in 1985 my sister had a healthy five-month-old baby boy fall from her womb like a stone, carrying her heart with it, because her cervix did not seal properly holding the baby in. (DES daughters are twice as likely to be at risk for a premature birth as unexposed daughters.) Subsequently she had a little girl, after literally being sewn shut, a leaky, scary pregnancy.

My mother's records indicate that she did not take DES with me, but I am skeptical, so freely was it handed out back when, and as the minutes tick away until I can leave, I rerun our family medical inventory, the gynecological ineptness running through our female family tree, through many a family tree, realizing though that my mother's hunger was every match for my own and if they'd told her to drink snake oil she would have. Lying there, I think of her with love, of her own long-ago longing to be a mother and her tenacity in satisfying that hunger. Will I quit where she didn't? And musing so, I move thankfully out of the present and into the past and see her as she was then—a small-boned, large-breasted blonde beauty in an ultimately doomed marriage who was willing to stay in bed for months at a time to hold on to us, my sister and me—and I am back there, in the 1950s, beside her.

4

THE FIFTIES:
THE KITTENS OF SUBURBIA

Her body in profile, her face smiling into the camera, she's a knockout, curvaceous and coy in her tight-fitting sweater, Lana Turner's lusciously wholesome younger sister. This is my mother in a 1953 photo spread in *The TV Star Parade*. She is featured because she is the costar of *The Ray Milland Show*—a bona fide sitcom wife. My sister and I, ages four and three respectively, smile out from adjacent photos, her "tiny tintypes," as the copy reads, the little white suburban princesses being fussed over and tended to by our glamorous mom. There is also a picture of her with my baby-faced father, the pretty young actor-parents out for a night on the town, he in suit and tie, a cocky lopsided smile on his face, she in cleavage-revealing sheath with a mink stole around her shoulders. My pretty, pretty parents. What could be sweeter, more hopeful, more dashing than our little family unit, our fifties family unit. The entire issue of the magazine, in fact, is a page-by-page paean to family life. There are stories about Lucy and Desi at home with their little girl, and about Dean Martin's new baby effecting a reconciliation in his troubled marriage, and a real tearjerker about some long-forgotten actress entitled "Her Heart Craves a Home." There is also an open letter to Dr. Kinsey, of sex fame, whose survey of American sexual habits had just been published. The female author of the letter writes to say that the doctor has missed the beat by ignoring women on TV who, far from being sex-crazed and on-the-loose, are on the whole a wholesome, faithful breed (as opposed to the "26 percent of the women you questioned who had extramarital relations"). Certainly that was an accurate description of my mother's role on TV where she was playing the adoring, slightly patronizing—make that matronizing—wife to Ray Milland's absent-minded professor. She got him out of scrapes and set things right while fussing over him and winking at the audience, ever so gently, about his ineptness. That was the sitcom chemistry, Dad as breadwinning bumbler, Mom, the manipulative, slightly superior "better half." He had the money and power, she had the sexual favors to give or withhold and the right to ridicule him a little for his failings. Call it the perverse equality of inequality. At the time though, watching my mother bustling about up there on the TV screen in her robe, hair all simple and softly curled, her

face so smooth and shiny and hopeful, baiting and bantering with her
significant other, I thought I would die for love of her, of her sweetness
and prettiness and motherliness (even if it was directed at a man). I
wanted to crawl into the screen and be her daughter in that other world,
especially since at home, photo spreads to the contrary, our real family
was loudly coming apart. The conjugal center was not holding. We would
be gone, my mother, my sister and I, within a year and a half.

That, of course, was the thing about the fifties with all their patina of
familial bliss: A lot of the memories were not happy, not mine, not my
friends'. That's probably why the myth so endures, because of the disso-
nance in our lives between what actually went on at home and what went
on up there on those TV screens where we were allegedly seeing ourselves
reflected back. The perfect sitcom family—Mom, Dad, the kids, the dog,
everything in place, ordered, understood. The roles were clear, clean,
unimpeachable. There were designated gender stations, clearly marked
turf. Mom in her station wagon ferrying the kids around, Dad at work,
Mom doing the housework, Dad taking out the trash, Mom at the stove,
Dad at the barbecue. How many mitts and tongs and sturdy outdoor
aprons were those dads given, on how many birthdays and Christmases
over the years? The barbecue was center stage of their summertime
theater. That's where fathers did their only high-spirited culinary thing,
drink in one hand, tongs in the other, barking out into the warm night
at our happy flame-lit little faces, "Who wants it rare?" Things get wedged
in memory. After all the years of learning to do practically everything else,
deliberately appropriating other "male" chores like changing fuses and
hauling out garbage, I still defer to my husband when it comes to
barbecuing.

As I began to listen to other grown-up girls of the fifties, middle-class
white girls, I should specify, using their memories as a goad to my own,
particularly those who, like me, "forgot to have children" or managed to
have them just under the wire, I was to hear the same kind of stories.
There were some variations certainly, depending on circumstances and
geography, but underneath often there was a startling overlap of remem-
brance, of too many backyard barbecues and too much booze and Sinatra
forever crooning over the flushed faces of our dreamy-eyed parents as
they sought to kindle or rekindle romance on the back patios of postwar
America, Updike Country. And underneath it all, for us little girls watch-

ing in our pajamas, there were pointed lessons, a palpable feeling of unassuageable longings, male and female. Everybody seemed to want something more but nobody seemed to know what it was, and watching, we held our breaths, after the optimism of the first drink was long passed, waiting for the denouement, the sodden set-tos, the sorrow-filled recriminations.

"You know, I honestly don't know how big a deal the drinking was," a new acquaintance of mine, Jane Allen, said of her parents. "They didn't stand out in the crowd in any way at all. Nobody thought of it as a drinking problem, nobody ever fell down or drove into a tree, but drinking was always a big part of their lives, and our lives."

I smiled listening to her. I remembered. Jane is a small, elegant blonde, on the Diane Sawyer order, a decade divorced and, yes, childless, who runs her own public relations/environmental fund-raising firm, one, she assured me proudly when we first talked in her beige Manhattan office, that handles only socially responsible causes. She is one of those high-earning, gym-going, big-city businesswomen who run things with directness and wit and wear quiet makeup and elegantly subdued scarves tethered around their trench coats. But beneath her forty-two-year-old facade and chic short hair, she retains a shyness, a leftover girlish intensity that causes her to blush when she swears. At a dinner of friends, we were drawn together by the symmetry of our memories. It was those parties she, too, remembered most, not the parties themselves so much as the early evenings that preceded them. That's when things were at their best, their big old house on the Hudson outside New York City lurching to life for a minute, her parents getting pretty, the silver being polished, she and her younger sister being dressed up in their party clothes and shiny new black patent Mary Janes. They would watch it all, she says, with tremulous enchantment, waiting for it to start, waiting for it to end. On the way to school in the morning she would take note of the stale disarray, the glasses and ashtrays. By afternoon, when she and her sister came home, it was all cleaned up, everything back in place.

"For days afterwards, no one would say a word," she told me. "Everything would get cold and quiet and I hated the house even more then. It seemed so big and empty most of the time. My father was very attractive and very charming and sometimes he wouldn't come home at all. I don't know when I got it, that he was off screwing around. You know, at some point you just get it. I don't remember talking to my sister about it even. Most of the time my parents just went on as is, in this cool truce. He was a lawyer in the family firm, not very happily, and my mother stayed home and did the housework and fussed over us children, even though we had a maid. I remember watching her even on vacation compulsively vacuuming the rental house while my father had a small tantrum about something—that was always his prerogative—and I said, 'No way.' She always had to beg him for money and I said to myself, 'That'll never happen to me.' And I'm true to the goals I set myself. That's what blows my mind."

"Those goals being?" I asked.

"Financial independence, and I don't vacuum on vacation, and I never, ever drink too much," she said with a determined smile. "It was just always clear to me that my mother was not enough. There was this unspoken family assumption that she wasn't bright. She'd been a secretary when she and my father met and hadn't gone to college. She was pretty and did her bit and put on the parties. But she was not enough and I was determined to do it differently when it came my turn. I became my father's daughter instead. I became good at sports, skiing, even ice hockey. I not only went to college but got an MBA and finally started my own business—so that I could be independent. I think a lot of us women coming out of those fifties families did that."

Listening to Jane, I remembered my own fledgling resolves, not articulated on any level in those early years, but they were certainly taking root then as I watched—we all watched—the often strained arrangement of our parents' lives and marriages. Oh no, we didn't want to duplicate that. Oh yes, we were going to do it differently. Down the road we were going to be, not our mothers' daughters, but our fathers', as Jane said, even going them one better when our turn came as she had done, going to Yale, starting her own business. There was pathos in that, and revenge. In fact, our favorite children's books, as she reminded me, were Nancy Drew mysteries. She was our heroine of choice, a pert, blonde sleuth with a heart of gold, an adoring father and a long-since deceased mother. They were kindred souls, the Drews, the perfect mystery-solving Oedipal pair. And like her, we were going to be independent. We were going to get the education most of our mothers didn't get (in the 1950s, only 20 percent of college undergraduates were women and only a third of those graduated, most dropping out to marry) if only to command the respect of our oversized, in-charge-of-everything dads. We were going to make our own money because that was the only route to independence. That lesson was clear and I have heard it time and again from my baby-boom contemporaries, women who watched their moms ask for money, beg for money, perform for money, those moms with their migraine headaches or their sub rosa bitterness, or not so sub rosa as the case may be. There were girls I knew then and certainly later—women I met when I became a writer—whose childhoods were darkened by real craziness, whose mothers were truly damaged by the choreography of the times and whose memories make Jane's and mine look rosy and suburban by comparison.

As one told me, a tall, dark-haired political consultant in Washington, D.C., Ann Rubinstein, a recent first-time mom at age forty-two: "Oh Christ, my parents were very unhappy in their poverty. I come from this very left-wing Jewish family, very volatile. We lived in a small apartment in Philadelphia. My mother taught history in grammar school and then when I was about nine she went and got a Ph.D. so she could teach in college. She was immensely capable but very unhappy trying to maintain it all, a career and a family and deal with my father. He was a social worker, very demanding in that male way, and there was no money and it just dragged her down. She would come home exhausted and many days she would simply retreat to her bedroom and just lie there crying. I took care of my younger brother and made dinner and took on all those responsibilities. My mother felt that my father didn't carry enough weight, and her way of saying that was, 'Men are good for making babies and supporting them but after that it's yours.' But they were very intertwined, always yelling and carrying on. I have no idea what their sexual relationship was. I know they had to get married when she got pregnant with me because her puritanism would not let her do otherwise. I also think she loved him at that point but I don't know if she ever had an orgasm in her life. She certainly wouldn't tell me if she had."

Ah yes, the elusive female orgasm haunting our imaginations. There was so much sexual subtext rumbling through these childhoods of ours, unmistakable and covert all at the same time. Nobody was talking about it, but it was there. So that was the other thing we were going to demand, along with money and respect: our own sexual pleasure, and that resolve informed, I think, the tenacity with which we would later cling to our birth control and our sexual prerogatives at the cost of motherhood.

Something just felt elementally askew in those households, our households, where many of us found those years our fathers' and brothers' secreted stashes of *Playboy*s tucked in briefcases and desk drawers and slid under beds. What titillating queasiness they occasioned, those naked female bodies, our bodies-to-be, those great big, teasingly wholesome girls with their robust breasts and pointy nipples (pubic areas were still off limits). I remember vividly the sort of nauseated arousal with which I first beheld a centerfold, wondering what it all meant. The message was that sex for women somehow had to do with a kind of seductive passivity and that for men it was about voyeurism. Looking at those pictures, we weren't just confronting the bunnies themselves, but also the mental picture of our fathers looking at them, doing what, thinking what, wanting what, wanting, wanting out, wanting more, wanting to do to them what would later be done to us. It was palpable all that wanting: Mother wanting something more, Dad wanting something more, everyone wanting something more. This wasn't going to do for us fifties girls; we were going to have to change the equation even if it meant—in my case this took root way back then, I am now convinced—abstaining from motherhood because clearly that was where Mother got caught. We were the kidlets of doom, tying her by the apron strings to manifold tasks, keeping her not only from her own dreams, from making her own money to buy those dreams, but also from being one of those creamy centerfolds Dad so clearly wanted.

My MOTHER SAID she gulped when she first saw my father in civilian clothes, that he looked so young, so not-altogether-formed. They were already married by then and she had never seen him out of uniform. It was 1945. They had met two years earlier in New York as young actors in the play "Winged Victory," which would be my father's shining thespian moment. My mother was the only daughter of a screenwriter father and a somewhat sophisticated ingenue from Los Angeles, via the American Academy of Dramatic Arts in New York City, he a handsome baby-faced young man from a small town in the sooty industrial valley of Western Pennsylvania. A mismatch? Who's to say about them any more than about the other fifties parents, though their joint pursuit of success, even stardom, was certainly a rarity then, a foretaste of marriages to come.

But there was an imbalance, a sense of father-knows-best that rankled my equally hard-working mother. Glimpsed backward, it seems as if they had the toughest of both worlds: trying to balance ambitions within the fifties imbalance, the given fifties roles—like the one my mother herself portrayed up there beside Ray Milland—which doomed them to trouble right from the word go.

Neither childhood had been idyllic. My mother's mother had virtually abandoned her when she was five, running off to Europe with her second husband to cavort with the likes of the Duke and Duchess of Windsor, returning years later to be taken care of for the last twenty-five years of her life, which my mother dutifully did. A proud, spoiled Southern belle with a college degree and an unto-the-grave vanity and wit, my grandmother was clearly capable of lives she had not led, and the stories she told us upon her return from Europe affected my sister and me, invigorating whatever fledgling resolve we might have had in those early years to make something of ourselves. We did not want to end up like Grammie, on the daughterly dole with nothing more to show for her life than faded elegance and a pronounced martini habit.

My father's mother also served as a cautionary tale. His father, my grandfather, was a sweet-tempered civil and mining engineer who had been content to go day after day, year in and year out to the same second-story corner office in their small town and come home for meals. But his mother, also a college graduate, was full of angry, unrealized dreams. So much nagging disappointment coursed through their white clapboard house on the hill—I remember it from visits there as a small child—and indeed through her tall, wide-hipped body that she could literally laugh and cry at the same time, full tears and full laughter, as if all her feelings were crowded up there right at the surface and could not be differentiated. My father felt keenly the press of her longings and set out to satisfy them, as later I would set out to satisfy his.

It was a lot to carry out of a childhood—all those textured layers of thwarted dreams rumbling under the fifties patina—but a lot of us did it. In those manicured lives and choreographed marriages there was an often-pronounced loneliness, an emptiness that we would try to fill with our own accomplishments. And our role, the one we would have so much trouble trying to shed later, was simply to be the best little girls in the world, the high-achieving, make-no-waves, properly behaved little kittens ready to seduce our households into happiness. In effect we became the premature peacemakers, the family nurturers, the clowns, the cheerleaders, so many of us, and that, too, went into the non-motherhood mix. It was a weird inversion: infantilized in their circumscribed roles, our moms sometimes became the coquettish girls wheedling either money or tenderness or both out of Daddy, leaving us little girls to assume the adult role, looking after Mom, playing to Dad, smoothing the waters, dancing over their disappointments with our impish charm. Our brothers, on the other hand, if we had them, didn't have to do any of that, didn't have to concern themselves with the feelings of others. That was also a given. They were of the world and could get dirty, talk dirty and act out, within reason, pursuing their own goals or boyish dreams. But that was not our lot. We were the hothouse flowers of suburbia—Mother's little helpers, Dad's coy little kittens, hopping on his knee at day's end, making him laugh, making him proud with our report cards and clean fingernails—and I remember even as a diminutive five-year-old rattling around our big, old, cold-to-the-bone house in my nightly insomnia that the overwhelming feeling was one of trying to be something I was not, of enforced cheerfulness, enforced inauthenticity, of claustrophobia, of, dare I borrow the metaphor, being in the closet, which is why, I'm convinced looking back, I had a terror of actual closets or elevators or being in tight places. I already carried a kind of choking feeling with me and would scream frantically when I got accidentally shut in anywhere. When my sister and I once locked ourselves in the bathroom—I must have been five, she six—she had to forcibly restrain me from breaking the glass part of the door with my small, frantic fist, so desperate was I to get out.

I have a picture of my parents from a year or two after they were married. They are a very photogenic pair, my father tall and handsome, my mother small and blonde in a fur-trimmed coat. They look young but mature in the way young postwar parents looked. Their marriage would last eleven years and produce two children, my sister and me, and in the deconstruction and reconstruction of both of their lives there would be a lot of discordant and boozy melodrama. So this was one of those calm-before-the-storm photos, two people who look attractive and hopeful, poised for what happiness the world has in store for them. At least that's the way it's always looked to me all these years, even after I was aware that their union was difficult in many ways from the beginning—

fraught with fault lines—and this picture then was a best-foot-forward effort or maybe just one of those moments when they believed it might all work, that they might pull it off and have a rich, full life together. There is a certain sympathy in their posture; they look inclined toward each other.

By the time this photograph was taken—I can see sun and big old cars in the background—my parents had already moved to Los Angeles after "Winged Victory." My mother had not wanted to make the move. She wanted to stay in the East and have a go at a New York stage-acting life. She knew the vagaries of Hollywood, having grown up there with her father. But my father was insistent. The big studios still held sway then, and he was offered a contract with Metro Goldwyn Mayer. Over the next couple of years he would appear in a number of movies, (*Stalag 17,* with William Holden, *Father of the Bride,* in which he played Elizabeth Taylor's groom) and television shows, big-time stardom just always a little bit out of reach, while my mother, putting work aside, set about trying to get pregnant—a long ordeal that would prefigure mine some thirty-five years later. Operations and miscarriages and months in bed taking that pernicious DES, and finally she had two little girls who would, in due course, as she resumed her own acting career, appear beside her in those fan-magazine publicity spreads. On ponies, in straw hats, in starchy little white dresses, in blue-and-white-check bathing suits that matched our mom's—a sunburned trio—we were the stuff of someone's dreams, I suspect, someone out there envying our blonde, blue-eyed good fortune.

But if we were part of the pop culture pro-family propaganda, at home the real marriage was almost at end. My mother wanted out. My father was trying to keep her and in doing so, the larger-than-life, custodial maleness that he always carried flared explosively, pushing her even farther away and driving me, in the bedroom next to theirs, into the sheltered cubbyholes for my dolls and stuffed animals, among whom, night after night, I finally fell asleep listening to their loud anger. We moved out in 1955. I was five, my sister was six, and my mother was thirty-one. She would never marry again. There was nothing obdurate in her resolve, nothing overtly "feminist" in the sense we all came to understand it. The years went by, that's all. She never cast her personal story in political terms. She went about making money and making a life for the three of us. She did not take alimony, probably more out of guilt at having splintered the family than out of conviction. After all, divorce was uncommon in the 1950s. In a decade when 70 percent of American families were still intact, with a breadwinner dad and a stay-at-home mom and 3.2 kids, we were an anomaly, a bruised forerunner of things to come. Of course, the fifties themselves, with their tenacious grip on our fantasies of family life—fed in no small part by TV shows like my mother's—would turn out to be an anomaly, an aberrant time when marriage age dropped and the birth rate soared. Between 1940 and 1957, roughly the years my contemporaries were born, we of the so-called Sacrificial Generation, there was a breeding frenzy as the fertility rate actually increased 50 percent and one-third of American women had their first babies before they were twenty, a population growth nearing that of India's. Apparently the triple whammy of the Great Depression, the Second World War and subsequent Cold War with its threat of a nuclear finale and rot from within encouraged Americans to hunker in and celebrate hearth and home. That meant, among other things, a return to sharply etched male-female roles, which had been eroding in the twenties and thirties, a renewed effort to redignify American manhood and redomesticate or "contain" (that was the word used about communism: containment) the American female after her escape from the house into the wartime economy. We first-wave baby-boom women would be the bridge between the two manly decades, the 1950s and the 1980s, spawned by one, provocateurs in good measure of the other. Clinging to the pendulum, we would swing with the culture as it lurched from pro-family decade to pro-family decade with a sharp detour through the sixties and seventies, the heyday of liberation when we daughters of the fifties would infiltrate the work force again and dramatically postpone marriage and certainly motherhood. But during the fifties, most women were at home and most families were intact, meaning that my sister and I were more decisively outside the happy family dream, even as our very own mother was up there on the screen portraying one of those yummily wholesome sitcom wives. I learned the lesson early: Things were not as they appeared in the swell houses of suburbia.

It was my father who stayed in the big, old mock-Tudor house near the ocean in Santa Monica we had shared, nursing his broken heart and waiting for work. It was odd seeing such a large, demonstrative man so doubled-up, so silenced by loss, odd and, I suppose, instructive, my first inkling of a symmetry between the sexes, my first intimation that men were as hurtable underneath it all as any female. We watched him, my sister and I, when we were dropped off there on the weekends, stricken by the sadness our absence and our mother's absence seemed to be causing him. We were lucky in one major way. My parents, when it came down to it, divorced with a rare grace and we were never batted around between them or made pawns in any leftover business of theirs. We were shuttled back and forth from house to house with relative ease on everyone's part, carrying no coded messages between the adults. Nonetheless, the dissolution of our family was not easy. On our visits my father, still in his terry-cloth bathrobe, perennially between engagements, would sit for hours, it seemed, in his upstairs study while we tiptoed around the big, empty house that was no longer home. Then he would come to and off we'd go to Sears to buy tools and eat hot dogs. He was large in sorrow as in everything. But our own sadness, my sister's and mine—certainly mine—at the turn of events was mixed with relief. The anger had stopped. He married again eight years later, finding a good measure of happiness if not exactly peace. And in our turn, or so it now seems to me, my sister and I would push off in effect, like our mother before us, against his maleness, his complicated, not-altogether-realized dreams and oversized anguish, finding pockets of deep tenderness beneath the bluster—like swimming into a wonderfully warm spot in a lake. The love was never in question; he held on to us post-divorce with rare paternal tenacity. But the way it played itself out sometimes was, what I heard from other daughters of the fifties who felt either cuffed about by or put down by or somehow cut off from paternal love, by demeaning quips or off-color jokes or the simple assumption on the part of these men that they were a superior sex and destined by God to be in charge. My father carried about him a sense of male destiny, that he was part of a world order, a functioning, achievement-oriented world order that was beyond the female scope. He didn't mean it meanly. It was just part of the time and place, his legacy, reenforced by everything around him. These fathers were not all ogres or jerks. What they often were were men without the habit of kindness, men weaned on the notion of male dominance. Some would later make journeys toward some sense of mutuality with women and tenderness toward them, prompted either by those daughters—who had made their own journeys by that point toward self-assertion—or often by a younger second wife. But back in the fifties they formed a kind of remote and formidable short-haired brigade. Notable to us small, impressionable girls was the way they dealt with working women—secretaries, waitresses, maids in hotels, the big-voiced, patronizing expectation of service that made us squirm with identification and embarrassment. Do this, get me that. And yet what we did in answer to them, ironically, or maybe not so ironically, was to switch allegiance, just as Jane said, jump ship, jump genders and go over to our fathers. That's when we began to identify with the aggressor, all the way back then. That's what we did and who wouldn't have done it? Not that any of it was conscious; back then, when we were children, none of it was. You were little, female, hopeful. You watched and you saw what happened and in the accumulation of episodes you saw the pattern: Daddy ruled the roost, called the shots, made the money, made the decisions, so you signed up on his side, and fifteen years later when the women's movement came along with its incendiary manifestos telling you to avoid marriage and motherhood, it was as if somebody put a match to a pile of dry kindling.

But it came at cost, our baby-faced resolve. Very early we parted sympathy, it seems looking back, with our own sex, with our own mothers on some level, and therefore with a part of ourselves, the mothering part, precisely what made us both receptive to feminism with its adamant anti-maternalisms and later to the reactive pro-family pendulum swing. I don't like to use "pro-family" because it somehow belongs to those on the right. Let's just call what happened in the eighties the reclamation of motherhood, and it was done, yes, with the gleeful urgings of the backlash brigade who blanketed the eighties with their pro-family propaganda, but also by women I knew and loved, hard-driving women with major careers who were after not just babies per se or motherhood per se, but after a reconciliation with their memories of their own mothers. So having a baby wasn't just having a baby. It became a major healing. That is part of the reason I felt so bereft when pregnancy continued to elude me. I was denied that particular kind of healing, and so set me out on this literary kind instead.

I remembered something a friend had said to me a few years earlier, a great, big garrulous woman, Julie Templeton, who was a talk-show host when I was a green reporter back in the mid-seventies. I adored her on sight, she seemed so out-front, so adamantly single and childless, possessed of a brightly colored, hippie chic. Her parents also had divorced early, her attractive ad man dad moving out of their Brooklyn apartment and into Manhattan, leaving her and her wildly embittered mom to tough it out alone. Periodically she would be dressed up and sent into the city to get money out of him, and they'd do the town and stay in a fancy hotel and then she'd go home and, as she described it, turn back into a pumpkin.

"You have to understand," she had told me when we talked about it, "I made up my mind right then when I was nine or ten, whatever it was, that I would never, ever have to ask a man for money. But you also have to understand that it was my mom I hated for putting me in that position and I just never wanted to get stuck with a baby to support and no man and no money. And then later, way later, when my mom was old and moved out here to be near me, and we became friends finally, I was divorced and it was too late to have a baby, and I think we both regretted it because it was something we were finally ready to share."

It was that I remembered, that something-to-share part. That's what I was after, I realized: a way back. That's what the elusive baby somehow promised, a way finally to heal the childhood wounds, come full circle, be reconciled to one's own sex, to mothers and motherhood. It would be a long road back for many of us because as we left the 1950s, we young girls, we pampered suburban kittens, we did so with the pronounced beginnings of ambivalence, not just a love-hate relationship with men, or maybe it was more envy-anger in many cases, but a love-hate relationship with our own sex, the limitations and constraints implied by it. There were the clearly telegraphed messages: that sex and motherhood were contradictory, that a woman had to choose between one or the other, between husband and children, between passion and procreation—there was your mom and there were the beckoning bunnies hiding under your father's bed, or perhaps the girl in town—and finally between all of that, between family and yourself or your work. That was the message I certainly picked up as we sailed out into the new world, a blonde threesome, my mother, my sister and I, borne out on a wave of recriminations and hope, and I watched her increasingly struggle with making a living at her chosen craft of acting. Adolescence would only intensify my sense of being divided against myself, as it would for many of my fifties sisters. We had miles to go before the sexual revolution and the women's movement offered their healing balm—even though that balm would, in effect, compound the ambivalence first—and miles more, in many cases, until good therapy and decent relationships augmented that healing even further. Meanwhile we moved on into the 1960s with the traditional notion of a woman's domestic role still pretty much extant while within our prepubescent psyches roiled around that chorus of female disappointments that extended back through our mothers and grandmothers and their grandmothers, and which many of us were determined, in our pre-articulated, pre-feminist resolve, to try to redress. So had begun, I could see now, my journey away from motherhood, begun ironically in the decade that would be known as "The Golden Age of Families."

A GIFT?

A GIFT it will be. There was never any question that I would fall by the wayside, not yet, for surely I can do no less than my mother did all those years ago. Surely we are women of the same tenacious fiber, my brave, intrepid mother sailing out into the world with two little girls to make a life alone long before that was routinely done. Surely I am her daughter, and my sister's sister, for she too had a pregnancy ordeal, and will avail myself of all the high-tech tricks before I am done trying to have a baby. I am fated to go forward and am now strangely relieved to arrive finally in the full-blown arms of manipulative breeding. No more halfway measures, no more inseminations, no more reluctant eggs hugging my smarting ovaries. This is the big time, the three-ring circus of conception, and I am now, recovered from all those failed inseminations, an eager acrobat, ready to go the distance. Now it's time for the GIFT, the latest best hope of the wizards. The procedure involves out-patient surgery done through a laparoscope—a long seeing-eye instrument inserted into the abdomen through a slit at the base of the navel. Minor surgery in that sense, but surgery nonetheless, replete with general anesthetic and price tag of $8,000. Through that small slit in the belly button, my eggs will be retrieved and, via a catheter, put immediately back into the top of my fallopian tubes along with my husband's sperm, therein to do, God willing, their fertilizing dance.

The thinking behind it is simple: Since normally fertilization takes place in the tubes, why not approximate that as closely as possible? This is the closest to nature the wizards can get, and I am excited to have arrived at this point. First done in 1984, GIFT is still fairly newborn. This year of 1988, only 3,080 have been done nationwide (resulting in 654 actual babies) so I am indeed a guinea pig, or, as on one of my better days I cast it, a procreative pioneer operating out in some brave, new baby-making world where everything is new and untried. I am excited to be plowing down this new road, all my previous failures momentarily forgotten. The more invasive GIFT so far is showing a better success rate than straight IVF (in which eggs and sperm are left to fertilize outside the body, the resultant embryos inseminated back into the uterus twenty-four to forty-eight hours later). Dr. Marrs, for example, whose numbers tend to com-

pare favorably with the best clinics around the country, has a 23 percent
live birth rate per GIFT procedure as compared to 10 percent for IVF
(for women over forty, the numbers drop to 19 percent for a GIFT, a
paltry 8 percent for an IVF). The chance for twins with IVF is 15 percent,
with GIFT, 18 percent. To talk to infertile women about the scary
prospects of multiple births is like telling a man in the desert that too
much water might suddenly spout from some given oasis. We will gladly
court the risk of twins or triplets—there's slightly less than a 1 percent
chance of those with either procedure—or quads or quints, knowing also
that there is something called "selective abortion" available (not the
loveliest of phrases, I grant you) in which some of the embryos can be,
as it says, selectively terminated in utero. But the prospect of too many
babies is nothing compared to the prospect of too few, make that: none.

The process begins the same way as the insemination cycle. Sonograms
and shots, sonograms and shots—for me, three vials of Pergonal a day
starting on day two (day one is the first day you bleed). I am now up to
$150 a day plus $50 for every sonogram, and as the days go along, my
shot-giving gets worse not better. I grow squeamish and inept as the days
pass, raising little bruises right and left until my hips look like some
half-baked tattooer ran amok over them. Finally I surrender the task first
to my husband, but not wishing to take my wrath out on him, I enlist my
intrepid friend from up the block, another veteran of the infertility wars,
and she is quick and unhesitant, rarely drawing a wince or spurt of blood.
The process makes a bit of a mockery of any emotional steadiness and
toys with one's optimism. Nevertheless, I surrender to the drugs unresist-
ingly, hopefully, determinedly, teetering all the time on a kind of hyper,
volatile edge. By day nine, ten, eleven, I am going to the clinic every other
day for blood tests and sonograms. I am tethered to it by an invisible
umbilical thread of hope. The monitoring this time is much more intense,
since more is at stake. With surgery looming and a certain do-or-die
quality to these high-tech attempts, the whole process is more intense,
and we women going through them are ourselves more intense, giddier,
a little more wild-eyed than the others as we await our turns in the
stirrups. One doesn't want to bomb out of this process by having inade-
quate hormone levels or too few eggs—they won't go in after them unless
you have at least four, preferably more—or by ovulating prematurely and
blowing the whole thing so that every new sonogram or blood test is a

hurdle to be gotten over. So far things are looking good. I am showing eight follicles of roughly the same size—which is important, that they ripen at the same rate—and with luck at least five or six of the eggs will make it to full maturity. All systems are go and I keep jabbing away, three shots a day now, my entire life otherwise on hold, in hock to this quest. I have never known anything like this, so consuming, so derailing. Work has been like that at times. Love has, the swimmy self-absorption that comes with intense emotion. But this is an even more primal absorption, a complete physiological and psychological stranglehold. I feel for days as if I've been swallowed by my own body and am peering out at the world through my own womb. I live in a hyper-stimulated closet of longing, my mood lurching between hope and despair within days, hours, minutes, moments, and I realize I am the life-making analog to someone, say, making regular visits to a clinic for radiation or chemotherapy.

In fact, the husband of a close friend is doing that and at the end of the day, over a glass of wine, she and I compare the tenor of the respective waiting rooms: the faces of the patients, their demeanors and body language—the slump, the smile, the pallor, the pain—and the perverse symmetry of hope that haunts those who are trying to make a life or to preserve one. I try to cheer her up, she tries to cheer me up. A few years older than I, she, too, married an older man with children and has none of her own, but reminds me that a few years before, when her husband had prostate surgery, he put away some frozen sperm in case she wanted to have a baby. Much ado about sperm—at least we are able to laugh at that. But she has a long, dark road ahead and we know it. There will be time enough after that to decide whether or not to use that sperm. That's the world we live in now, she and I, one where even posthumous procreation is possible, and we shiver and giggle at the thought. So far, apparently, no one has actually done this: avail themselves of their dead spouse's sperm. No doubt it will happen.

D-Day nears. I am given my last shot, the hCG, on a Friday, and on Sunday morning my husband and I dutifully arrive at the hospital in downtown LA at seven. It is fall but I realize as I sign in and hand over my $1,450 for the hospital and $650 for the anesthesiologist—I have already written checks totaling close to $5,000 to Dr. Marrs, everything payable up front, before they'll touch you in the operating room—that I have not noticed the season at all, any of the seasons over the past six or more months. I am skimming through them, living on top of the weather, unattached, unmoored from all physical sensations save that of my immediate body. I sometimes find myself out and about ill equipped for the weather at hand—a T-shirt in the rain, a heavy sweater when the hot Santa Ana winds blow—so oblivious am I. All other hungers are on hold, the hunger for food or warmth or work or sex, beside the hunger for a baby. My husband gives me a hug and goes off to give his sperm sample and I go off and get ready for surgery. Strip down, put on gown and paper cap and booties—hardly the garb for a sexual encounter. Hardly the way to get pregnant. Oh, but I am far from home, from the comfort of my conjugal bed, and I smile at all the years, all the passionate and contested years in that bed. It's been a long road to this hospital cot where I now lie trying to consummate our long union.

An icy sensation shivers through the IV and up into my arm and I am out cold, awakening in the recovery room, I gather from looking at the clock, a couple of hours later feeling groggy and punched in the belly. I am sore all over, my shoulder and neck ache from the gas that has been pumped into my abdomen in order for the doctor to have easier access to my fallopian tubes. He comes by, boyish and soft-voiced as always. It's the good news, bad news joke. He has retrieved eight eggs and put three of them back in one of my tubes, the only good one, as it turns out. I have more scar tissue and adhesions everywhere and my left tube is once again bound down and inaccessible as it was before the "corrective" surgery I had in 1985, surgery, he explains, which probably left me with more scarring than I had going in. Terrific. Medical science once more making things worse. I groan inwardly—how many times will this card be played? The surgery I had is now routinely done through a laser procedure, which is much less invasive, less costly and less inclined to leave one scarred. I missed it by a year or two. What can I say; who can I rail at? I took my chances and am now irrefutably a one-tube woman. But that's good enough, the doctor gently assures me, though I realize my odds for pregnancy have now been reduced. Nothing I didn't somehow suspect. But the four eggs are in the other tube, the sperm swimming in there with them, and I must bring good will to their meeting, remembering in my fog that my mother conceived with only one ovary and one tube. Perhaps I will follow in her footsteps.

The two weeks that follow are useless. I give over to the watch. I am constantly running my hands over my belly and breasts, taking the measure of their roundness—are they swelling with life?—knowing on one level that my vigil is absurd. What's done is done. What's there is there. Who's there is there . . . or isn't there. But once again I cannot detach. I have a blood test seven days in, which looks fine—the hormones continue to be appropriately rising—and then begin the agonizingly slow day-by-day crawl to the pregnancy test seven more days down the road. I pray, I make bargains, I send up more mea culpas to anyone and everyone, those station-wagon moms again and the moms in the neighborhood, not the suburban wives like me, but the other mothers, the Latina women who leave their own babies on the other side of town—or, for that matter, all the way back in their own countries—to come look after the babies on mine. Tender of tummy and hobbled of ambition, incapable of any serious work, I sit many an afternoon on the front stoop, waiting for their parade, the dark-eyed women pushing the towheads up my pricey, tree-lined street, chatting in their easy, soft tongue. Motherhood in the neighborhood. I want no part of it. I want every part of it.

But once again it is not to be. I don't even make it to the pregnancy test, spotting by day thirteen, hanging over the toilet bowl and willing away the blood even as it falls. Stop, don't come, don't continue. But there is no gift here and I curl up around my drug-bloated abdomen.

Would that the hunger would go away, that I could somehow come to my senses, get off the track, but in fact it's the opposite: The baby hunger grows as it is thwarted. Of the five other eggs he retrieved this time, only one fertilized, but did not go on dividing—not an auspicious indicator of the quality of my eggs. He thinks all that PCOD business is implicated. I can make lots of eggs, but not necessarily good, mature ones. Nevertheless, I know I will plow ahead as soon as possible. Another GIFT perhaps. The doctor assures me that it could still work, though out beyond three attempts the returns make no sense. I am nearing my thirty-ninth birthday and am fully aware that after age forty, the odds get even worse. A do-or-die upcoming year then. As I lie in the yard recovering from the failed attempt, life-size menstrual cramps washing over my body from head to toe and back again, the thin sunshine of late autumn in Southern California whispering over the pain, I think of timing, of history, of the years I have been on the earth, the marvels and perils of technology. If all this wasn't available to me, this weight of technology, could I just turn around and get on with my life? Must I avail myself of it, of this revolution in conception, just as years earlier I eagerly availed myself of the revolution in contraception—an adolescent beach bunny longing for love and swallowing birth control pills with mindless diligence? I have been twice cursed and blessed, and lying here, the cramps easing up finally under the onslaught of painkillers, I remember those sensual sunny Southern California days, circa 1966. We baked away many a summer afternoon, my adolescent girlfriends and I, greased up on our towels, rotating our bodies for even brownness like birds on a spit, our sharp hipbones jutting up into the cloudless sky. Coppertone filled the air and the Rolling Stones growled sexily on our transistors as we pondered life and love, not knowing at that point that we were destined to be the eager sacrificial virgins of the sexual revolution then breaking out all over America. The prissy postwar fifties were over; the sixties were beginning.

6

NOT QUITE THE SIXTIES

The sixties weren't really the sixties for a long time, certainly not for those of us who were still young girls as the decade began. But indeed something did happen in 1960 that set the decade in motion, something that would dramatically change my life and that of every other woman. Of course I didn't know it then. I was still too young to get it, to understand what the introduction of the birth control pill would mean for all of us and for the culture at large. It was the bomb, or certainly one of the bombs, that was going to blow the fifties nuclear nest to smithereens and would decisively aid and abet my journey—many of our journeys—away from motherhood. And it was making its appearance, poetically enough, the same year John F. Kennedy won the presidency.

What a potent, sexy combo—the charismatic young president with his beautiful wife and, for the first time in history, female contraception that was virtually 100 percent effective if used right. Here was the means of escape from our mothers' destinies. Again, none of this was articulated then by those of us who were still relatively young girls in the beginning of the decade. Certainly I, for one, was unconscious of the great shift that had taken place in my own destiny with the advent of that pill, though I would be ingesting it nightly by decade's end along with 10 million other American women. But in 1960 I was still only on the cusp of adolescence, filled with hero worship for the young president, a kind of puppy crush. What we didn't know, what few knew except for a few male cronies and followers of the Kennedys, was that for all his seeming modernity, this president was the quintessential fifties male, fifties Catholic male with a pronounced whore-madonna complex—there were women you wed and women you bedded—so that he was as much a throwback as a new beginning, more so, as was his martyred, cheated-on and ultimately widowed young bride. But at the time they seemed dreamy, delicious, beautiful—the ideal couple to preside over the swinging new decade the pill was ushering in. By the year of the pill and Kennedy's election, one out of three American wives was already in the work force, the divorce rates were already creeping up—my own mother was less and less an aberration—and rock and roll was certainly thumping through the culture. Elvis, in fact, had been doing his seditiously sensual thing since the mid-fifties, offering us a hip-swiveling counterpoint to the sitcom niceties. Here was something to pierce our good-girl armor. I do remember watching mesmerized as he strutted his stuff on *The Ed Sullivan Show.*

But for the most part, for those of us turning into the 1960s, as preadolescents, the message about women and their place in the world was pretty much the same old fifties message: Women were clean and pure and loving homebodies who were supposed to hold on to their virginity until marriage and thereafter tend children and husbands. That was to be our lot, and our education, both formal and informal, continued to push us in that direction, even as that seldom-discussed but always-under-there current of sexuality—the bunnies, the Beats, the rock and rollers—increasingly smoldered through the culture. But down the corridors of my preteen years, the word I remember hearing the most was "hush" or some variation on it, a quashing chorus of "shhs" that inevitably greeted one of my characteristically high-decibel riffs on the world and served to intensify my feeling of choking. Diminutive, as I would be until my last years of high school, alternately shy and outspoken, I had a sharp eye, a sharp tongue (I had already gotten the message loud and clear: that things were not what they seemed, that all the nicey niceness of my suburban world was a bit of canard) and a high-decibel delivery for someone so little, which sometimes met with amusement on the part of the adults, but more often seemed to bring forth that dreaded "shh." By this time we were a firmly established female household, living in a succession of rental houses near the ocean. There was my mother, my sister and I, and Nana, the tough Swedish woman who'd been living with us and scrubbing behind our ears since we were two and three. She had with us a very resolute hand, not unloving, but emphatic, which, by the time we were eight or nine, had already worked its molding magic. We were upstanding citizens, diligent students and more: perfectly socialized little females, the best little girls in the world. And this in a household of women. There was no daddy to mind. But we had our substitute in effect, our Nana in her white uniform, object of so much love and so much fear, the stanchion in our disrupted childhood. She used to tell us that she had eyes in the back of her head. So we could never, no matter where we were in a room, escape her appraising gaze. The idea was that we would behave in a decorous, feminine way at all times, that our nails, indeed our entire beings including our vocabularies, would be scrubbed and clean. She once actually washed my mouth out with soap because I had said a supposedly bad word. Whatever it was, it would have been inadvertent, child's play, certainly not something said in anger or rebellion. Yet she grabbed me and whisked me off to scrub my mouth, filling my small soul with a sudsy rage memorable still after thirty-odd years.

I did not react at the time (the women's movement, when it came, would feel like the culmination of a fifteen-year delayed take). That would have been unthinkable since it was also against her firm bosom that I often sought solace from the world's injustices, even as she, or so it certainly seemed to me, occasionally meted them out herself. Nor did I go off to my mother seeking redress. That too would have been unthinkable. We were not to cause trouble; there had been trouble enough in our family already. That was clear. My mother was working and invariably picking up the pieces of some romance or another and she was not to be tattled to or embroiled in our daily domestic dramas. As I saw it, my job with her, as with my heart-stung father, was to go on being a pint-sized cheerleader, a soother of wounds. Which is not to say she didn't adore us—and motherhood, for that matter. She did. She made no secret of it and was outspoken in her pleasure at our company. On weekend mornings we took refuge—my mother, my sister and I—in dressing-room cubicles and at drugstore cosmetic counters where my mother sought to put a shiny new spin on our common lot. Hair dyes and half slips and lipstick. I loved watching her go through the beauty rituals, blotting her lips and buttoning up dresses and sniffing appraisingly at her perfumed wrist, my valiant, my beautiful, my ever-so-tan and ever-so-divorced mother.

But our daily management clearly belonged to Nana. It was she who was in charge of us. She was our surrogate, the schoolmarm and principal and Sunday school teacher all rolled into one—a woman who loved us but existed to tame us, muffle us, mold us and, above all, keep us clean in body and soul.

There was that residual part of me still alive, though, still chafing against Nana's dictates and the dictates of socially correct female behavior, a tomboyish part, if you will, a word I have heard time and again from my contemporaries. Tomboy. I was a tomboy. And that's because any freedom, any physical freedom or chance to get mussed up we identified with the opposite sex. Late afternoons in our Santa Monica neighborhood full of two-story Spanish houses and intact families, my sister and I would canter around in the enlivening chill in our plaid shorts and cotton blouses, faces flushed with exercise and exuberance, a "boyish" part of us girded for fun and combat. In an unwieldy mixed-sex pack, we boys and girls roamed the streets and vacant lots, playing fierce games of tag or, in semi-careful warfare, lobbing dirt clods at each other. This was OK, we were more or less given to understand, as a vestige of childhood, though we were scrubbed from head to toe in the aftermath. But such hooligan behavior was certainly not part of the repertoire of the young ladies into which we were being transformed.

Years later, Harvard professor of education Carol Gilligan would put together a book, *Making Connections,* about adolescence in which she would talk about the bustling confidence of young girls, eleven- and twelve-year-olds (and not children of the fifties, mind you, but girls of the late eighties), about how they were up front and full of self-assertion and self-esteem, qualities that started to erode once they crossed the Rubicon of puberty, once they got it that the world was of men's making and taking so that they were in effect left out of the major equation, taken less seriously. Their response was to hide, bury a part of themselves, lose their footing so that by sixteen or seventeen, their sureties of self had dissolved into confusion.

I do remember feeling like that, feeling at war with myself as I slid further toward and into adolescence, because I didn't know what to do with all the zest that seized me on those afternoons, a buoyant, careless, fly-in-the-face-of-the-wind joy that, once allowed, had subsequently been deemed improper, in part because it was laced with a dangerously prema-ture sexual energy. That was the implication though no one said it directly. And I did what so many young women apparently did, and do, for that matter, if Gilligan's study is right—and my own informal one, for that matter—I turned inward, lost part of my sense of assertion. Nana, in effect, became my internalized superego and I directed my energies to-ward socially sanctioned feminine achievement, that is, good report cards and proper deportment. Like so many women I know and have talked to, I sabotaged my irreverence and creativity way back then, so that it would take me many years to tap back into that early unalloyed aliveness, many years to feel free, free as a writer, just free in general, unhindered by the expectations of the world at large, all those expectations of correct female behavior (even the later expectations of correct feminist female behavior).

I did kick. We all kicked some in those years, had our little stubborn moments of rebellion, the last hurrah before being damped down. I vividly remember the triumphant queasiness my own rebellious moments sent through my prepubescent soul. In my eighth-grade year at a private school in the foothills of Bel Air, the same year, in fact, of the Cuban missile crisis, I alone, in a class of maybe ten other girls, refused to run for May Queen. To this day I don't know what truly prompted me to resist. Fear of not being elected as my year-older sister had been the year before? Was it that, the unwillingness to match myself against both her and my mother, beauties both, I thought, beside whom I felt decidedly small and scrawny with my dutch bob and emphatically flat chest? Was I rejecting the whole glamorous Hollywood world in which my mother was increasingly struggling to make a living, after her successful sitcom days, rejecting the whole beauty tyranny that women suffered from? That's to credit me, I feel certain, with way too much conscious thought. My decision was reflexive; I did not want to be matched up against my friends. I just said no that day when they called for us to sign up and was as abashed at myself as the homeroom teacher, who immediately marched me across the well-manicured lawn in my little navy blue pinafore to the principal's office, a patrician-looking woman in her sixties whom we all called Aunty Cathryn. She was not pleased. I had never, in five years at the school, caused the slightest stir, done anything that was not absolutely by the book, but now I dug in. I remember a cool chill up the back of my neck as she lectured me. This was a lovely ceremony, she said, time-honored. What could I mean by my refusal to participate? What indeed? All I knew was that I could not do it, and a film of defiance settled over me; I will remember that feeling all my life for the newness of it, the unexpected thrill of resistance. My mother thought I was making a big deal out of the whole thing, but she did not try to talk me out of my position, and that was that until the end of the year when I did not receive the school's big award, the one they gave to the outstanding pupil/ exemplar of the school's spirit, an award that I probably assumed would be mine given my good grades and all of my basic obedience. But no, I had stepped out of the chorus line for a minute and would be penalized. I did not win. Arriving home with my diploma, I flung myself on my small canopy bed and wept at the injustice of it all, at what my self had wrought,

not with regret but with angry resignation. So this is the way it works;
so be it. But for the most part, for the foreseeable years, I simply fell back
into line, balking only occasionally and really quite mildly at the prevailing
strictures.

The fondness mid-life women have for their first moments of resistance is amazing to behold. The years drop away and a girlish bravado
takes over as they remember, something altogether different, more virginal than the hard-won competence and independence that characterize
many of their adult lives. I saw it time and again as I talked to my
fortysomething friends and other women—a private elation at a remembered moment of early assertion or affront given the world. Ah yes, so
that's who I was way back then. That was in there, that chutzpah, that
irreverence, even then. Girls sneaking off and having their ears pierced—
that was a big one, daring but ultimately not too punishable; girls suddenly
balking at taking a given test, deliberately flunking; girls daring to speak
up to fathers for the first time. For my friend Jane, growing up in that big
house on the Hudson, rebellion came in her refusal to go to church with
the family when she was twelve. She simply decided one spring Sunday,
as she told it to me, that she had had enough of the hypocritical happy
family picture her parents, particularly her mother, was intent on present-
ing to the world.

"I was all dressed up and scrubbed and ready to go and I said to my
parents: 'I'm not going.' They were shocked. My mother got very upset
and tried to talk me out of it—no one was going to hit me or anything—
but I was adamant. I announced that I felt God was in the garden and
that's where I was going to be. I know I hurt my mom—to her our church
appearance was vindication of a hard week's work—but I guess I meant
to. I wanted my distance from all that she represented. Meanwhile I
continued to do all these things to please my father, the sports, the grades.
My achievement was also hard on my mother. She was jealous of it and
resentful. She was always saying, 'I wish I could read as much as you'—I
read voraciously from early on—and she was always making me feel like
I had to apologize for succeeding. And I know, in my compassionate
moments, that she was just lonesome, afraid that I was getting away from
her, ahead of her and siding with my father, which, of course, is exactly
what I was doing."

That's what we were trying to do, all right, elude our mothers' fates, sometimes wounding them unwittingly in the bargain, getting it all turned around. I did it, reading voraciously and making surrogate mothers of my teachers in an effort to carve myself out a new life, a new female space, where my frantic articulateness would be rewarded and I would be taken seriously. As we got older and closer to hard-core adolescence, the tougher it got and the more torn we got, the more conflicted about achievement. What good was it, after all? What were you going to do with it? What was your future—a home, some babies and a husband with a Playboy Bunny habit of his own? Or if you did plow on trying to succeed, you risked losing the love of those you bested, be they mothers or friends or boyfriends. We were certainly being warned about that, big time, about the delicate egos of men. You couldn't go plowing into their self-esteem with your smarts. No, best to keep your brain under wraps and your girlishness out front. A typical article in *Seventeen* magazine, which I was dutifully reading as a preteen, this one circa 1962, warned us not to beat boys at sports. "Fellows like girls who can play tennis or ice skate, or swim or climb rocks, or walk or paddle or toss a football . . . a little," a young man wrote in the "From a Boy's Point of View" column. "Of course, it's not considered good form by anybody but her coach for a girl to beat her guy at tennis or swim him out so far that she has to bring him back under her arm—that kind of thing could upset our whole social order, as well as upset a fellow's natural pride." Call it managed competition, call it choking another part of yourself off. Call it maddening. But we did it, we learned to tiptoe around the egos of the young male inheritors of the earth.

From fathers, too, came the same lesson. As a friend of mine, a high-powered entertainment lawyer who came late to motherhood, said to me: "My father was always telling me, 'Boys don't like smart girls, so keep your mouth shut.' I believed him. I was filled with self-loathing but I was determined. I was such a talented, bright young person, but I had to scratch and crawl for everything I got. And, of course, my brother was the prince who could do no wrong."

These brothers loom. I didn't have one, but the sixties girls who did, viscerally remember the disparity, the encouragement given to brothers, the perks, the preferences. I heard numbers of stories about IQ tests— girls wanting to find out their scores, wondering if they were smarter than their brothers. "I just know mine was higher than my older brother's and that's why my father wouldn't tell me, I just know it," a dark-eyed, fragile-looking mother of three told me. "After all these years I can still hate him for it, for not telling me."

Another friend remembers throwing a full-out tantrum—her first act of family rebellion—when her father refused to take her to a baseball game when she was around ten. "He was taking my two brothers but not me and I was crying and screaming and saying, 'But why not, why not me, why shouldn't I go, too?' My mother tried to distract me, we would do our own female thing, but I held on, absolutely adamant. I see myself sitting on those stairs, this ugly worn green carpet, and just raging on and crying until he relented. I didn't want to do the female thing with my mother; I wanted to do the male thing with the boys."

That's what we wanted, all right, but then into our already-conflicted adolescent lives came the harbinger of our female fate, menstruation, brazenly announcing that all our intentions to the contrary, we were indeed our mothers' daughters, destined to follow in their footsteps. Here was the bloody proof that we were inescapably female after all. So much for identifying with the aggressor. Like most of my friends, I vividly remember the day I first bled—such an odd introduction to one's fate, really, blood, the sign heretofore only of a wound. It was summer and I had been asked by one of the pretty "fast" girls in my class to a beach club. I was small enough and fast enough on my feet, or with my mouth, that I could cross into the ranks of the popular even though I was seriously studious. I went that day, the thick pad chafing under my none-too-scanty, two-piece bathing suit, shyly but proudly mumbling: "I can't swim, I have my period."

For those of us coming of age in those first years of the 1960s, menstruation came not only with the reiterated recognition of one's otherness, which meant secondariness, but also with all the old prohibitions against sex. If the times they were indeed a changin', or beginning to change, many of us teenage girls in the early sixties were still very virginal, still supposed to regard boys as the sticky-fingered enemy who might try to get at us, stir us up and pry us open, might try to get to first base (a kiss), second base (touching above the waist), third base (touching below) or even slide home (intercourse). It was incumbent upon us to resist, deflect their approaches, stay chaste and pure, which I adamantly did, doing no more than exchanging a few grudging, tight-lipped kisses with boys who had taken me to dances. So again it all had the feeling of stuffing part of yourself down. It was another form of "shh." No wonder we exploded later.

By the time puberty hit, my sister and I were ensconced at the Westlake School for Girls, then a sprawl of comfortable old Spanish buildings in the foothills of West Los Angeles. It felt safe, incubative, a place to compete with other women, to achieve without remorse—even at boy things, at math and science—and not worry about being popular with boys. As girls we were being imbued with a heady sense of tempered outspokenness. I say "tempered" because there was still the sense that we had to toe certain lines, behave in decorous ways, even as we were certainly goaded to exercise our intellectual gifts, such as they were.

I took another rebellious shot my first year there, 1963, as a still tiny, bobbed ninth-grader. I submitted a love poem to the school literary magazine about a white girl and a black boy being forced apart "by those all-knowing people, those omnipotent bodies of society, who would not let me be of him or him of me." It was wrought, precocious, an object totally of my inflamed imagination and of being peripherally aware of the burgeoning civil rights movement. From the safety of our white suburbs we sixties girls looked across a racial and sexual divide at the black world with both longing and guilt. That's where the women lived who came to do the laundry, or sometimes to live in our houses, carrying with them an aura of a different world, harder, jazzier, sexier, the world where the music came from, Little Richard and Chuck Berry and all those thumping rhythms that made such an odd counterpoint to our relatively prim upbringings. It was the world Hattie came from, the big, vibrant black woman who came to stay when Nana left, Nana with her austere Scandinavian love. What a contrast Hattie was, spirited and enveloping, teaching me to make lemon meringue pies and letting me lie curled up beside her in the little downstairs bedroom where we fell asleep listening to the Dodger games on her portable radio. Six months of lying nightly beside her big, burnished body, taking in the miraculous warmth, and then she was gone, shot to death one Saturday by her ex-husband when she went home to Pasadena for the weekend. I think my poem, written a couple of years later, was an epitaph for Hattie, for my feeling forcibly wrenched from her—my first major loss—for I knew not a whit about romance, interracial or otherwise.

After much ado and much lobbying on my behalf by my sister students, the poem was rejected by the powers that be, the tough old ladies that ran the academy. Once again I was somewhat abashed at the stir I had caused—obedient straight-A student that I was—but secretly pleased. I was trying to carve out some place for myself, some voice, cause some trouble even as, especially as, we were dutifully plowing, at that point, through the male literary canon, the canon of high male romance, of Hemingway and Fitzgerald. Men were the writers, the world travelers, the moralists and dreamers who could put an elegantly tight-lipped spin on their monstrous male sentimentality, leaving women authors, it seemed, in the sweet domestic dust to write about tea parties and village romances. I didn't want to be left there, left behind, left out of the equation. On some level I guess I was already fancying myself as a writer, a protester, however sheltered and naive.

All over the country, as it would turn out, young girls like me, well-behaved, high-achieving fifties children turned sixties kids, were being unwittingly groomed for the cadres of the upcoming revolutions, particularly the feminist revolution, though certainly none of us knew it then. Women's lib was not something I was truly conscious of until I graduated in 1967, but I did know, from watching my mother, that I would have to take on the world in some capacity as she had done. There were no guarantees. Marriage didn't last and love was treacherous and you had to be prepared to look out for yourself. That was the message. I had watched my mother, determinedly and bravely independent, buying and selling houses and intrepidly moving us around as fortunes rose and fell, fall in love or certainly in thrall to men who wreaked havoc with her heart. Front-lawn dramas full of threats and tears had reached my adolescent ears on many a night, even as, in the daylight, she was buoyantly maternal and raggedly optimistic.

Watching my own mother and my friends' mothers—who were almost all married and not working outside the house—I began to develop the "two-out-of-three rule," not articulated really for years down the road but certainly intuited, that a woman can have two out of the three big pieces of life: love, work, children. All three were impossible, so you had to content yourself with two. My mother had us and work. Most of my friends' mothers had marriage and children. I would later try the third variation: work and love. I don't think my resolve was anywhere as conscious as it sounds, though it was taking shape. And then something did happen to make my fears of motherhood very definitely conscious. When I was around fourteen, my mother, having gone from theater to sitcoms to soap operas, finally gave up her acting career to sell real estate. She needed to make steady money, something Hollywood couldn't provide. She would go on to have a hugely successful second career, but at the time the house absolutely vibrated with her sense of loss, and watching her with my adolescent eyes, I determined never to have to abandon my life's work—how grand that sounds, even though I had no idea what my life's work might be—in order to support my children. In a house that had known heartbreak, divorce and dissolution, this registered as the worst somehow, the end of my mother's own dream. I hated her pain and myself for being implicated in it, and I hated men, for whatever their part was in her unhappiness. They seemed to be a large part of it.

Jane told me that it was right at this point that she too was finally hating men, turning the equation around, no longer trying to please her father and instead feeling bad for her mother. "I think I was aware in my teens, somewhere from around sixteen on," she said with a half-laugh, "that I really hated men and that I really wanted to make them suffer. That really felt like fun. I mean, it felt like it was going to be fun. I had terrible anger and I remember not knowing what to do with that feeling and not knowing where it came from but feeling that my father was the cause of a lot of my mother's unhappiness and would he please just straighten up so we could all be a happy family. And I remember that I was going to nail some men. Unfortunately I turned out not to be as good at it as they were. Not so long ago I came across this picture of my father in an old scrapbook. He was very Hemingwayesque. He really did try to play the big macho papa. In this picture we're all off on a camping trip somewhere, my sister and my mother and me, and he's there with his fishing tackle, in his shorts, standing there with all the arrogance of the ruler of the world, the master of the universe. I mean, who is he trying to impress, just us?"

My father, too, had that big American male quality that became harder to deal with when my sister and I became adolescents. By turns tender and abrasive, he moved in a milieu of loud, sometimes vulgar men, men in lightweight summer jackets and casual shoes, Hollywood men who made jokes about women just needing a good bang. I heard them, how could I not have heard them? My impulse was to hide, starve myself away, what a lot of us young weight-conscious girls were doing even then. I had finally learned, after a childhood of being intense and scrawny and verbal, to settle in and eat. Hattie helped but so did a trip to Europe with my father just before puberty struck. I ate from one country to another, fillets of sole and rich sauces and salami sandwiches on hard, crusty bread. I ate till my zippers wouldn't zip and my snaps wouldn't snap and everyone started to tease me. I ate joyously and completely unself-consciously for the first and probably last time in my life, coming home fifteen pounds heavier, launching into my first diet, my first and only diet because after that, with puberty imminent, I simply backed off, shut down and controlled my eating from then on. It was all too scary, the body, the pleasure, the adding of flesh, the odd leers and the hardy-har high-decibel jokes that warned you off the repercussions of your own budding roundness, your own nascent sexuality.

There were girls having a much tougher time than I right then, girls I knew who had jagged, repressed fathers who went absolutely nuts when their daughters got interested in sex. There was so much undercurrent, so much dissatisfaction, so much sexual stuff floating around under the surface as always. Ann Rubinstein told me both of her parents came unglued when she hit puberty.

"I remember my mother pulling me into the den where my parents had been fighting. She pushed me into a chair opposite my father and was saying to him, 'Go on, tell her, tell her what you think.' I was thirteen and I couldn't have been more innocent. And she said to him, yelling now, 'Tell her.' But my father wouldn't say anything. So she finally said to me, 'He thinks you're not a virgin.' I didn't even know what the word meant."

Within a year Ann—already tall and precociously sophisticated—fulfilled their fears, taking up with a nineteen-year-old musician from the neighborhood, plunging into both sex and drugs with a vengeance.

"I showed them," she told me, laughing a little darkly. "I took up with this guy who himself turned out to be very abusive. I saw him constantly then and off and on for the next ten years. And he started a pattern of flying into rages that would grow to the point of him finally hitting me. Just like my father. Then I would run away and it would settle down again. I understood I should not be a victim but didn't know how to get out of the cycle of struggling for understanding and independence and acceptance from men who were incapable of giving it to me. My father was the absolute prototype of these men and I continued for years after to seek them out. I wasn't interested in the sex. I was interested in being nurtured but I didn't really know anything about that, about how to ask for it. So we were in this constant struggle. And it was all made worse by drugs. I took everything in pill form but I never went near a needle or psychedelics. But I took Dexedrine and Benzedrine—I liked all the uppers because they fought the depression and helped get me through high school."

I looked at her as she talked, the freckles across her pale skin, and could see the girl she once was, tall and scrappy and abused and determined to survive. We were part of our particular historical time, the fifties–early sixties, and yet in some senses generically adolescently female, with all that implied, the desire to burst forth somehow even as the constraints get tighter and the sexual reckoning nearer. With the drugs and sex, Ann had gotten ahead of many of the rest of us, moving on into the hard-core sixties, which didn't happen to me and most of my friends until we left home to go to college toward the end of the decade. In my relatively chaste girls' school, I didn't know anyone who was sleeping with a boyfriend and I certainly never heard of anyone having an abortion (our own mothers didn't confide theirs, as it turned out, till much later, till deep into the days of liberation).

But for the girls who were at the top end of our so-called birth cohort, the Sacrificial Generation pioneers, women like my talk-show friend Julie, the sixties had indeed already begun. Seven years older than I, she had hit into them early. She was already seventeen when Kennedy was elected, seventeen and pregnant. Julie had never told me the story until I went looking for her again as I began my own infertile reckoning. And when I found her, living in Chicago, big and vibrant and noisy as I had remembered her, she told me a far different story than the one I expected to hear. Way back in 1960 she had turned up pregnant and had given the baby away. She was seventeen, on her own in Los Angeles—not so far from where I was growing up as a gawky ten-year-old repressed beach bunny. She had fled the East Coast and her mother's anger and was doing "a million jobs"—waitressing, teaching dance, typing—to pay the rent and keep herself in school at San Fernando Valley College. Her first boyfriend had followed her west on his motorcycle, a tough, handsome guy, as she describes him, who later became an automobile mechanic.

And by the time he was gone six weeks later, she was pregnant. And terrified.

"I was deathly afraid my parents would find out," she told me in her elegant Chicago lakeside apartment where we talked until two in the morning. "I felt so humiliated. My mother had always accused me of being sexual when I was in high school. I had big tits and loved Marlon Brando and I did carry myself in a rebellious way. I was in the change of the change of the change. It was the first true years of rock and roll, of Elvis—'Heartbreak Hotel' and 'Rock Around the Clock.' And Brando. I can tell you if you talk to women my age they'll all tell you about seeing him in *The Wild One*. It was an epiphany for me, a turning point in my sexuality. That movie turned me on so that it ruined my life. That's why I fell for this guy with his motorcycle. And the sex was just great. He was very gentle and it was just great. And later on, because I enjoyed the sex so much, I thought I had this wild woman in me that would get out of control if I didn't put a clamp on it—she would get out and screw me. That's why all my relationships after a brief time end up becoming quite sexless. I tried everything to get rid of the baby. I took pills and stuck things up me, everything, but of course nothing worked. I had no idea how to go about getting an abortion, so I found the social services people and I became very responsible about finding the baby a good home. The minute I was out of the hospital, I found a therapist and I told her, 'This is going to bother me for the rest of my life and I'm going to try to work it out now.' I never told anybody else. It became the hidden secret, the humiliation—getting pregnant—the scarlet letter, and I held my breath, some part of me always waiting for the phone to ring, waiting for her to come find me, waiting for my secret to get out."

So much female guilt. So much repression. So many mixed signals, about sex, about achievement, the constant push-me-pull-you. Like Julie, I too became shut down, sealed off from something, some elemental part of myself. I did very well in school—I did have the sense that achievement might somehow rescue me—and had a handful of intense, jubilant female friendships that endure to this day. And I learned to dance—by myself, in front of the mirror, in front of the TV, twisting and surfing and stomping to Dick Clark and the other dance programs—cutting loose at proms in a way wholly out of character, causing my friends to watch with amused encouragement as I adroitly spun and shuffled, eyes closed, in some rhythmic dream. For girls weaned on cotillions and father-daughter dances, to gyrate solo in a throbbing auditorium was liberating beyond belief, intoxicating, more so for me than the booze or drugs that were just beginning to be part of our party-going. I was afraid of drugs and alcohol—I'd seen plenty of the latter—and of boys, or in a pre-feminist rage at them, which I couldn't articulate. Edgy and verbal and in my last year of high school, I rebuffed the deep tenderness of a first boyfriend because I had no understanding of that kind of sweetness. His gentleness unnerved me and after about a month of excruciatingly soft kisses, I went dead inside, turning him away. I just couldn't handle it, couldn't imagine what lay ahead, what sort of life. My mother's? My friends' mothers'? Whose? What was the model? Was I destined to hook up with some man and be a wife and mother, after all, all my ambitions notwithstanding? I certainly felt groomed to be a caretaker through those adolescent years, even to look after the adults who went so ineptly around toying with each other's love, another reason why I and women like me, women like Jane and Ann and Julie, women growing up in tumultuous homes, would so long delay motherhood, not just because of some ferocious ambition, as the family values propagandists would later have it, but ironically precisely the opposite: because so many of us had already done so much caretaking, so much peacemaking, so much "woman's work" in our childhood homes.

Confused and depressed, I spent the last couple of years of high school in withdrawal more or less, hiding in books—except for my dancing jags. I spent my free time with my friends ricocheting around town and to and from the beach in our hand-me-down cars while off on stage-left the sexual revolution was finally in fairly high gear, while off on stage right the feminists were tuning up their rhetoric, sharpening their pens, and we suntanned, weight-conscious, high-achieving young women of the Westlake School for Girls in our now thigh-high uniforms were heading into their warmly vitriolic embrace without yet knowing it and with a detour, of course, through the sexual revolution first. I was given birth control pills by my childhood doctor when I was seventeen because my period was irregular, so without knowing it, or without seeking it, I was signed on to be a participant, my timidities notwithstanding. One thing for certain: I would not be burdened by an unwanted baby like Julie. In a swift seven years, between 1960 and 1967, the year I finished high school, there had indeed been a revolution. By graduation day it was clear to me and my friends that a woman's place was changing, thankfully, but to what we weren't sure. To the simple question, Where is a woman's place? the answer was no longer "In the home." The consternatingly exhilarating new answer seemed to be: in bed. That would bring both new freedom and new tyrannies and decisively nudge us farther along our path away from motherhood as we evolved into the eroticized generation.

7

MAKING EMBRYOS

I am still in the flush of exuberance over this out-of-body breeding, still game to plow ahead, try the next procedure despite the accumulating failures. Thus, I do not balk even slightly when the doctor proposes I next try a ZIFT instead of another GIFT. I am a few months past that attempt and into a new year. It is early 1989 and we are moving down to the dead end of the alphabet here, running out of acronyms.

ZIFT (zygote intrafallopian transfer) is the latest of the latest of the latest, the newest promised panacea, and I am helpless to resist its lure. Only about thirty cases have been done so far around the country, Dr. Marrs tells me, seducing me with the image of the two of us in some cutting-edge conspiracy against my quirky physiology. Oh yes, we can do this together, his calm explanation seems to suggest.

ZIFT is a real wallop, a real endurance test, a combination of IVF and GIFT, a procedure in which eggs and sperm meet first in a dish. The resultant embryos (or zygotes, which are technically one-cell "pre-embryos") are put back into the fallopian tubes the next day, left to make their way down into the uterus. The idea again is simple, elegant: Make the embryos first, then instead of just shooting them into an unsuspecting uterus (as in IVF), put them into the top of the fallopian tubes so they can move on their own down into the womb, telegraphing their imminent arrival as they go. That's the idea. It's logical, it makes sense as everything seems to in this world. I'm game even as what I am looking at here is two back-to-back outpatient hospital procedures, one to get the eggs, one to put them back, or rather put the zygotes back should there be any. This is the marathon of the high-tech world, an even more grueling ordeal than GIFT, and I am amused, as I sign on willingly to do it, at how undaunted I am by the fact there are no statistics yet to prove whether this procedure is effective. I'm amused at how completely I am able to block the memory of the last failed attempt to conceive, as women block, I am told, the experience of childbirth in order to do it again.

It is not the physical discomfort that is so daunting, though there will be a certain amount of discomfort involved—the endless blood tests, the endless shots, needles, needles everywhere. Nor is it just the apprehension of being put to sleep, though that's always there—the fear that I will drift

off and never come back. No, the real fear this time is that I am about
to discover whether my husband and I can make embryos. They will be
there in that dish together, his sperm, my eggs, for twenty-four hours, and
we will see point-blank whether this union of ours is, on the most basic
level, sterile. That's the unnerving part, beside which the physical assault
is minor. If we can't make embryos, we are out of the baby-making
business altogether, no ifs, ands or buts. There will never be a piece of
us together, and I push away for the one hundred and fiftieth time, the
one thousandth time, the memory of this man, this big oversized in-your-
face American man crooning to me in the glow of our early passion about
wanting to have a baby with me back then when I was eighteen, nineteen,
twenty, and he was twice that.

Young, hopeful, nubile and presumably fertile at that long-ago point
but ineluctably wedded to contraception, I did not hear him. I could not
hear him. I would not hear him. I had too much to do, too much to be.
I am now the age he was then and am full of an ex post facto tenderness
for his early procreative ardor that I could not reciprocate. I hear it now
but he has moved on. We are planets in a different generational solar
system. At sixty-one, he is growing weary of my obsession. Will I stop?
When? How? After this ZIFT fails or the next one or the next? I have
no idea how to get off this track. Worse, I have no desire to, not even a
twinge, no matter how punishing this quest is—to soul, psyche and
marriage.

Luckily—and this is the good news and bad—the process itself takes
over and becomes so involving, I forget the long-range fears. I live in the
needleful present, in a twilight of hormonal stimulation, my mood floating around me like an extra being, as if there are at least two me's
(sometimes it feels as if there are twenty, all crowded into my flushed skin
doing some willful dance with my normally steady personality). This time
there is an added irritant: in addition to the Pergonal, I am taking something called Lupron, two more shots a day, little jabs into the thigh, which
are supposed to help control ovulation by reining in my hyperactive
system. The Lupron is supposed to act as a control mechanism, slowing
the process down and allowing the maximum number of eggs to mature
at the same time, keeping one or two follicles from racing ahead of the
rest and blowing the whole cycle. In effect, what it's doing is shutting you
down as the Pergonal is jacking you up—a one-two punch that has me

living on a giddy, tear-stained edge. I burst into tears the other night when the man on *Jeopardy* didn't know the answer. "What's wrong with him?" I wailed at my husband, whose sympathetic scrutiny only made me more irritable. I glare at the other drivers on the freeway and sulk when asked what we should have for dinner. My shot-giving grows sloppy. A misplaced jab elicits a huge bruise that stains my thigh and causes people who see it to wince.

The days slide on in a blur—shots, sonograms, blood tests, shots, sonograms, blood tests—I poise every afternoon near a phone to get the results, to see if I am continuing to make the cut, if all systems are still go. I don't even try to work anymore during these stretches. I have given it up. I submit to the obsessional nature of this quest as if I were in some envelopingly demonic love affair.

The other good news is that once again I am making plenty of follicles, close to a dozen this time, clustered like grapes on my two plucky ovaries. Not for the first time and certainly not for the last, I brood about the possible eventual repercussions of this hyperstimulation. How can it be good—all this frantic egg making, all this stirring up of extra hormones? The doctors all assure us that there is no downside, that Pergonal has been around since the early sixties, but who can count on that given the wreckage caused by the likes of DES and the IUD and the untreated PIDs. We all know this, but we plow on, my infertile sisters and I, because the drive to reproduce has stunned us, I think, beyond the point of no return, beyond the point of rationality, certainly beyond the point of considering later repercussions. The only repercussion we see is the abject loneliness of non-motherhood, all right, nonbiological motherhood. That's the drive, to have a baby of one's own, as if the very survival of the species somehow depended on it. The quest feels that urgent, that basic, that animalistic—indeed, beyond rationality—and I continue to be stunned, in my lucid moments, at the depth of this urgency. Where could it have been all those earlier years?

D-Day comes again, this time with another reckoning. Before any of these embryo-making procedures, both husbands and wives must sign forms specifying the fate of our extra embryos. The doctors will put only three back in one tube at a time and the extra ones—should there be any—will be frozen for future pregnancy attempts. There are more than 20,000 embryos on ice around the country, by-products of these high-tech attempts. But what happens to those embryos if you tire of the chase or if something happens to either of you? These are supposed to be joint-custody embryos, not usable by one partner alone in case of divorce; so far the courts have upheld this position. So there they sit, in liquid nitrogen, your suspended children, frozen in some twilight zone.

The choices are daunting and I sit with the form late into the night pondering what to do. Should we give the embryos to another infertile couple? Or should we let them be used for research? Or should we simply allow them to be thawed and die? And is that the right word, anyway? Die? Isn't that too big a word? Finally, I sign, consigning my unused pre-pre-pre babies to someone else, dazzled and bedeviled both, by the thought that down the road some stranger could bring them to life, suckle them, raise them, teach them to laugh and dance and look at the moon.

Cattle embryos, I read in the literature, stored for seven years have produced healthy offspring. Human embryos stored three years have turned into healthy babies and there is no reason to think they could not last perhaps hundreds of years, being carried to term by some wholly new evolved female centuries down the road, though the American Fertility Society is strongly against the transfer of embryos from one generation to another, in part to keep siblings from ending up carrying each other—a weird thought. It's all a little weird out here where for the first time in human history scientists know that women can carry each other's babies and give each other eggs. Doctors were skeptical about this, thinking there was some inviolable connection between a mother and her embryo. But no, those embryos can be moved around and have been since 1980, when doctors performed the first human uterine lavage—a technique used since the late nineteenth century on a dozen mammals like cows— flushing a pre-embryo from the womb of a fertile woman and transferring it into the womb of an infertile one, an immensely delicate procedure with a very low success rate. The latest answer is simply to take eggs from the fertile and give them to the infertile. I can buy donor eggs now as if they were sperm, which have been brokered for thirty-odd years, younger, friskier donor eggs. They would be put in a petri dish with my husband's sperm and then I would carry the embryo—an embryo, a baby, with no genetic link to me. Conceptual adultery? I don't know.

Reading all this stuff as I assiduously do, I ask myself over and over: Could I do this; is it sweet, the height of sisterliness, all this sharing of bodies and body parts? Or is it a transgression of some basic order, of nature itself, herself, and of the very notion of maternity? My soul seesaws and I am grateful as yet not to have to confront those possibilities, of borrowed wombs (official name: gestational surrogacy) or purchased eggs (official name: oocyte donation), so intent am I as yet on trying to conjure up and carry an embryo of our own. Of course, there is also the more controversial straight surrogacy (vs. gestational), in which a fertile woman would, to the tune of $10,000, be inseminated with my husband's sperm and then nine months later hand over the baby. In short, we would be borrowing not only her womb, but also buying her egg. This, at least this, I realize I cannot do. It just comes too close to baby-buying, though I don't rule out the other two yet—buying eggs or renting a womb— realizing that these lines might seem fine indeed to those not faced with these decisions. This high-tech baby-making world is indeed a moral mine field and we must reckon, each and every one of us, about our own choices, ones I am still desperately hoping I will not have to confront.

The eggs come out on the morning of February 8. I am woozed out with a sedative, wheeled into the operating room, draped over the stirrups in a dreamy stupor, and the eggs are sucked out of the follicles by a long needle inserted up through my vagina alongside the transducer (the proper word for the visioned dildo). I come to a couple of hours later, feeling only slightly invaded, and am allowed to leave after I shuffle about for a minute and prove the earthworthiness of my legs, leaving behind all my hope in the world, riveting it on that petri dish where my nine retrieved eggs now lie amid a sea of my husband's carefully culled and washed sperm.

My anxiety level rises, on the yeast of hope, to an entirely new pitch. I pace and pace, knowing they will call the next morning to tell me whether any of the eggs fertilized. If not, well then . . . If so, I must rush back to face a second surgery. What a choice. I don't even bother trying to sleep, riffling again, as always, through my past, letting memories float around, sweet memories full of sand and sunshine, my mother, my sister and I in our matching swimsuits, a blonde, blue-eyed troika with sun-burned noses all those summer days long ago.

The nurse finally calls at nine the next morning. "There are four of them," she says, "come get them," words that send shards of elation through my body. Can it be, can I do this thing, can I carry these zygotes now that they're here, one toe on the earth, one cell on the earth? That's all they are. I dress carefully, as if for some important meeting or interview, shaving my legs and washing my hair in some sort of time-honored feminine ritual, and then off we go, the proud parents of four thriving pre-embryos. Our union is apparently not sterile after all. I am giddy, allowing myself a momentary pang for the non-survivors, the cells that did not flourish (why so many of them?), trying to be grateful for those that did.

At the hospital it is the same routine: the paying of the money, stripping down, lying on the gurney, having temperature taken and blood drawn and then the IV inserted, and bang, I'm out and back again, and three of the zygotes have been deposited at the top of my one good fallopian tube through the laparoscope; so the fourth has been frozen. Waking, I finally feel completely beat up, exhausted, achy all over and anxious to get home and tend to my zygotes.

For two weeks, every day, I have another shot—these, in fact, are the worst—a big, oily dose of progesterone, the pregnancy-supporting hormone. Just in case. For two weeks I tiptoe on the earth's surface, afraid to laugh or cry or have a bowel movement, lest I dislodge anyone. This is silly. They will have made their way to the uterus and will be flourishing—the zygotes implant about five to seven days after fertilization—or they will already be gone, evaporated, a footnote in my personal history book. Nonetheless, I cannot help myself. I keep constant vigilance over the possibility of them, moving slowly, scarcely leaving the house, barely able even to muster the concentration for reading, my longtime pleasure. Television makes me jumpy, more so than usual, and I'm not fond of it much in my normal state, whatever that was. In fits of nostalgia, I play them the old tunes, Janis Joplin at very low decibel—don't want to stir them up—and James Taylor crooning "Sweet Baby James." That is inevitably where I go for remembered joy, to the late 1960s, more specifically to Santa Cruz, California, in the late sixties where I was in college when the country was dissolving into messy personal and political passions and I was falling in love with the father of my embryos, my husband, my forever, my earnest husband who, the day of the pregnancy test, when it's finally over—all the waiting, the minute-by-minute countdown—muffles my sobs with the full weight of his commiseration, because once again they have called to tell me I am not pregnant.

8

THE REAL SIXTIES

By September of 1967, when I began college, *Newsweek* magazine was saying that with regards to sex, candor and general permissiveness, the country "had changed more dramatically in the past year than in the preceding fifty." And indeed that felt right. It felt as if someone had simply reached up and flipped a big switch in the sky. After all those well-mannered years when being clean and honing our feminine manners and protecting our virginity were tantamount, the sexual revolution was hard upon us. The pages of *Vogue* were now full of girls in Courrèges minidresses: big-eyed, stork-legged, androgynous nymphets like Twiggy and Penelope Tree, sexed-up tomboys—appropriately enough—who pointed the way to the new sexuality. Gone were the maternal bosoms. We women were now to be the sexual play pals of the Age of Aquarius. *Hair* was playing in New York and there was a general explosion of nudity and profanity, a pent-up explosion after all the fifties containment. It was quite a change for us college-bound sixties good girls.

That summer I attended the Monterey Pop Festival with friends, a gentle bacchanal of dreamy-eyed, dope-smoking, sleeping bag–hopping kids who swayed ecstatically to Otis Redding and Janis Joplin. We camped in a meadow, high and unafraid, among thousands of other new-world pilgrims in beads and beards. There was a sensual sweetness to that momentary community—anchored, for some, already with a heady moral outrage over Vietnam—that I have not known since and which is hard to remember given all the mythologizing and counter-mythologizing that's gone on about that decade, really the end of that decade.

As the sexual rules abruptly changed, and with them the whole underpinning of female upbringing, i.e., the preservation of one's sanctity until marriage, the whole notion of female purity with which we all had been so inculcated, I felt grateful for the shift, but also miffed, dislocated, bewildered. I hated the world we had all come from, the sexually punitive world of the fifties–early sixties, the puritanical weight of American culture, all that conditioning, all that repression, all those "shhs." But even so, I had complicated feelings when the rules seemed to switch so suddenly, tiptoeing tremulously into the libidinous new world of the late 1960s. For those of us who were heading off to college those years armed with blue jeans, boxes of books, and birth control pills, sex itself—and how embracive you could or should be of it—would still be an issue and not one easily resolved in a bedding or two. This was new turf and having tried to define ourselves against the culture, to stand up to its restrictions, we now had to reckon with its sudden lack of them, and that wouldn't be easy either.

My personal solution to the general confusion at that point was quite simple and very complicated: I fell in love with a man twice my age and started trying to find myself, define myself under his impassioned if heavy-handed tutelage. So much for independence, going it alone, being a brazenly solo young woman. I embarked into coupledom, serious, hard-core coupledom.

A handsome and distinguished journalist, head of the *Newsweek* bureau in Los Angeles, Karl Fleming was arrogant and edged and passionate about everything—newspapers and George Orwell, Mexican food and motorcycles and me—and the package was irresistible. He was the colleague of one of my best friends' fathers, and we had met on their tennis court when I was sixteen and he was thirty-eight. The married father of four, he was then sporting a crew cut and a visibly wired-up broken jaw, which he had gotten covering the Watts riots. An inveterate Southerner, he had then been in Los Angeles less than a year and was destined, as were so many, to have his California experience. Little did I suspect that I would be it. But when he announced very suddenly, two years after our first meeting, that I was the love of his life, the light of his soul, showering me with both compliments and books of straight-ahead, plainspoken American poetry, that was that.

We seemed elementally in synch, primordially tethered, mutually disdainful of pomp and pieties, mutually besotted by California, specifically Santa Cruz, where I was then happily ensconced in college, mutually taken with strong, clean English sentences—which he would later help me to fashion out of my characteristically dense acadamese (the rough-hewn, homespun Sartre to my miniskirted de Beauvoir, I liked to imagine in my happier moments)—and mutually committed to his young children. I had no resistance to them. On most days it truly did not seem like a daunting proposition, hard as that might be to imagine. The times were different, messier—families coming apart and being refashioned—though I did inherit children well ahead of the trend. But I myself had been a child of divorce well ahead of the trend, and had inherited a stepmother who had taught me a lot about loving someone else's children. I had my own scars and was determined to help minimize theirs, the ones I, of course, having fallen in love with their father, had helped cause. I was so young and they were so young and were all sun-streaked and wounded and I loved them because they were his and because I understood what had happened to them. They would turn out to be one of the great joys of my life; having them around a lot probably did siphon off some of my maternal energy—nudge me farther along my non-motherhood road— though, in truth, it often felt less as if I were a parent figure and much more as if were were growing up together.

But the love between their father and me was no easy thing and never would be. We came from diametrically opposed worlds, he raised in an orphanage in the bleakly beautiful tobacco country of eastern North Carolina, me, of course, from the sunny west side of Los Angeles. He was all rough edges and abrasive charm, a traditional fifties Southern male, raised in an atmosphere where the dominant attitude toward women had been, as he later told me to my chagrin, "To find 'em, fuck 'em, and for- get 'em." But he did have a determined sense of fairness—not male-female fairness, because that he'd never been exposed to—but baseline fairness, and a sense of outrage that infused his coverage of the civil rights movement. A college dropout, he became a newspaper man and made his way from North Carolina, through Atlanta and Houston, ending up in Los Angeles in 1965, just in time for all the upheaval, just in time to find me running around my home turf with my inchoate ambitions and sunstreaked hair longer than my skirts. And from the bruising shelter of my own childhood, I looked out and saw this giddy quasi-grown-up full of all this Hollywood-sized macho moral zest, a self-created man, not self-made—that always somehow had to do with money—but a self- imagined man, a rude, crusading, easy-to-affront-and-give-affront hand- some American man who had conjured himself up out of a Dickensian orphanage childhood, and I was hooked. He had had a real life while I had been incubated, sheltered, pampered. I wanted out, I wanted in, to the main event, the grungy, exhilarating road show of life. He seemed like the ticket.

To say he was a father figure/mentor is to point out the obvious. To say that the disparity in our ages and experience made my slide toward womanhood and the independence I longed for even harder to achieve is also obvious. He wanted to see me every weekend and talk to me every night, to pry into every nook and cranny of my mind and heart—and body—crowding into my college life with adamant devotion, materializing beside me at every moment. We got off to a blissfully jagged start, he smothering me with both his sexual and professional expertise, me eager for that while recoiling at the same time. Ours was a complicated transgenerational dance, carried on in the small aquamarine-and-white apartment he had rented on the beach in Malibu, in woodsy motels along the California coastline, and in my small dorm room, where we tucked in like the other collegiate sexual pioneers in the now free-flowing, no-rules dormitories. Boys came and went; strangers stayed the night with strangers. Amid the sex, love cropped up every now and again, true love, though you would not have known it from the media, which had us all pegged as frantic fornicators. In truth, nobody had quite prepared many of us young women for this. We hadn't heard anything about sex at all growing up, most of us, except for girlish speculations and matter-of-fact biology books, which in no way could prepare you for seeing an erect penis for the first time, all that saluting desire, all that potentially vindictive desire. There was no precedent for the messy disturbance sex could cause in your soul, and indeed there were times I felt as if I were being fucked by—there is no other way to put it—the entire weight of male culture, groaning and sweating and arching and longing atop my pierceable, fragile frame. I alternately loved the heft of this male body and resented it, its arrogant intrusion into mine.

At the time, for all the sexual stuff going on, I don't really remember talking to other young women about this wealth of feelings. I was privy to a few graphic chats about what went where and who did what to whom, but nothing about this complex of feelings. On the road from repression to liberation/exploitation, we had somehow bypassed the poetry. There was no pause button. From one injunction we had switched abruptly to another: Don't do it; do it. And suddenly we young women were all part of some redefining American upheaval. It was scary and thrilling, liberating and nerve-racking all at the same time.

A few of my friends tumbled into the new world with ease, plowing through a succession of men with good humor and easy hunger and apparent pleasure, not to mention the occasional venereal infection that would later make pregnancy difficult, if not impossible. None of us thought about that then. You trooped down to the student health services or to your gynecologist and they handed you some antibiotics or some suppositories and off you went, never thinking of possible long-term damage. No one was talking about that then. The reckoning would come later for many of us. Meanwhile we were busy dealing with a whole new psychedelic swirl of emotions. I certainly was. An inner cacophony of feelings routinely swirled through me as I made my way through the ancient Northern California redwoods to my seminars on political philosophy, on Karl Marx and Thomas Paine, Herbert Marcuse and Hannah Arendt, seminars that, along with Vietnam, roiled my political passions as certainly as love roiled my other ones.

Everything was sharp and vivid then, on that beautiful haven of a campus with its heart-stopping view of Monterey Bay, glistening in the sun on many a day. The sixties were in full force by then, especially in a place like Santa Cruz, a kind of intellectual summer camp full of long-haired boys in hiking boots and long-haired girls in flowing dresses amid whom my older suitor and I in our unisex jeans and T-shirts didn't stand out very much. Nobody even seemed to notice, or care, that he was twice my age since any number of long-haired, graying male professors were loping around among us in their blue jeans. We just blended into the free-love, antiwar atmosphere that was hanging over much of America at that point—along with a kind of permanent cloud of marijuana smoke—certainly over its campuses, though Santa Cruz itself was a little isolated, a little removed from the hard-core protests.

My friends at bigger schools like Stanford and Berkeley were more in the line of fire, both sexual and political, more hard-pressed to sort out all the bewildering new messages. As one of them said to me: "God, I remember those days so vividly because I was so confused all the time. I was a nice little girl from Seattle who expected to find a husband at college and have kids. I mean, my mother never worked a day in her life. And suddenly there I was at Stanford in the late sixties and all the rules were changing. It was all happening so fast. I remember David Harris was student-body president and there was this woman, Vicki Drake, who was a topless dancer in Palo Alto, and she ran against him and her slogan was 'A vote for Vicki Drake is a Vote for VD.' I didn't do drugs and I didn't protest and I didn't sleep around. I think I was just totally repressed because it was all too much for me. I'm the class of sixty-nine and my friends and I—we're now mid-forty-year-old women—we didn't know what hit us. We got swept on a wave that was happening and didn't know how to get to shore, and most of us didn't marry until way late and most of us don't have children. This whole group of women just got stuck because the rules changed right when we would have gotten out of college and gotten married, but we couldn't quite do that anymore. The nice, boring provider types we thought we were supposed to marry would no longer do. But nor were we really prepared to have full-fledged careers. That hadn't really sunk in yet either. We were just on the cusp of this exciting, horrible thing. Clearly there was more out there than we'd been led to believe growing up, but it would take us a long time to find it."

The women I knew at Berkeley were having an even more complicated experience, having plunged headlong, after our tidy, well-mannered childhoods, into the world of big-time protests, of macrobiotic food and communal sex and whatever drugs you wanted. As Todd Gitlin said in his book *The Sixties: Years of Hope, Days of Rage*: "The radicals were hipper in Berkeley, the hippies more combative, and there were enough of each, all the possible hybrids, to feed any utopian vision imaginable." I remember feeling all that hopeful, exotic, erotic tension when I visited Berkeley in those days and being personally thankful that I wasn't in school there. It was all just a little too much, too heady, too dislocating, especially for women.

An escapee at long last from her crazed Philadelphia apartment, Ann Rubinstein landed there just as the People's Park protests happened in the spring of 1969. With her masses of dark hair, she was turning into a wily if damaged survivor, working to put herself through school and partaking of the protests but from a safe distance, maneuvering her way out of a volatile situation by flirting with one of the National Guardsmen whom Ronald Reagan, then governor of California, had sent into Berkeley to quell the protest.

"I think all those years were such a struggle emotionally to find out what you were supposed to be and what mattered and what didn't matter and what you could handle," she told me. "Luckily I'd done all the drugs already and gotten that out of my system. You know, those were the years that if you dressed neatly, they told you you were too straight. At home in Philadelphia I was too hippie and in Berkeley I was too straight. I remember guys coming down on me for wearing a bra and I'd say, 'Look, I'm fighting gravity and I'm starting now.' I was sleeping with this guy, one of these counterculture studs with a ponytail and real undercurrent of misogyny, who had this funky house in the Oakland hills that was open all around and he'd set the bed up high, perched in the windows so it was completely exposed. Nobody was around but the chipmunks, but it struck me as so corny and arrogant. And the sex wasn't any good. People weren't talking about orgasms quite then. The women's movement hadn't hit them with the idea of oral sex yet. I remember the first time I brought that up to a guy—it must have been 1971, I think that's when all that stuff about the clitoris started to hit—and I remember the look on his face. By that time finally, you could take the pill. It'd been around for ten or so years but they'd finally gotten the dosage down so we could all stand it and that's why the women's movement really took off when it did—I'm convinced of it—that and then, of course, the legalizing of abortion. Those years just before all this, the years I'm talking about in Berkeley, 1968 to 1971, those were three of the worst years in terms of the subjugation of women. We were supposed to be these flower children willing to whip off our tops and sway naked in the forest. We were their old ladies, their antiwar Madonnas. The media loved it and played it big, those pictures of girls putting flowers in the barrels of guns. I wanted no part of it. I was very ambitious. I was driven toward independence. It was that or be one of these pliant doormats. And you just knew the men were only dabbling, having a holiday before getting serious about reembracing power, whether they were going back to the university or back to their political left movement or even back to being carpenters or running construction businesses. They were going back and where were we going?"

Where indeed? There were still no arrows pointing the way and we were already, in this eroticized new world, running headlong into old-line machismo, machismo moreover with the added moral twist provided by Vietnam. "Girls say yes to boys who say no." That was the line. It was your patriotic duty to sleep with resisters. It was all getting twisted around, coopted, manhandled, our newfound sexual freedom. The phallic under-tow was already beginning, though for a long time it would continue to masquerade as liberation. I was luckier in some ways to be with a man out of this generation where there was this twisted, intact machismo (Karl's maleness was more old school, more grounded in old manners, more straightforward, less devious, if you will, a kind of perverse blessing), a machismo that permeated the counterculture and the antiwar movement and was in large part responsible for the incipient women's movement. One of my friends was at the infamous 1969 antiwar rally in Washington when an activist named Marilyn Webb, attempting to talk about female oppression in the New Left, was taunted from the crowd with cries of "Take her off the stage and fuck her!"

Leaders like Webb would shortly take center stage in our collective female consciousness—be the heroines of our rage—but at that moment in the late sixties, Ann Rubinstein said the only role models she found were among the folk singers, Joan Baez and Judy Collins and Laura Nyro, women, as she says, of grace, women who were both sexual and had dignity and were writing songs with tough, ethical cores. Movies were still a role-model wasteland full of childish women like Julie Christie in *Darling* or *Georgy Girl* galumphing around coveting her best friend's boyishly roguish husband and baby.

The so-called New Man, as the media dubbed him, was a charmingly off-putting sexual revolution hybrid with a kind of passive-aggressive masculinity. In a *Mademoiselle* magazine of January 1968, I read that this "New American Male" was someone who dealt with women straight on. "Because the New Man sees women in the round rather than pornographically, sex becomes like money, simply one of his stakes in life." Something to deposit. It was sometimes cold here in the turned-on new world with these new American men—these cool-eyed, newfangled studs—but for girls long repressed, it was still a perverse advancement, a chance for air even though you still had to fight to get it from under those sometimes suffocatingly heavy male bodies. There were times when I'd awaken in some cabin in some beautiful secluded valley south of Santa Cruz and hear the heavy breathing beside me and want to jump up and run away, be unmussed and free. But I stayed put, learning the ropes of love at the hands of a scarred teacher who, like my father, clearly loved me but was awkward at the small intimacies, the small courtesies. But I had no words for any of that then and, high on our May-December passion, we carried our romance up and down the coast of California all through those days of the late 1960s, a coastline itself redolent of marijuana and thickly lined with hippie hitchhikers with their dogs and bandannas and hastily scrawled destination signs. S.F., L.A., BIG SUR, NORTH, SOUTH, they read, take me everywhere, take me anywhere. It was a free-floating circus, up and down the coast it went, carrying us along with it, dropping us off at one end or the other for a while, until we got back in the caravan.

Our romance was clearly heightened by Karl's professional involvement in the times. He was covering the antiwar marches and the assassinations, that of Martin Luther King, Jr., and Bobby Kennedy, coming to rest in my arms, post-midnight, when his deadlines had been met, exhausted and overwrought, and we would cling to each other amid the extraordinary, unnerving events. We ended up at the infamous Democratic convention in Chicago in 1968, for example, when the streets were aswirl with rage and sorrow, already the writer-in-training, the always somewhat timid, if outraged voyeur watching people only slightly older than I throwing rocks and having their heads cracked by billy club–wielding police—make that "pigs." I was there as a magazine intern and it was becoming fairly clear to me that my own activism would be confined to paper, if I could manage it. That's what I wondered, whether I could do what my older lover did, plunge out into the world, asking questions, taking the pulse, writing what I saw. By and large his was a man's world, full of hard-talking, hard-drinking men with Hemingway complexes. Almost everybody I met through him, his colleagues, were male. On those newsmagazines then, women were still the secretaries and the researchers. Was that where I was heading after all my high-flown education, to some desk somewhere, to get someone coffee or do their research? We didn't talk about it. And again, I don't remember talking to my women friends about it either at that point, as about the sex. Most of us were taken up with surviving the tumultuous present moment, trying to figure out how we fit into the scheme of things and how much, as Ann said, we could handle.

My friends at schools on the East Coast were having pretty much the same experiences, trying to maneuver through the heady new waters, inevitably coping with boyfriends of one description or another, often the Ivy League princes of upper-crust America who were themselves trying to cope with Vietnam. At Yale, Jane had fallen in love her first year with one of the big men on campus, one of the pedigreed anti-warriors with a last name for a first name and piercing blue eyes, and she, too, was having trouble making the turnaround: letting go, hanging loose, getting down, getting high. Driven in school, determined to be somebody and something, she had nonetheless been sideswiped by love and was having a hard time making good on her resolves while trying to have a tender, intimate life. Like many of us, she was trying to find her way after a lifetime of feeling suppressed, carrying with her from her childhood an anger at men that caused a kink in her soul.

"Dawson was bright and funny and terribly arrogant," she said of her boyfriend, "and I have to confess I thought he was a real jerk at first, but then we started dating and that was pretty much it. We shared a bed for a long time before we actually slept together, six months or more as I remember. We were giddy and elated about the attraction we felt for each other, but confused by the performance standards set by movies and books and the popular culture where everyone seemed to be having great sex every three hours."

I have heard a lot of that from women in the years since, a lot of us trying to unbuckle in this new highly sexualized world after a lifetime of other messages, of timidities gained in complicated households. Like Jane, I was clearly carrying a lot of unarticulated anger at men beneath my sunny, blond exterior, anger left over from the previous years, anger being both quieted and fomented by my unweighted romance and my confusion over what lay ahead. I didn't know how to take a sexual lead, how to ask for things, how to refuse things. I didn't have the vocabulary for that with men. Many of us didn't. I'm not even sure I knew I was missing the vocabulary, though I often felt tongue-tied and prickly, unlike in the classroom where I had no fear, a testament to my girls' school. Some of my friends with younger men fared easier, groping together with their equally virginal boyfriends toward some mutual place and pleasure. I contented myself with the idea that I was in a high-voltage romance. Not for nothing was I a child of Hollywood, weaned on my parents' drama, on-screen and off. There were girls I knew at Santa Cruz, some of those wavy-haired flower children, who did seem to flow into the new world with more ease and less anger than the rest of us, bedding randomly and cheerfully and without guilt, virtually shacking up in mini hippie-pads right there in the dorm. I would see them stumble forth into the sunlight, messy and euphoric, maybe heading for class, maybe one given by an equally long-haired left-wing mythology professor or the like. But even there, I couldn't tell what was actually going on. There was a girl who lived down the hall with her boyfriend who was to me the essence of counter-culture cool, a beautiful girl with tawny skin and knee-length dark hair out of which emanated always the smell of pot and incense. She and her boyfriend did fight; we would hear the noise. And then one day she appeared on the threshold of the dorm in one of her Indian-print bed-spread dresses. She stood there blinking into the bright morning through a blackened eye and I shivered with the déjà vu of it all. So we weren't in some sweet new world after all, at least we women weren't, not yet anyway. And how would we get there? How would I be my whole own person—part centerfold, part Hannah Arendt—now that I was in the firm grip of love? I certainly no longer felt I was on some predestined train heading into marriage and motherhood. The fifties scenario was over for me and most of my friends, done in by a sensual conspiracy of dope, birth control pills, and rock and roll—they were indeed a heady brew. Did I get it when Mick sang "Under My Thumb"? No, I was completely unconscious of the lyrics even though I mumbled them by heart as strobe-lit auditoriums full of us did our intoxicated, jangly thing, a blissed-out ensemble of gyrating soloists. It was hard to see your way around all these things—men and sex and the often retrogressive musical messages—to who you were and what you wanted to be, just you, without any of the rest of it, any of the rest of them. So hard because none of us had been programmed to think that way. We had been programmed to think of other people first, to be caretakers. Now we were stumbling along trying to be more, figure out what that "more" was, trying to stumble away from the paths of our mothers but down what other paths no one was sure. What exactly were the contours now of a woman's life, a happy woman's life?

I was studying hard, eagerly digesting the great works of political philosophy, mindful with some small part of my soul that almost all of it was written by men. So where was I heading? Graduate school? Law school? Many of my friends, women and men, were heading that way, but I had had enough of school. I wanted at life, whatever that meant, and I was beginning to think I could be a writer, clearly part of the attraction of my larger-than-life suitor.

Given the peculiar romance in which I found myself, my sixties were not "The Sixties," but then again, whose were? We all had our own pieces of it—more or less sex, more or less dope, more or less political grand-standing. For the boys who were sleeping with my friends, nice boys mostly, not the counterculture studs or the New Left Leaders with their morally laced machismo, Vietnam was a real crisis of conscience. For the sons of World War II vets, the task of putting a heroic spin on non-service while less fortunate men were dying, not to mention trying to get out of the draft in the first place, was no small psychic task, one that continues to reverberate through their ideas of maleness. There were losses for these men, too, with the assassination of the Kennedys and Martin Luther King, but the Kennedys in the main because they were, for these young men, the conscriptingly charismatic male figures whom they wanted to emulate, to follow, so that years later, no matter how much negative stuff has come out about Jack and Bobby, they continue to loom in the hearts of men. (Witness Oliver Stone's 1991 movie *JFK,* which tried to turn the slain leader into an ex post facto peacenik.)

At the time, we young women wept too, certainly, and felt an enor-mous sense of uncertainty. In retrospect, though, those assassinations helped clear away the father figures, so that women, trying to sort out the old and new messages, the old and new mystiques, were finally freed up by decade's end to have their moment. We female baby boomers had reached a critical mass on college campuses during the sixties, as Todd Gitlin points out in his book. Between 1950 and 1960, the number of college women eighteen to twenty-four increased by 47 percent and then by another 168 percent between 1960 and 1970. And these women were staying in school and graduating, unlike so many of our mothers had done. Oh yes, we had gone a long teasing way in a short time. Near the beginning of the decade I had flown across the country for the first time sitting primly beside Nana in a velvet-trimmed coat and gloves, and by the end I was braless and blue-jeaned, like all my friends, a change of clothes that certainly bespoke our coming change of consciousness, as did the shift in our language. No more washed-out mouths. Four-letter words were now part and parcel of many a female vocabulary, and it was not uncommon, among the pristine redwoods, to hear the refrain "Go fuck yourself" out of a coed's mouth. This was, as it turned out, an exhilarating teaser of what was to come as we continued our uncharted path away from the traditional course of female lives.

TIME-OUT

I am on an enforced sabbatical from my quest. A body can take only so much, and they have told me to go home and chill out, in so many words. The overheated mechanism must be given a chance to cool down, get back to normal, take a deep breath. All is quiet below. No hormones, no shots, no cumbersome ovaries. And while there is relief in the respite, in many ways this time-out is harder. Untethered from the clinic, I feel adrift, unmoored, as if I might float away, and though we make love on the odd, miraculous chance that something might connect, some lucky egg and some wildly perseverant sperm, it is a perfunctory, arid kind of sex, driven for me only by the underlying procreative urge.

I still faithfully use those little drugstore ovulation kits, waiting for the stick to turn blue—the sign of impending ovulation—and then and only then can I manage sex. Hope will not leave me alone even as increasingly I am convinced that something is essentially wrong, something beyond the one bad tube, the scarring from the PID and the subsequent surgery. Something doesn't work here. There's an elemental or hormonal hitch. As far as I can see, I have some explained infertility—that tube, my penchant for making unrupturing follicles—and some unexplained fertility. Enough of my system does seem to work just fine. But now there's an added quirk: My husband's sperm is a little mercurial, a little more sluggish as time passes. And the count is not terrific. But there are dazzling new techniques for this problem too, the doctor assures me. Another acronym, of course: PZD, or partial zona dissection, in which a hole is literally drilled into the egg (more specifically, into its covering, the zona pellucida) allowing a man's weak-swimming sperm to get in more easily. There is also something called microinjection of sperm, where one lonesome fertilizer is shot headfirst through the zona pellucida. So far we have not had to avail ourselves of these sperm-enhancing techniques—which are showing real promise—but who knows, what with the way things are going.

Still, the doctors remain cockeyed optimists. That is their role, their right, their need, dispositionally and financially, and I continue to alternate between gratefulness and full-tilt anger at their high-priced hold over me, over any of us going through this. They want us, they need us, and they've got us. We are the most obedient and desperate of clients, willing to sign on for anything, take anything. I am a rational, educated woman who cannot stop walking down this road, even as it seems I am throwing good money after bad. And yet I am simply marking time until they let me back in, let me start up again, let me plunge ahead mindless of the increasingly decreasing odds. After all, I've been through a slew of inseminations, one GIFT, one ZIFT. What's left? How many times can I do this? What fancy new procedure will they dream up when my back is turned to reseduce me with? I hear rumors out of the place about newfangled inseminations, intratubal inseminations, ITI, in which the sperm are whooshed not just up into the uterus, but up and beyond actually into the bottom of the fallopian tubes via a long, curvy catheter that goes up through the cervix and uterus into the tube. Oh boy, something new. Again, there are no statistics, just a flurry of hope among practitioners and patients, as always.

I miss them, my infertile sisters, their faces, their little white paper bags, their stories, their mordant humor. I just don't feel right out here among the living where people eat and sleep and go about their business. I watch them, interested at their everydayness, their small vanities. My husband brushes his teeth, my friend buys a new car, people eat huge greasy meals in restaurants and I study them like an alien from another planet, peering at humankind through the eyes of a stranger.

Is it just my paranoia induced by the lingering aftereffects of the drugs or do "normal" people look amiss at me too? No question, I am fragile and high strung in ways I never was, off center. I feel defective. I know that's crazy, that my failure—and isn't that a pejoratively loaded word to throw at oneself—is a quirk of fate, of nature, of bad biological luck and, yes, bad medical care, maybe my mother's, certainly my own. And yet it is hard not to carry a stigma of shame, of failure, even as my liberated self, my always-struggling-to-be-liberated self, categorically rejects the label. But many of us in this world—we high-achievers turned late baby-makers—are used to judging ourselves harshly, measuring our successes and failures as if the fate of womankind itself were ours to bear. And this is no different, I'm afraid. Of course, I am sure the drugs themselves, lingering in my psyche if not in my system, up the ante on all these feelings, make everything seem exaggerated. The doctors deny there is any hangover from these drugs; they say they dissipate quickly. But that's not the way it feels. They seem to have their claws in me even during this time off.

Friends delicately nudge me to give up the search, get back to my normal self, take a vacation, adopt. They are well meaning, gentle, sympathetic, implying that if I just relax and/or adopt, well then, maybe I will turn up pregnant. You know, unwind a little, lighten up and perhaps you'll get knocked up. Maybe you are just pushing too much, trying too hard— that is the clear inference, of course. Even relative strangers—since I have been public about my baby-longing in print—lean forward at parties and urge me to adopt or remind me in one way or another that I am blessed and have a good life and could I please just get on with it. I smile back, as if, yes, I will certainly consider their advice, even as in my secret soul I am angrily deflecting their nosy goodwill and counting down the days till I can reclaim my rightful position in the stirrups. It is there I seek redemption. I see forty dead ahead and everything in me wishes to cheat time and turn up pregnant before that birthday. I don't mind getting older. In fact, I like it, the sense of self, the cessation of certain worries, certain felt obligations. It is only this that I mind: turning forty without a baby. Even as I say it one more time, I laugh at the absurdity of this enormously late procreating. Is it fair, after all, to have a twenty-year-old when one is sixty, not to mention the age of the father? I imagine us at our child's graduation from college, elderly parents of a no-doubt embarrassed young person in mortarboard. That's what's so unnerving about this time-out. It forces one to reexamine the entire quest. I ask myself again and again: What's the drive, the need? Is it to be a mother to my own offspring only, or to mother? That I can do easily. All around me the worn-out infertiles, the clinic dropouts, are adopting and their smiles are genuine, relieved. I see them with their newborns and wonder: Why not? Is my desire simply to nurture a small soul and bring some joy into his or her life? If so, then let's adopt, as the Greek chorus of the concerned would have me do, and get on with it. Or is it something more basic, all right, more narcissistic, to have a baby of one's own genes, to see across an infant's face the play of one's own features and to imagine within the flowering of a personality akin to one's own, or at least derived from it, to contribute to one's familial tribe a biologically connected baby? Am I simply suffering from some sort of genetic narcissism, as some feminists maintain, a dupe of patriarchy and technology that makes me want to produce a child of my own? In my masochistic moments I read their books—*Recreating Motherhood* and *Beyond Conception*—their tirades against this high-tech breeding. It is a violation, they assert, and I am reminded of how different things look from the inside. One thing to rant about situations—as I indeed have done myself—another to be in them.

I do get it. I am deeply aware of the manipulative, money-making, heartbreaking, elitist and, yes, patriarchal slant of the whole business. In deference to the delicate egos of men, any defect of sperm, for example, comes under the rubric of "the male factor," while our female biological quirks are itemized and demonized. We have "hostile mucus," "incompetent cervixes" and "irritable uteruses." How's that for a malevolent trio, as if our biology itself had a demonic personality—like those rapacious vaginas that wander through the male imagination threatening to swallow them up. Yes, I get it, but I cannot back out, no way, not yet. Am I simply suffering from demented gene-lust, precisely what these same critics accused William Stern of in the Baby M case back in 1987? I covered that trial for *The New York Times Magazine* and while I came down against the idea of surrogacy, finding it a form of baby-buying, I have to confess that Bill Stern's longing in that courtroom did not feel so different finally from my own. Wasn't he, in fact, on some level, the kind of man the women's movement envisioned, a man tender to the point of tears about the baby he'd fathered? No way, they all shouted. He was a womb-renting patriarch of the worst order, and I realized that like a quizzical Catholic who rankled under some of the tenets of his or her faith, I rankled under some of the tenets of feminism and always had, trying all along the way to carve my own new faith out of the old. A feminist existentialist. It occurred to me that that's what I was and had always been and now, with every fiber of my being I wanted not only to be a mother but to give birth, to be pregnant, to feel that second pulse thumping inside. That cannot be discounted, the feminist theoreticians notwithstanding. There is a sense of a space unused and I hate that, hate the idea of never once being pregnant, of carrying with me into menopause and old age that never-once-occupied space. It riles my imagination, my internal never-occupied condo-womb where no one ever took up residence, knocked on my belly from the inside out. How can this be? How can those embryos have not taken hold, not taken root? Where did they go, those zygotes, those bare beginnings of life floating off and turning my uterus into a cemetery? Am

I woman enough to throw up my hands and walk away and stop trying to make more embryos? I cannot stop, not yet. The teasing ability to make these embryos is too irresistible, if heartbreaking. The process forces much philosophizing.

Does life begin at conception? Oh, the old devil question. I must think no with part of my soul—else I could not do this; and yet I must think yes with another—else I could not do this—and there are many days I wish I had been born before any of this technology was available. Then I would have just had to make my peace. Get a baby, not get a baby and get on with it. There are days, too, when I actively wish I was from a different time—how about those "repressive" fifties, for example—when women had babies at age twenty. How about that? I could have a twenty-year-old now. Or I wish sometimes that my husband and I could not make these embryos at all, that our sperm and egg would simply lie inert in a petri-dish Mexican standoff or that the doctor or doctors would somehow agree that I was beyond their help (try to find a fertility doctor who will tell you that; in fairness, some do, but usually only after the patient is well nigh broke and broken). Sometimes I wish I just had the guts to junk the quest myself. But alas, on my resolute days I am able to face forward again, eyes on the embryonic prize, knowing I will plow ahead, contenting myself with the thought that perhaps some young woman down the road will get pregnant via technology that is being tried out on my weary body. Not weary enough, as it turns out. And as at so many pivotal points in my life, as at the long-ago juncture when as a baby-faced twenty-two-year-old I said a reluctant "I do" to my outsized suitor even as the feminist manifestos flew warning me against precisely that, I am not sure that what I am doing is the better part of courage or the better part of cowardice. Maybe a bit of both. Maybe that's the lesson, that an act of courage might contain the seed of cowardice just as an act of seeming cowardice might contain the seed of courage. Certainly, marrying as I did, when I did, when the chorus of liberation was bidding me be free, felt like a hopeful and courageous step forward and a capitulation. Both. Truth is: I don't make a very good ideologue and I didn't right from day one when, in the first giddy years of marriage, I began to add my own voice to the feminist upheaval.

10

THE SEVENTIES:
HOT TUBS AND HOT MANIFESTOS

They crashed against the shores of our consciousness in the first years of the 1970s, wave after wave of them, the manifestos of women's liberation. What a concept. What a lifeline. No, what a context. That's what they did, they put us in context, after so many years of trying to figure out what had felt so elementally askew, in those heavy-breathing beds and earlier, in our angst-filled adolescent days, and all the way back, watching our moms, our beloved, repudiated moms. We had done it, too, repudiated them, and were regrettably destined, in the throes of liberationist euphoria, to do it more, to castigate some of the bargains they had made, before, of course, we realized in the postliberation doldrums that we had done it too: made bargains, different ones, but often the same ones. But that is to get too far ahead, to preempt the euphoria my friends and I felt poring over those angry, defiant words of the feminist firebrands. Germaine Greer and Kate Millett and Robin Morgan and Matina Horner and Sally Kempton with her brave, sad piece. It was like awakening in a new country with a new declaration of independence. Our declaration. Our independence. Though we would be caricatured in hindsight as eager acolytes sprung from the dreams of some ferocious (translation: man-hating, lesbian-leaning) females, that was not at all what it felt like, or what it was, given our history, given where we had come from. It felt like the beginning of a long overdue, if overwrought, healing. On an intellectual, personal and political level, I was never to feel so giddy, so hopeful, even as the new manifestos with their often high-handed injunctions against marriage and motherhood were a little scary, a little dauntingly rage-filled. It was a lot to take in, to assimilate, for us fifties kids, right on the heels of our grappling with the mixed blessings of the now ongoing sexual upheaval. This was the next wave to ride. I pored over all those fierce words feeling elated, hopeful—all that stuff about obligatory screws and marital enslavement and clitoral orgasms—all those manifestos that I dutifully underlined in my studently fashion. At last we would be free; we would throw off the shackles; we would chart a new path, define a new world in which men and women would be equal partners, tender and strong and proud, everybody entitled to the full range of their emotional, sexual and productive selves. For one bright, shining moment, in those days of the early 1970s, it truly seemed possible, irrefutable. Who would want anything less?

So what did you do, then, as a young, ambitious, determined-to-succeed, manifesto-devouring but adamantly tethered young woman? I got married is what I did, which made my liberation all the more difficult. I simply could not see a way around it. I was not able to leave the gruff, earnest and sometimes endearing lover/mentor I had taken up with. Here I had been enlightened, hit over the head with my oppression, had it spelled out for me in chapter and verse—the superior attitude of men that had nagged me all my life from my earliest conscious days as a pampered kitten in my fifties household—and yet I turned around and signed on for marriage, a unit that would prove intransigent, weighted down with traditions and prejudices, hard to renegotiate despite all one's efforts to the contrary. There was now a bloodbath of retrogressive sex manuals telling (the newly freed-up) women how to please men—Dr. David Reuben, for example, advising us in his 1971 best-seller, *Any Woman Can,* that "the most effective way for a woman to guarantee happiness in marriage is to refuse complete sexual satisfaction before marriage and *never* refuse it after marriage."

In short, obligatory sex was of the essence, no matter what those libbers said, not just obligatory sex but now you were supposed to be friskily multiorgasmic to prove to your man how effective a lover he was. As "J," the explicitly cooing author of *The Sensuous Woman* (1969) reminded us: "Pin up on your bed, your mirror, your wall, a sign, lady, until you know it in every part of your being: We were designed to delight, excite and satisfy the male of the species." J offered a list of "sensuality exercises" on the order of licking your own fingertips with your eyes closed, and reading her manualette, I wasn't sure whether to laugh or cry or grumble angrily. No question, the phallic undertow was already snaking its way through the culture, and those of us who married at that point would learn the same thing, that the male-female balance, particularly the marital arrangement, would be very resistant to change. There were so many built-in expectations that would be hard to shake, to reform. The hardest to change would be the notion that we women were responsible for the nest, making it and certainly keeping it clean, not to mention tending to everyone's emotional and sexual needs. But on we plowed.

Having come through our repressed fifties childhoods, on into strained teenhoods that gave way to the sexual upheaval of the late sixties, with its new tyrannies, then into the heady heyday of liberation, we sailed with a kind of hopeful resignation into marriage, putting the accent, depending on the week or the day or the minute, on hope or resignation. A lot of my close friends married then, marrying their college boyfriends in simple ceremonies in rabbis' offices or in summer meadows, hoping to do it differently than their parents had done, the weight of the institution notwithstanding. The pared-down marriage ceremonies were an indication of their intentions: no vast church extravaganzas with umpteen bridesmaids in satin dresses; no vows to honor and obey; no taking of their husbands' names. When it came my turn, I did, in fact, add my husband's name to my own, thus becoming a three-namer. It felt more liberated to me, more adult than simply going through life as Daddy's little girl—after all, it was our fathers' names we had all been carrying here—though my choice put me into immediate tension with my heartier feminist acquaintances, sending up my spine that old chill I had felt when confronted by an irate Aunty Cathryn when I chose to forswear that long-ago beauty pageant.

By January of 1971, having rushed through college in three years because I thought it would keep me from being bored and because I was more or less anxious to get on with my life, I was back living with the man I loved in his Malibu apartment trying, in fact, not to get married. I had called off one wedding as my mother was literally on the way to the post office with the invitations. I was too young, too unfinished, too out of my depth. While we had blurred into the carnival of late-sixties Santa Cruz, back in LA, on Karl's home working turf, I was often treated like an unwelcome Lolita. At one black-tie party he took me to in Beverly Hills, the coiffed and bejeweled women in their floor-length gowns glared at me in my thigh-high mini-frock with daisies all over it. At the sound of the dinner bell, one materialized beside me, cooing, "Oh honey, I thought they were going to put you to bed with the other children before dinner."

There were other parties, backyard get-togethers in what, in retrospect, was clearly the height of the suburban sexual revolution. I knew these couples; I knew the women and I knew their husbands. They were in their thirties, recent arrivals usually from somewhere else. They didn't stand a chance. There was just too much sun and too much temptation. I watched the wives on these evenings, learning to smoke dope and gamely getting in and out of hot tubs, these pretty heartland moms with their Breck hair and maternal flesh, dimpled in the moonlight. I watched them watching their husbands watch the younger, saucier girls and it was like watching an impending train wreck.

Some couples did make it through all this unscathed, or not completely unscathed, but with a few manageable infidelities and the women went on, after their children were in school, to have major careers of their own. But some went too far to get back, ending up divorced and angry and broke. There were lessons everywhere. It was a mine field, being a woman, and that's what the manifestos were all saying, or shouting, reiterating what you had felt from your earliest days. You had to have your own life; you had to have your own money. But like my friends, I married hopefully, figuring somehow it would all be OK. I was just too smitten with the idea of love to walk away, too taken with the idea that I was an object of rapture to some big grown-up man. All those male romance novels, on top of all the childhood fairy tales of rescued damsels, not to mention all those dreamy rock-and-roll ballads about being Johnny's girl, had done their work, which no number of Germaine Greers could easily undo. No, that's not right. It wasn't being loved that thrilled me, but the reverse. I was so pleased to love; that was the unexpected part, given how scratchy I often felt, certainly toward men. There was something else, I think: the recognition that for women marriage could provide freedom, enough security to cut loose both sexually and professionally, if it worked right, that it could be a kind of expansive cocoon. I think that was my hope, that I would find liberation within marriage, that I would bloom into a fulsome, highly functioning female, no matter how steeply I had been warned against that idea.

So on an unseasonably warm March day in 1972, the year I was exactly half Karl's age, we were married on the tented terrace of my father's house in Santa Monica, the one my mother, my sister and I had left him in almost two decades earlier. The ceremony was a high-spirited, homespun one, typical of the times. We wrote our own vows. We served fried chicken. And I, a twenty-two-year-old baby-faced bride in a form-fitting, cream-colored Rudi Gernreich dress (he was famous for his topless knit bathing suit) was yielded unto marriage by both my father and my mother. Vestiges of the new (the downplayed pomp) and of the old (why was anyone giving me away at all?), exactly what marriage in general felt like.

What was palpably obvious was that no flurry of feminist outrage could so easily contradict all that other conditioning. The forms were tenacious, the male-female forms, try as we might to change them.

Being a young wife in the early seventies was, at least for me, a highly conflicted state. Among my wedding shower presents were both a pair of black crotchless panties bestowed by some salivating distant relative and a slender book called *Advice to a Young Wife from an Old Mistress*, a chatty admonishment to us young brides not to get tangled up in conjugal drudgery but to remain attentive and attractive, frolicsome and flirtatious, in short, mistressy. ("Wives," the book states, "might be amazed to know how much time a mistress spends listening; cooking favorite dishes; selecting a gift or her own clothes to please; developing her own knowledge of many things from medieval art to fly-casting; seeking out new places to go; caring.") That was also the message of the popular *Cosmopolitan* magazines I sometimes read or skimmed. Helen Gurley Brown was and would continue to be the perverse pamphleteer of quasi-liberation urging young women to get theirs by sucking up to men (quite literally). It was manipulation with a brassy, updated sexual spin, which said nothing finally about finding your own voluptuous self—hardly what the indefatigably scrawny and coquettish Ms. Gurley Brown was all about. But young and eager to be happy, to be loved and loving, I processed all this retro-advice from Gurley Brown and Dr. David Reuben right along with that of the radical feminists, just as I alternated between eager new brideisms—lacy nightgowns (white in the early years, black to come later as I matriculated from child-bride to temptress) and three-course meals—and an agitated determination to avoid all that prescripted wifely behavior, all the flirtatious attentiveness of the hard-to-shake feminine mystique, and get on with my as-yet-undefined life's work.

I was often giddy with passion and hope. I loved having a little house of my own, our little white cottage with its messy, sprawling back garden. I loved cooking and having a kitchen of my own. It was, as far as I could see, the only creative or sensual aspect of housework. We spent hours making meals together, my new husband and I, elaborate dinners of stews and homemade bread and the fried fare of his Southern home turf. On sunny days we rode our big Triumph motorcycle into the coastal hills to gather wildflowers, driving home at dusk chilly and pressed together, inhaling their sweetness. There were happy times, too, when my four young stepsons spent the weekend and we made a noisy slumber party out of our reconstituted family, for me, an unaccustomed spill of maleness. The boys were so lifeful, so loud, so hopeful, so forgiving, and I loved them as survivors of the same great romantic upheaval in which we all seemed to be costarring. Their father had drawn clean lines for all of us, something very rare, I was to learn later from my other friends who inherited stepchildren. He made it clear that he loved them, but that they could and would not come between the two of us, just as I could and would not come between him and them. Clean. There would be no games, no guilt. I loved him for that.

But there were also times when I felt like Sally Kempton in her *Esquire* piece. The man I married sometimes just seemed so big, so furry, so phallic, so crowding, so certain, and there were nights I lay down next to him in a rage. There were mornings when I awoke abashed to find I had scratched my thighs the night before in the frenzy of not being able to make myself understood, even my love understood, by a hard-driving, hard-drinking, hard-talking Southern orphan boy who had no business being in my life nor I in his. It felt as if we were clawing our way across that gulf between us, a gender gulf, a geographic gulf, a generational gulf, any and every gulf you can name. Both sensitive and insecure, he glared at me when I contradicted him at parties and was brusque when my college friends came to stay. I simply didn't know how to take him on over these things, didn't know how to stick up for myself, to tell him to knock it off. It was hard to be liberated. You just didn't get it overnight, not after all the other training, the shh's and self-abnegations, the maternal examples, the paternal put-downs. You didn't just, in the wake of some rousing literary vehemence, turn around and be strong and self-assured and authentically independent—not the brittle, defiant, tough-jawed defiance some of us women did seem to adopt, but authentic independence, a solid sense of self-worth and strength, especially within the confines of love and marriage. It was too quick a turnaround, though many of us tried to make it in that giddy, hopeful shrill moment.

My friends Julie and Jane also married in the early seventies, even as they, too, were feeling emboldened by the women's movement. Nearing thirty, with her gypsy/hippie look at its flagrantly sensual height, Julie had had a succession of wounding romances with hotshot businessmen who, as she says, couldn't be monogamous. Bruised by men and determined to make it on her own, she turned heart and soul toward career.

"Can I tell you the rage, not just from the affairs, but from always knowing you were second class?" she said to me. "I was enraged at the choreography of life, that men and women are simply not treated equally. It was a joke to go to college between 1960 and sixty-eight. You were going to get out with a degree and become a secretary. A lot of women majored in psych or education or social welfare—caretaking stuff. Those were the jobs you could get that weren't secretarial. I was absolutely ripe for the women's movement when it came along. I got hired as a summer producer at this radio station. When it was up, this old crusty guy who was my boss was going to replace me on some pretext or another. He gave me some nonsense about the union objecting because I'd been a replacement. So I went to the union meeting with my own little petition and got them all to sign and went back to him and said, 'See. You're wrong.' And he gave me the job and later he told me, after we'd become friends, that he saw himself in me at that moment. I thought I was the prototype of the new woman, strong but feminine. I liked the idea that I was part of a movement, part of history, though I did think some of the rhetoric was silly, like that line about women needing men like fish need bicycles. Crap like that. But I would not have gotten my job except for the women's movement and the government pushing people at that point to hire women. And my friends were getting in the door too. We just saw ourselves climbing this wonderful ladder, so I was able to ignore the other urges. I don't even know what other urges were in there.

"I did marry in 1973 when I was almost thirty, a hospital administrator. It was easy and comfortable. He was a sweet man, very supportive of my career, and for a while, like my pattern, we were passionate and then it went away. I didn't even think about children in that marriage. The career was so satisfying, so satiating, almost in a sexual way. It was just so exciting to think that you were going to be more than your mother was. Maybe we did end up being selfish somehow."

Selfish seems a strong self-indictment. What we were was fierce out of fear, given where we had come from, afraid always of ending up under the male thumb, afraid of not being independent, afraid, too, of the passion because it came at such cost. But we went ahead and married, gamely walking down the aisle, thus fulfilling the old notions of a woman's place even as the manifestos flew.

Jane Allen, graduated from college and heading toward business school, did the same as Julie and I. On an August evening in 1971, just as the day's heavy heat was abating a little, wearing a high-necked Victorian dress, she married her fellow Yalie, Dawson Cooper, in a fairly traditional wedding in a field in New Hampshire while a friend played the guitar and sang folk songs.

"I woke up very early that morning and went downstairs to be alone before everything started," she said in her soft, earnest voice. "I remember listening to Rachmaninoff's 'Rhapsody on a Theme of Paganini' on the record player—it's very sad and lilting—and I was in the living room and I just cried when I heard it, and I had this overwhelming notion of terrible regret for the childhood and adolescence that had never been fun. It had all been deadly serious and hard work, bone-crushing hard work, all maneuvering and negotiating, nothing ever discussed that really needed discussing, my parents just circling each other. I was very clear that what was offered to women wasn't enough, though I was often shocked or provoked or surprised or baffled by the feminist proclamations. It did seem awfully definite: You shouldn't do this, you shouldn't do that. Men are all shits. On the other hand, I think that the urge I had to go out and make my own living and never ask for a dime from a man is very much at the heart of it. I mean, that's independence by a standard that has always been considered male. And I think it has changed my life from what it would have been. I don't think I foresaw the consequences, but it's very clear that it would have been harder for me to learn to be dependent than to learn to be independent. But I also wanted to be married. I loved the beginning. We had every intention of going to graduate school and then going into business together before having children, which we just assumed we would have. Three actually. We discussed the name for the first one a lot, if it was a boy we would call him this, if a girl, that."

I, too, loved the beginning of marriage, the hope of it, and in my innocence and egotism I, too, wanted to improve the world, and the only means I had at hand were words. Always words. So shortly after I married I began in earnest to try to become a writer. My first printed piece, "Up from Slavery—to What?" was a manifesto/counter-manifesto urging women to hold on to their uniqueness even as they sought liberation. It appeared as a "My Turn" essay in the *Newsweek* magazine of January 21, 1974. Day after day I sat at the dining room table pounding along on my old Smith Corona typewriter, eagerly thrusting my words under the acute editorial eye of my husband at day's end. He had left *Newsweek* right after we were married to start a small weekly newspaper on which I got my start, writing recipes and restaurant reviews. When it folded nine months later for lack of funds, he felt professionally unmoored for the first time in his life. I felt implicated in his unmooring, as if he had abandoned his whole life trajectory to start anew with me. I soothed him as best I knew how while trying to find my own voice and enlist his aid in that search and it wasn't easy, any of it. Our shared passion for words, for journalism, would be one of our greatest bonds and he would be my most astute editor, a tough and tenacious mentor though I know it wasn't easy, me muscling in on his turf, and especially since this was uncharted territory then. Women had worked before, certainly. My mother had. But this was new, we were a frisky, emboldened lot who were collectively threatening to men. Many of us, far from being the caricatured bra-burning man-haters of those days were bending over backward in our marriages to soothe the blow of our ambition. Most of us went right on doing "womanly" or "wifely" things: shaving our legs and fixing dinners even more elaborate than the ones our casserole-baking moms had turned out. That's essentially what that first piece of mine was all about—women trying to be liberated without being mean and male in the bargain. I was already staking out the irreverent middleland, already worrying about giving up one set of tyrannies, the old female ones, for another set, the traditionally competitive, work-till-you-drop-dead-of-a-coronary male ones, already worried that if feminism did not somehow celebrate female-ness—not femininity, but femaleness—it would lose something grand, something elemental, some source of strength, of originality. Equality had started to seem like a false goal because on certain primal levels—sex, for example—equality was impossible as I had learned in my maiden bed. We were the entered, they did the entering and no amount of theorizing, no amount of clitorizing sex, i.e., making it external, as it were, would alter that fact. I liked the subversive wisdom I saw in the women around me, cherished it, the chutzpah of the perennial outsider, and I feared losing it, being cramped again into some small space, some small male-defined, pin-striped space where you slogged away until they handed you the proverbial gold watch at the end of the line. Was that life, the one we wanted? I certainly didn't. Nor did I want to identify with the aggressor—go on identifying with the aggressor, I should say, since I had been doing that for a long time. I wanted to be liberated from that too. In the *Newsweek* piece this is how my own personal feminism was already shaking out:

For a long time now I've been going to parties and hearing that creative people in America are—like gasoline, raisins and happily married couples—becoming scarcer and scarcer. To which I always reply, "Just wait until we 'new' women find our voices. Then you'll see the real stuff again."

Apparently, my boast was hasty and naive. We may have come a long way, baby, but if our first creative efforts—the books, the magazines, the films, the canvases, the TV shows, the plays and the poems—are any indication, it isn't nearly far enough. The sad truth is that the words women are writing, the magazines they're editing, the shows they're producing sound almost exactly like what their husbands, lovers, or masters, if you will, have been turning out for years. . . . In fact, women are going men one better: they're running faster, swinging harder, playing rougher.

This female toughness may be excused as an entrance fee, a survival device that women feel they have to use. But what it really is, it seems to me, is a capitulation and a copout. It's as if we were all sticking our thumbs under our overall straps and saying, "See. See how sharp and quick our little minds are. We can think like men after all. We can even outplay you at your own game."

A word of caution. I am a women's liberationist, a feminist. Like any other halfway sane woman in this country, I have to be. I want it, and I want it all, and I want it now. And I concede that this wanting of mine has been made a lot easier by the efforts of some hard-thinking and hard-talking women who have gone before.

What I want is equal rights—professional, emotional, and sexual. What I don't want is that good old American brand of equality that insists that we're all equal not only in rights but in body and soul as well. What I don't want is to give up my specialness, my female ethnicity. The trouble is, there seems to be only one game in town. And like blacks who had to take the kinks out of their hair and the jive out of their language—their recent attempts to put both back in being symbolic not substantial victories—to get into the game, there will be enormous pressure on me to lay aside my frills of body and mind at the entrance gate. I don't want to think, eat, sleep, talk, laugh, act or write like a man. I don't want to wear a handsome suit, carry a briefcase and anticipate clogged arteries at age 40. I don't even want to wear blue jeans all the time. I don't want to make, in short, all the same mistakes men have been making for years. I don't want to hate homosexuals, coworkers or beautiful women just because they threaten me.

What I worry about as I enter the real world is how much of my fantasizing, my craziness, my intuition I'll have to leave at home in order to be successful out there. I strongly believe that it is our much-mocked feminine intuition that will make us better doctors, lawyers and Indian chiefs. With that intuition, we can operate out of an instinctive wisdom, not out of the pragmatic reflex that propels our men to Watergate and other such sinkholes.

I worry that I've already been seduced, that I'll also do anything to earn an extra buck or an extra pat on the head. I worry that I'll push and pull whatever small talents I have to suit the market. I worry that I'll round off my corners so I can slip into the game unnoticed, that I'll play for "their" stakes—a jazzy job, a jazzy husband and jazzy kids— and abide by their rules. I worry that I'll learn to be clever, to take all the short cuts, to steal all the bases. All of which makes me worry that I'll never hit a home run, or that I may never even try. And if you don't try to hit home runs, why play ball?

Again, some stricter feminist souls, including friends of mine, angrily said that I was a seditious sellout, betraying the cause of female emancipation by falling back into notions of gender differences. I was adamantly in favor of equal rights and eternally grateful to women like Julie Templeton who were knocking down the barriers in front of me, all those women in those magazine and newspaper offices who were meeting and filing lawsuits. I just worried that in our zeal for so-called equality we were buying into male definitions of success, big-time, mainstream, capitalistic, male notions of achievement and that that would be the death knell not only of true liberation, of any truly alternative political or economic class consciousness, but also of the sweet sorority that had been the upside of my childhood experience, both at home and in my girls' school. I didn't want to lose the chatty, commiserative female community that had supported me, and yes, I liked looking pretty, and yes, I liked being seductive when it didn't seem obligatory. And above all, I wanted to go on being a dissident, certainly if I was going to be a decent writer and/or social commentator. I distrusted orthodoxy, even feminist orthodoxy. Having so recently found my voice, I lived in absolute fear of somehow losing it anew, having it whittled into ideologically correct platitudes that were at odds sometimes with the goal of liberation. Even as I embraced feminism and, yes, felt saved by it, I was pushing against it because it accentuated the sense I had of being divided against myself—at war with my own sex—and so began my ongoing intimate literary wrestle with a movement and a philosophy that were at the center of my young life. I worried then about what I would continue to worry about, that with the careers we would end up parroting the worshipful male attitude toward fame and fortune (as opposed to honest, creative work), the dismissive attitude toward femaleness, and the capitalistic, count-up-your-orgasms version of sexuality the new manuals were all espousing, make that clitoral orgasms. Germaine Greer had spotted the tyranny in that, saying that "if we localize female response in the clitoris, we impose on women the same limitations of response which has stunted the male response." And if we said we were equal, who was going to give us child care, if and when we needed it, and across-the-board maternity leave? We should have insisted on it right then.

The movement mothers, like the leaders of NOW (the National Organization for Women) did try to insist on it, but we eager young women plowing into the work force did not have babies on our minds. Oh no, anything but. When my husband would talk tenderly about wanting to have a beautiful little girl with me, I would freeze in terror beneath him. Marriage was one thing. That I had succumbed to, with hope; that I could walk away from if need be. But motherhood, no. That's where I would draw the line. I remembered too much from my own history, from the fifties and the sixties and now here in the swinging early seventies, when the message to educated young women was being reiterated everywhere we looked, the message that motherhood was a desexualizing trap. I had been at those evenings and in those hot tubs—I'm not talking about sex parties, just sloppily charged summer evenings—and it was the men (not the women's libbers) who, if I am not mistaken, made their wives feel dislocated, unhip, and made me shiver at the thought of being in their place. No, not for us, my contemporaries and I. We would be a different breed, sexually adroit and professionally intent. We would find work and cling to it. Certainly that was my intent. No babies for me, not then, if ever. That, in fact, was the theme of my follow-up essay for *Newsweek* written the year after the first. "Making Babies," it was called, a prophetically inelegant title since down the road that's precisely what I would end up doing, making babies, or trying to, in test tubes and petri dishes. Call it the piece that came back to haunt:

Four years ago, when I was 21 and newly school-sprung, many of the women I knew—myself included—were agonizing about whether to marry. Most of us finally did. Now a lot of my friends and other women of my generation are agonizing about whether to get pregnant. Many of us haven't so far. And the troubling thought has crept into our souls and our wombs (presuming they are separate places and sometimes I'm not so sure they are) that we just might never make babies, that we might enter middle age alone—perhaps divorced or widowed—childless, womb-tight and woebegone. Why, if women face this almost certain aloneness later on, are so many of us so strangely steeled against pregnancy? . . . The most oft-given answer is: "Well, I have a career to pursue and I can't risk dividing my loyalties between work and a baby." How stern and unlovely and downright corny that sounds. Yet I myself have said it many a time and will undoubtedly say it many more. I believe it. I believe that I am not put together enough right now to cope with dishes and diapers and postpartum depressions while trying to carry on what I imagine to be a life's work.

A baby was never going to fill my me-need, my what-am-I-going-to-do-when-I-grow-up-need. I always knew that. And then the women's movement came along and firmed up my resolve to work and the resolves of women like me. Also, many of us had watched our mothers try, at 40, to pick up the pieces of some long-abandoned life and work when our fathers had left them. Their example was not lost on us. I have many times said to myself and heard other women say: "That won't happen to me. I'll always have my work. Nobody—but nobody—can take that away from me."

And so, rather fiercely, we cling to our work as to a life raft, hoping that it will keep us afloat in good times and bad. Though we might in private moments yearn sometimes to trade in our full heads and empty wombs for empty heads and full wombs, we cannot now. Having committed ourselves so early and so firmly to our so-called careers, we are afraid to commit also to a baby. We're afraid to risk failing twice. It is, in fact, precisely because we take motherhood so seriously—as, God help us, we seem to take everything these days—that we're staying away from it, at least for the moment.

There is something, though, deeper than our work that is keeping many of us from making babies, something to do with sex. What has happened to many young women, I think, is that effective contraceptives—which we have used faithfully for a decade—are now so much a part of our bodies, and of our consciousness, that we are scared to set them aside, scared to get pregnant, not physically scared, some other kind of scared, a bigger kind. Before the recent arrival of failsafe contraceptives, lovemaking for women was baby-making, pure and simple. But these new contraceptives put women on an equal footing—rather, on an equal bedding—with men, so that for us, sexual pleasure is now no longer an accidental by-product of procreation, just as a baby is now no longer the by-product of accidental afternoon lust. The very urges themselves, the lovemaking urge and the baby-making urge, have become separated in women. Now we can, like men, bed at will, without being physically or psychologically penalized, without having the moment complicated, or dignified, by the possibility of procreation. What a relief! What a joy! . . . Many of the women I know long to tumble into pregnancy, like their mothers and grandmothers before them, with no agony aforethought, long to pledge allegiance with their wombs to the men they love. But they can't. They're stuck in a holding pattern. So am I. I'm feeling willful and wobbly and—oh, why do we women feel the need to soft-peddle it?—I'm competitive and ambitious and confused a lot and I don't think any baby ought to be subjected to me right now. At least no baby of mine.

After reading the essay, a friend called. "Sounds like you are protesting too much," he said. "It sounds like you really do want a baby." I was stunned. I reread the piece as I would do a hundred times in the years ahead, studying the head shot of the still baby-faced, twenty-five-year-old woman that accompanied it. Was he right? Did I want a baby but was steeled against it? I can't answer. I couldn't then. I was a product of my time, a typically fear-filled, chutzpah-filled beneficiary/victim of feminism, contraception and ambition, a young woman trying to find her way, trying to hold on to some irreverence, not be subsumed by competitive male culture, on the one hand, or domestic female culture on the other, while trying to have the best, least punitive aspects of both. With my editors I was outspoken, savvy and emphatic, ever eager to defend the slightest comma, but I continued to tiptoe around the man whom I loved and with whom I could not quite imagine having a baby. I couldn't imagine trying to do it all, be a serious writer, a wife and a mother. That violated my two-out-of-three rule. I put my head down over my typewriter and did not look up again for a decade, didn't even consider having a baby as I went about trying to grow up within the confines of marriage and learn to write at the same time. It was a collision or a collusion of so many things, my non-motherhood and that of many women I knew: the childhood memories, the non-fail contraceptives that had transformed our lives, the women's liberation movement hitting us right in our early twenties, the age when so many of our mothers had nested and bred. We were the making of a revolution, the unmaking of the idea that biology had to be destiny, and it was thrilling, thrilling to think that you had a purpose on earth beyond biology, beyond caretaking, beyond the traditional "female" role. The joy of those early writing years, pounding away in the dining room, has stayed with me always. It felt like a celebration, a coming home, an un-choking after all the years. I never felt lonely again in the same way. I was determined to remain a free-lance writer for as long as possible and was certainly gratefully aware that my professional liberation from a nine-to-five job was made possible by a man and his willing support of my quest. I did not want to have a regular job if I could help it because I figured I would learn to bend my voice for publication and because I figured I would be angry all the time, angry at the constraints, the editing, the men who ran things. I wanted to stay out of the fold, away from the power games inevitable on professional turf because I was afraid I would learn to play them all too well. So I stayed home, sitting in the dining room for the next stretch of years, adding my revolutionary, or quasi-revolutionary, voice to the melee and trying with everything in me to turn my marriage into a passionate partnership. I began to understand the pleasure and the cost of trying to stand on my own. And the immense difficulty of doing that, of, indeed, making good on the idea, not of feminism per se, but of liberation, both personally and professionally. All those delicious manifestos ringing in my ears to the contrary, it would be far from easy and take many more years than many of us ever imagined at that luminously angry moment of the early 1970s.

11

SOULS ON ICE

How long has it been since I have been here in this clinic? I look around. I feel a little jaded and recycled, especially as I don't recognize practically anyone. There's been a decided turnover. A handful of my sister patients have gotten pregnant; but the vast majority have fallen by the wayside, gotten out of the loop and I miss them. Their abdication feels like a bad omen. It is a brand-new year and I am forty. Oh, I didn't want to be forty, not this way. I passed the big birthday, grief-struck and irritable, and have only now, these two months later, been able to face another go. It has been almost a year since I have done anything outlandishly high tech. The ZIFT, as it turned out, took much more out of me than I realized, and as the months mounted I could not climb back up on the proverbial horse, could not get back in the stirrups as I had planned. The embryos haunted me, the ones that (who?) had come to naught, my children manqué. My mourning danced around them as if they had been full-blown babes in arms and I didn't have the physical, psychic or moral energy to jump right back in and make more. As 1989 slid along, I did dial back and do a few old, trusty inseminations and ran headlong into my new/old problem: the unruptured-follicle syndrome. Time and again, even on cycles when I didn't take any fertility drugs, when I just ovulated on my own and we put some washed and culled sperm up there in the uterus, the egg clung, the follicle wouldn't rupture, the system was elementally out of whack, and I finally figured that I had compounded whatever endemic faults there were and had better cool it for a while longer.

Sex? In the cool-down months I tried it, we tried it, when I was ovulating. In my decompression I had temporarily even given up buying the little Ovustick kits, the ones that turned blue, but so attuned had I become to my body, so aware of its inner rhythms, that I knew to the minute practically when and if the egg did let go, as indeed they still occasionally did, especially as the months went on and my system seemed to be settling back down. The drugs had helped in my ovulatory detective work, leaving my ovaries a little hypersensitive so I had cramps now, not only when I menstruated but also when I ovulated, a kind of comforting twang deep within that assured me I might still, by some miraculous chance, turn up pregnant and/or that I was at least not yet out of the game and into the change, as everyone cutely called menopause.

But now I am ready to try again, ready for the next acronym, and indeed, they have one tailor-made for me, according to the doctor. FET—frozen embryo transfer. Oh boy—time-lag procreation, that's what we're talking about here. It is advertised to me as the latest, surefire antidote to my failure to conceive. The idea is that the fertility drugs so rev up my excitable system that it makes it well nigh impossible for me to carry my embryos during the same cycle I make them. There is just too much background noise, as Dr. Marrs describes it, even with the Lupron shutting down my own system. It is as if my hyperactive mind has literally infected my reproductive parts, though again the doctor smiles indulgently at my poetic suggestion, debunking it politely as nonsense. Oh no, my problems are systemic, biological, and he can surmount them if I just hang in long enough. Oh yes, he is still gung ho, still full of a maddening and seductive optimism, this technostud, as I have come to look upon him, soft-spoken but ego-full, tender enough but driven toward getting us, his infertile harem, pregnant by whatever means possible. It is he, Dr. Marrs, who did the first successful frozen embryo transfer in this country in the summer of 1986. By that point, more than two dozen babies had already been born from frozen embryos in other parts of the world, in Australia and Britain, the Netherlands, Israel and West Germany, and there had been no perceptible damage to the babies in the chilly manner of their suspended conception.

Stored like sperm in liquid nitrogen of −196 degrees centigrade, the embryos are thawed and then inseminated straight into the uterus in a version of tape-delayed in vitro fertilization. This is now what I am looking at, now that the GIFT and ZIFT have fallen short: I will make embryos in one cycle, we will freeze them and put them back two or three months later. This appeals. There is something to enchant a baby-starved soul in this time-lag procreation, because for those two or three months I will have a full-fledged frozen family, babysicles, souls on ice. It is an extraordinary thought, this ability to literally stop time, suspend life and start it up at some later date. It seems magical, and I confess I am taken with the idea of it, just as I am susceptible to the doctor's explanation about my overstimulated system. I am as starved for a seemingly logical explanation of my infertility as I am for a baby, and he offers up one.

Never mind that the explanations change as the procedures fail. I simply choose to ignore that fact, cheerfully swallowing the next explanation that comes along. I am also taken with the idea that this will be the first procedure in which we make no use of my tubes, which, for my money if not the doctor's, are implicated in my fertility problems. He swears that one right tube is good, but there is no proof; in fact, there is counter-proof, if you ask me, and this FET business will circumvent that tube as the frozen embryos, when thawed, will be inseminated directly into my womb. Never mind that the odds for this are even lower than for GIFT and ZIFT and straight IVF, in which fresh, non-frozen embryos are used. I look at the odds—at best, an 8 to 10 percent chance that one of these embryos will take hold, odds that increase only slightly the more embryos you produce—but I don't blanch. I put my head down, pay my money and start methodically taking my drugs, the Lupron first and then in tandem with the Pergonal, and there is, as always in the beginning, that lurching sense of hope.

Relocated friends visit in the middle of my shot-taking, an old high school classmate and her fifteen-year-older husband, and he and I discover that we are both taking Lupron to suppress our respective hormones. The drug works the same way for women and men. We laugh at the symmetry, at the turn our lives have taken since we were last together almost a decade ago when they moved away from Los Angeles. I am taking it, of course, to try to make a life; he is taking it to prolong one, to suppress his male hormones so they do not speed up the spread of his prostate cancer. We shoot up together, me jabbing daintily at my already bruised thigh, the one that still contains the fading map of my last mistaken shot, he, burly and unafraid, grabbing his belly and jamming the needle in with the mordant savoir faire of someone for whom minor discomfort has become completely incidental. Watching, I love him so, and feel my quest dwarfed by comparison. He had already given himself on the order of 600 shots and must continue doing so for the rest of his life. He has been chemically castrated and tells me that in and among the things his wife misses most is his smell, reminiscent to her of her father, which the drug has taken away.

She and I don't talk about that. Instead we laugh about the difference in our lives. Like me, she married right out of college, and as I launched into a work life, she became a kind of earth mother, baking bread and having children—two boys, now eleven and seventeen. She has a sturdy softness and insists on giving me my last shot, the hCG, and then they are gone and I am once more in the operating room, promising to name my embryos after her and her family.

They're in the dish again, some seven of my eggs, a passel of sperm and there is nothing to do but wait. Tomorrow they will call. I am suffering from a little minor postpartum depression and, as always, massive anticipatory fears. I wonder: Has the year been cruel, is forty some procreative Maginot Line as the studies suggest, or can I still make embryos? Can we? And if we can, there will still be no immediate resolution, no tortured two-week countdown. No, instead I will cede them to the deep freeze and get on with my life. There are days in this process, nights like these when I ruminate and can't sleep, when I am stunned again by what technology offers, moved on some level to think that throughout history, the women who walked the earth did not have this (perverse) opportunity that I have, not through the centuries of humankind was this freezing of babies-to-be any possibility, anything other than a sci-fi fantasy. But here I am and here they are: four shiny new embryos. That's the news from the nurse at nine the next morning, and finally content, I fall asleep in the bright morning dreaming of their later fruition. I dream constantly now of this process, dream of being pregnant, only to have my belly go "pfft" on the delivery room table of my nightmares.

At least as I awaken today I have some embryos on ice and there is a flash of animal joy, a frisson of elation that lasts but a second when I instantly realize how deeply tethered I am to them though our rendezvous is a couple of months down the road. I wanted to move freely, to crawl back into my "normal" life, but I can see already that they will not let me be, lurking always in the back of my mind. Funny to think they are already encoded, already who they are, destined to look a certain way, be a certain way, loud or soft, hirsute or prematurely bald. And a sense of humor—is that in there, too, I wonder, hardwired into the strands of DNA in the two cells of these embryos? When thawed—their passage back to earth, or more accurately, halfway back—they will be allowed to divide again, to the four-cell stage to see if indeed they're on the road to proper development, and then be returned to me. But the truth is: They don't need me at all. They already have a—suspended—life of their own. They could just as easily be thawed and put back into somebody else who would not ever need to tell them of my husband's and my original authorship. In fact, they might have a much better chance in someone else's proven womb instead of mine.

A fertile friend of mine, another of my old and cherished high school pals, has offered to try to carry them for me, but I'm not there yet. It's too weird, too lonesome. This batch I'll take. I am told that current freezing methods are good and that somewhere between 60 and 80 percent of frozen embryos thaw fine, like sperm. The real breakthrough, everyone suggests, will come when eggs themselves—or gametes, as they're called—can be successfully frozen and thawed. That would obviate all the moral dilemma of having full-fledged embryos in storage, and there is much work being done on the cryopreservation, as it's called, of eggs themselves. Much more delicate than sperm or embryos, they are more prone to damage in the freezing and thawing process, though the first human births, twins, from frozen eggs were reported in 1986 in Australia. When full-scale egg freezing is possible—still years in the future, most scientists agree—then young women will be able to have their untarnished eggs removed early and put on ice and then go about their lives until they are ready to put them to use.

Part of me wishes that I had some long-lost eggs to use, perfectly preserved back then when I was twenty-two, twenty-three, twenty-four, back when I was an emphatically non-procreating young bride. Full of high resolution and fear of being circumscribed in the domestic sphere, I had no time for motherhood. Would I, had the methods been available, have had my eggs extracted then and stored for the eventuality I now face? I probably would have, had it been part of the times, though it was unimaginable to me at that point that I would come to this—wanting a baby so—so intent was I in making my way in a culture in which liberation was proving increasingly hard.

12

THE OTHER SEVENTIES:
IMPOTENCE REARS ITS HEAD

I asked myself a thousand times then and later why indeed it was so hard. Here had been this vibrantly angry moment when the idea of the liberation of women was everywhere and seemed virtually unstoppable, a snowballing sentiment for equality. Yet that sense of liberation was still so personally elusive for so many of us. Was it our own failure of nerve, as author Colette Dowling would suggest in her 1981 book *The Cinderella Complex*?

In part, sure. We hadn't been raised to be independent, free, whole, untethered, especially within the bounds of love. Quite the contrary. From our earliest days in our postwar families, we were weaned to be polite, feminine, familial, attached, custodial, maternal. Certainly I was. All that training could not be shed like a winter coat. Not by most of us anyway. And then, of course, I had married as complicatedly as possible—a man that much older, more set in his masculine ways, used to being in charge. But even my friends who had married or were dating men of our generation were fighting the same battles, trying to redefine on the most elemental level how men and women related, while getting on with their careers and trying not to do the old female dance of dependency. But there was something else going on, right from the get-go, and that was the kickback of men. At some point Ann Rubinstein said something to me that stuck. "You know," she said, "feminism at base was fiercely romantic. We thought men were going to get it, to want it, to share, to have equal partners. We weren't prepared for how tough it was going to be. The roles were thousands of years in the making; it was romantic, or naive, to think we could undo it all in a couple of years."

Indeed. It just wasn't going to be undone that quickly. Ann was still solo and would be for a long time. She did it the other way, riding through the seventies as a single woman, living on her own in Berkeley, getting a law degree and dating a succession of noncommittal men. About half my friends were married like me and half were like Ann, living in big cities, getting advanced degrees or building careers and wondering when and if they would marry.

"I was running into these men who wanted nothing of marriage," she told me. "The law students were fairly straight so I hung around with these arty film students who turned out endless little nauseating movies of their girlfriends masturbating on top of Mount Tamalpais as the sun went down. The ones I went out with were doing a fair amount of cocaine—the drugs had shifted—and the sex was lousy and I was already saving money in case I ended up having a baby alone, which I thought was a very good possibility. What had my mother said about it all, that men could give you babies and possibly some money—although as it was turning out I was less and less sure of that part, too—but they won't show up for you emotionally. It's a bitter take on things, and I think the women's movement only confirmed it. It let a lot of men of our generation off the hook. I think they basically said, 'Fine, you want to be equal? You want to play your own part? Fine. Pay half the check.' They felt guilty because of their maleness, and what that turned them into is angry without knowing what the hell to do and more than willing to opt out of responsibility in relationships and it goes a lot deeper than not opening a car door. There was a ten-year period of no marriages and no babies, at least among the women I knew. You think that's entirely because women wanted careers? No way. That is not true. Men took a walk."

Many did indeed. By the seventies, marriage rates were down, as was fertility, in part, yes, because more and more women were working, but also because more and more men were opting out of the old roles. They did it out of anger and they did it out of fear, emotional, sexual and economic fear (the prosperity we baby boomers had been raised in was not holding). No question, the phallic undertow was clearly picking up steam in the wake of the lib din. And when legalized abortion was added to the combustible mix in 1973, allowing women the ultimate power of rejection over men, over their sperm, the phallic undertow turned even darker and more insidious. Not to put too fine a paranoid point on it, but from that point on, the political history of the country for the next twenty years, with its fundamental, pro-family conservative thrust, can be seen as nothing more or less than a concerted effort to put women back in their place or keep them in it and, conversely, restore men to theirs in the wake of the double hit (double humiliation, as many men clearly saw it) of Vietnam and the women's movement. The key attack point was our freed-up sexuality. Now the phallic undertowers set about remaking it in their own manly image, making it take off its clothes and strut its stuff, our magnified genitals suddenly floating across movie screens and center-folds, all slick and rosy and disembodied.

I don't think men understood what this said to us, nice men, decent men: how invasive, how fractionating, how lonesome, how perversely castrating—to see pieces of your anatomy unloosed from their moorings. What was happening here, in short, is that the sexual revolution was getting the better of the women's revolution.

I have often heard people say the two movements were the same, that once the pill came along and freed women to have sex, voilà: women's lib. But they were not the same, though they shared a brief overlap here in the early 1970s. In fact, the sexual revolution predated, coopted and outlasted the women's revolution in a deft manly sideswipe that left men in the driver's seat. In this we women played our own part. In the name of equality we got caught in an act of complicitous voyeurism, sexual machisma that would down the road reach its apex with someone like Madonna, or Sharon Stone flashing her crotch in *Basic Instinct*. In an effort to achieve parity, to air our grievances and unearth our sexuality, we women became the co-saboteurs of our own privacy. And with the sabotage of privacy went the chance for intimacy, which is only possible, after all, in private and for which we women would later so desperately clamor—tenderness, closeness, authentic lust, all of which got X-ed out of X-rated sex, which was, and is, in the main masturbatory even if there is another person involved. This left the pornographers, the sex doctors like Dr. Reuben and pals and the pseudo-feminists like Helen Gurley Brown to get their gleeful, grubby hands on our libidos, a salivating, profit-hungry phalanx poised over our beds aiming to redefine sex as a sport for which all kinds of expertise and equipment was needed rather than as an intimate act between lovers. So as we women—prodded by the dual hope of the sexual revolution and the women's revolution—tried to draw nigh unto men, those who would profit by the gulf between us stepped back into the hopefully narrowing breach. Thus the sexual back-lash of the 1970s lurched into full and sometimes sordid swing, the sweet revenge for us having at long last wrested away from men the procreative reigns and for trying to have sex on our terms and for refusing to have their children. Now men and the marketplace would turn the tables, degrade an act in which we could now be full-fledged protected partners, and put us back on the defensive, which is precisely the way I began to feel again so soon after the exhilaration of all those manifestos. On the defensive.

And they did it not just with the manuals and the pornography, but with a whole other tack, a kind of potent counter-tack at the same time: the threat of impotence. It was a great one-two punch: pornography and impotence (in a sense not contradictory, since the latter was the new excuse for the former). They went, so to speak, hand in hand.

Before 1972, impotence wasn't even an entry in *The Periodic Guide to Literature,* the book that lists all magazine articles for a given year. But starting in seventy-two, the year I married, I was aware of this sudden spate of articles about the so-called "New Impotence," the bottom line of all of them being that the brazen hussies of liberation were responsible for the rise of the fall of the phallus. No one had statistics exactly on this alleged epidemic of impotence, just theories, but practically all the magazines from *Esquire* to *Ladies' Home Journal* to *Mademoiselle* were warning us women to cool it, lest we scare them soft and end up with nothing: no pleasure, no partner, no procreation, none of it. Ballbreakers, castrators— that's what we were, and who wanted to be that? Those were the big, bad words. I had heard them as a child and here they were again, just as we were getting our legs. "Recently," went the party line in the *Good House-keeping* of July 1973, "psychiatrists have been reporting an upsurge of anxiety-based impotence in young men. One explanation offered is the increasing sexual demands of today's women. Time was (and not so long ago) when men could see themselves as aggressors and pursuers of today's women, who passively served their sexual needs. Now often, it's women who do the pursuing and make the advances and men who feel intimidated."

Talk about feeling damned if you do and damned if you don't. Even the "Zipless Fuck" in Erica Jong's jazzy 1973 novel *Fear of Flying,* which I received on my twenty-third birthday and giddily devoured, was impotent, a deflated, feminist-era Don Juan who left his liberated consort panting with dissatisfaction. Even John couldn't resist playing into the panic. And of course, not to be left out of the fun was the self-described Prisoner of Sex, the stormin' Norman of his day, Norman Mailer, adding his voice to the backlash, giving women a lascivious shove back up onto their pedestal where they could be wooed, won, claimed and climaxed by a worshipful, awestruck male who bowed down before their wombs, their "root in eternity."

Here is a motive that drives a man to scour his balls and his back until he is ready to die from the cannonading he has given his organs, the deaths through which he has dragged some future of his soul, it is a clue which all but says that somewhere in the insane passions of all men is a huge desire to drive forward into the seat of creation, grab some part of that creation in the hands, sink the cock to the hilt, sink it into as many hilts as will hold it; for man is alienated from the nature which brought him forth, he is not like a woman in possession of an inner space which gives her link to the future, so he must drive to possess it, he must if necessary come close to blowing his head off that he may possess it.

That was Mailer at his high-flown best, a frothing ejaculation of words, at the heart of which was an endorsement of male supremacy: Men need to dominate women because "dominance was the indispensable elevator which would raise [the] phallus to that height from which it might seek transcendence." In short, if we can't be in control we're not going to get it up. It was the New Impotence argument in poetic drag, a shrewd upending of the charge that men were all-powerful. "No, no, no," they were saying to women: "You're the powerful ones; we're the fragile ones. Go easy on us." This argument was made over and over in the popular literature of the early seventies; it came from doctors and writers and scientists. They hit us from all sides. The specter of a deflated phallus hung heavy over the dreams of liberation. With irritable heart, I read Lionel Tiger in the August 31, 1970, issue of *Time* magazine:

There's something that the feminists are going to have to cope with—that males are much more fragile sexually. It's often difficult for males to perform sexually if they don't feel the mood is just right. One of the problems here may be that primates physically have intercourse with females that they can dominate. It may just be that the phenomenon of sexual encounter depends on a sexual politic. And that without this politic, in the way it has been contrived for several million years, there may not be any sexual encounter.

On and on it went, a bludgeoning litany of sexual catastrophe. No, dominance wasn't enough for them. In a neat stroke, the boys of the undertow turned the dial a notch further and insisted that it was men, not women, who were the fragile sex. But they were not that. Women were, by every stretch of the imagination, the fragile ones. We were the enterable sex, the rapeable sex. What were the collywobbles of the cock compared to that? Not that they were not to be countenanced, those collywobbles; and not that every woman I knew then, especially the married ones, did not take them very seriously as part of the conjugal bargain, as part of the bargain of simply loving someone male, just as they did not spurn an obviously excited mate. In the give and take of a marriage, you looked at an erection with responsibility, solicitude, if not always lust or tenderness. That habit of solicitude had been silently handed down to us from preceding generations of women, long before the sex manuals and the counter-manifestos put an obligatory and ugly spin on it, before Norman Mailer and pals insisted that deference was the male due and dominance the biggest aphrodisiac.

The truce these sexual undertowers called for was a truce of non-truce, a mutual declaration to keep the war of the sexes alive and in that, the feminists played their angry unwitting part. It got all twisted up there in the early seventies. Things were not what they seemed, and when the dust finally settled and the hoopla died down within a couple of years, the idea of any real mutuality, by which I mean emotional, sexual and economic equal opportunity and enjoyment, had been buried under a lot of phallic pieties, biological sureties and gobbledygook about dominance and deference and the unbridgeable gulf between the sexes. What we lost right there, in the schism between the sexual revolution and the women's revolution, was the notion of a friendship between the sexes, of tenderness between men and women, in bed and out, and within a very few years, certainly by the greedy, grabby eighties, we would see the full fruit of this fatal schism: a highly marketable ferocious eroticism that made rape into prime video entertainment, turned every TV beer commercial into a female crotch-watch and left young women at sea sexually, insecure about the line between force and consent, all of which would be deftly blamed by the conservatives on us allegedly libidinous libbers. And indeed by not insisting right then on our own fragility—our violability—our femaleness, we eager-to-be-equal young women went down that path with them. In the name of equality, we forfeited a certain protective kindness from men, courtesies that were a lot more fundamental than opening a door and yet, in hindsight, not unlinked.

It was all this that I was trying to get at in my first essay, the notion of what was being lost even as much was being gained. I didn't want equality; I wanted something more, some delighted mutuality between men and women. I didn't want to go on identifying with the aggressor, though God knows I would for a long time. I wanted to be reconciled to my sex, to revel in it. I wanted to hit some grace note in the middle, I wanted to be a full-blown, high-achieving, robustly exuberant woman, instead of falling into a riven caricature, part throwback femininity in crotchless panties, part sharp-tongued, male-imitating harpy. And I think I knew, on some unarticulated level, that until that point, I couldn't or shouldn't or wouldn't have a baby. Maybe my friend was right. Maybe I did want one. Maybe many of us did. But in light of the undertow, you certainly didn't want to fall back into the old female roles. You didn't want to go around exalting your womb, your inner space of creation, your bloody link to eternity, or admitting that the sexual act itself had an inherent quality of inequality, not when you were trying to find your way as a young, liberated woman, trying to find your authentic self, your authentic voice and be a fully formed contributing member of society—as all my friends avidly wanted to be—capable of standing on your own two feet. And if you read Mailer just a little more carefully, you realized that buried in his love song to the womb was his rationale for seed-spilling promiscuity. A man didn't want to "sink the cock to the hilt," but rather to "sink it into as many hilts as will hold it," which couldn't help but put you in mind of the marriages that had washed up on the shores of your perverse paradise, leaving Mom alone with the kids while the errant breadwinner (there would be more and more of those) went off "to drive forward into the [new] seat of creation," seeing the kids on the weekend and sometimes, if you were lucky, sending money. No, far better to have the baby later when you were sure you could keep heart and hearth together should he take a walk or should you tire of your own anger or efforts at appeasement.

Indeed, I gyrated between those two, between anger and appeasement, all through the second half of the 1970s. The magazines I was writing for were still full of strong, gutsy, personal pieces by women—which was exciting—though I have to confess that after my baby-making manifesto, I turned around the next year and wrote another *Newsweek* "My Turn," this one a "Defense of Flirting," a conciliatory—some would say, reactionary—piece about the pleasures of the delicate eye-play, by-play, talk-play that went on between the sexes. At its best, the essay posited a sweet flirtatiousness between men and women and resisted the emphatic bedding of the sexual revolution; at its worst it strayed into Helen Gurley Brown territory. It was 1976 and in my own way I had become a handmaiden of the backlash, a sister of the undertow. Some days I felt as if I had never been anything but.

In my private life I also gyrated, alternating between flirtatiousness and furiousness, depression and hope, adamantly trying to hit that grace note, adamantly trying to befriend the man I had married even while much of the prevailing wisdom now held that to be a pipe dream. Months went by where I felt weighted down by a dark sorrow tinged with rage. What in the hell was wrong; why didn't men get it, this particular man? What was the big deal: Why couldn't he just exhale and let me in? Why didn't I just get it and get out, as Dowling would have it? Because love didn't work that way; it was always a fair amount more complicated than these thesis-driven books suggested.

There had been glimmers of that middle ground I sought. Laughter could do it, break down the ceremonial masculine-feminine barriers. I'd catch his eye, mid-laugh, and there would be an amused recognition of mutual humanness, of shared funny bones and flesh, no one on top, no one in charge. Ah, my giggling self said in tandem with his giggling self, so we aren't so different after all. But then it would be gone, the symmetry of laughter.

Sometimes in a dressing room, when we'd be shopping, there would be another glimmer: one of us hopefully trying on clothes, all exposed vanity, while the other peeked in the door, a smiling face in the mirror. What a relief; I had married a friend after all. I saw him in the mirror. But then he was gone, suited up again to do battle with the world and often with me, all full of judgments and swashbuckling intimacy. The biologically foreordained sexual dance? That's what they were all saying, the backlashers and their handmaidens, but nothing about it made me feel the least bit sexy, and I was haunted by the hope that the man in the mirror would come back. He was in there, under that Southern tough-guy, male crust, the honorable and tender suitor with whom I had ecstatically gypsied up and down the California coastline. Mailer and Tiger and all of them, they could take their backlash bravado, their biological sureties, their mumbo jumbo about wombs and phalluses, and vanish in the reactionary mist. It could be better, sweeter, fairer, freer, if you could just keep chipping away, just hang on long enough, which I was still intent upon doing. Pro-family? I was that to my core, always had been, the child of and wife of exploded nuclear families. I took great joy in my stepsons, two of whom lived with us at different times, in the angst-ridden, acne-prone throes of their adolescence, something I was close enough to in time to remember vividly. I watched them trying to fashion their egos and win girls and felt as tender toward them as I had toward my father those divorced Saturdays all those years ago, and I bitterly resented when the hostility of the culture and the difficulty of my marriage caused me to block my instinctive tenderness toward them, toward men, toward my husband. I would hold on. It would sort out. I would be damned if I would cause more dissolution.

JANE ALLEN did not have that same chance, to hold on, that is. A week before Easter of 1979, her husband, her best friend in life, her college boyfriend, left her for a younger woman. She had just turned thirty-one. In that sense she was ahead of her time, seemingly young for such desertion. After a professional crisis at his law firm, he left and went to Europe with a younger woman. When he came back the woman was gone. It wasn't about her. Jane's own career was kicking into high gear. With her MBA in hand, she had joined one of the first big, environmentally conscious design firms in the East as their marketing director and was routinely being featured in those "Women in Business" stories, all very tough, she says, on her ex-husband's ego.

"He'd started to make cracks in front of our friends about me being the star," she told me in her soft, modulated voice. "We had kept postponing the baby issue. He needed to get through school, I needed to get through school. But underneath all the delays was my own fear that, given my childhood, I would not be a good mother. But Dawson was very family-oriented and I'm sure if we had had a child he never would have left—or he would have come back—and in those hours and days and months after he left, I cried for the baby we hadn't had. I sat in the living room playing that music again, the Rachmaninoff I'd played the day of our wedding, tears streaming down my face, then I'd pull myself together and put on my suits—you know, those comical boxy things we were all wearing then with those shirts with ties at the neck—and try to make it through the day. I think these men were just knocked sideways by all of it, not just the women s movement but Vietnam, too. They just didn't have the rite of passage which is part of our culture and myth. They didn't get what their fathers got; they didn't come back from a war that they won. It was a weird evolutionary time, as if women were not just catching up with men but evolving way beyond them. We were so competent at everything—and I guess, damaged, too."

I was hearing that from a lot of women, women who like Jane were divorcing and women like me who were trying to hang in. We were all running into that subtext of competition. It was hard; you felt bad, torn—as always—angry. I did those nights on the road far away from home, trying to do precisely what my husband had done years before: be a first-rate journalist and writer. I ended the decade working for *The New York Times Magazine* doing long pieces, staying away from home for weeks at a time. The winter of 1979, I was on the East Coast for six weeks, working on a profile of Senator Edward Kennedy. Long days I spent flying around the Eastern seaboard interviewing old Kennedy hands, coming to rest at intervals in a small inn in Washington, D.C., where I would regroup and type up my interviews on a rented portable Smith Corona. There were afternoons when I would stand at the window watching the snow fall on the street outside, feeling as if my whole life had led me to that point, that window, and I would think of all the other women out there on the road encamped in strange motels and hotels, doing their work and phoning home at day's end like so many of their fathers had done, and I'd think, with a shiver of hope and pride, that indeed we were part of a revolution.

Between 1972, when I got married, and the end of the decade, the number of female lawyers and judges went from 4 percent to 13 percent of the whole, the number of women doctors from 10 percent to 13. True, women were still earning only 62.5 percent of the median weekly earning for men, a percentage that hadn't changed in almost twenty years, and most were still in low-wage service jobs. And yet there was still some hope. There must have been, I must have been feeling it standing at that window in 1979, the sense that if we just worked hard enough and hung in long enough we were going to transform the working world. It was going to shake out just like our marriages into one big equal-opportunity world. I knew it wasn't going to be easy. I was amused and sometimes irritated those winter months by the avuncular chauvinism of the old-line Kennedyites and by the pointedly lusty entreaties of my long-distance husband whose late-night phone calls inevitably made me feel guilty for being so far away and so full of work. It was all new enough still. I felt angry at him and angry at myself and angry at being a woman and knowing that I was always going to feel torn no matter how hard I tried, no matter how much feminist theory I sported like armor. I was beginning to realize that maybe I had pasted feminism over my soul-sickness like a Band-Aid and that what was under there—the childhood, the angry nights and mixed signals—had not yet been dealt with and would have to be sooner or later.

By the end of that year I was more despairing. The hostages had been taken. Carter was being lampooned as a wimp, the only president in memory with a real partnership marriage for which he had already been ridiculed, which should have told us not-so-young-anymore brides something, more than we wanted to know. "Wimp" was a code word for impotence, which was now being talked about again in the popular magazines after disappearing for a few years in the middle seventies. The women's magazines now offered a new rash of quizzes and columns about whether strong women, make that strong working women, threatened male libidos. The question was updated: If you earned more than he (which some women were finally beginning to do, in one out of ten marriages), would he still feel man enough in bed? Or: If he was potent enough to put up with your hard-charging ambition, was it fair to expect him to be a major wage earner, too? That was the new variation on the theme: male economic impotence. The magazines were full of it and some of the women I know were beginning to face it in their own lives as their husbands ceded to them, gratefully and/or grudgingly, the bread-winning role. At the same time impotence was making a comeback, "Women's Liberation Movement" was disappearing from *The Reader's Guide to Periodic Literature,* which, for one assignment or another, I was inevitably pawing through. By 1976, in fact, the number of listings under that title had shrunk dramatically since the beginning of the decade and taken a dark turn, with titles like: "Requiem for the Women's Movement," or "Trashing: The Dark Side of Sisterhood." By the next volume, "Women's Liberation Movement" was gone altogether. Granted, there were entries under "Feminism" and "Equal Rights," but, symbolically enough, "Liberation" was gone and the burgeoning new category was called "Women and Men," stories about "My Ideal Man" or "New Man/Woman Etiquette" or "Are You Too Assertive?" Hollywood was hitting the same note, offering us up these tantalizingly liberated, rather, pseudo-liberated, heroines like Ellen Burstyn in the 1974 *Alice Doesn't Live Here Anymore* and Jill Clayburgh in *An Unmarried Woman* (1978), women who break free of nasty men only to turn around and find dishy new Prince Charmings. It was Cinderella all over with a shiny, new veneer.

Then in 1977 there was another little pop culture tip-off that things were not evolving as we might have hoped: Those very popular Polaroid ads featuring Mariette Hartley and James Garner began, and the two had that same old sitcom chemistry, he the sweet bumbler, she the sort of motherly know-it-all, with an updated smart-ass twist. And that chemistry always said the same thing: The man's got the real power and, in compensation, the woman has the manipulative smarts. And indeed, as we young women did take on more and more roles in and out of the house, in the heady heyday of doing it all or having it all, we did tend to affect—I know I did—an air of emphatic, maternally edged competence. That competence, which extended to work, to housework, to the whole damn domestic thing, and even to sex, was a way of handling men. But it was ultimately not just fatiguing but disfiguring, to ourselves and to love itself. It distorted passion, just as the pornography did, unweighted it, but it would be a long time before I could root it out of my defensively managerial repertoire.

As for real maternity, I still had felt no twitches even as the first of my friends, all of us around thirty now, began to have babies. I watched them with awe as they cuddled and cooed, and wondered when, if ever, I would stray into that oozy, milky, soft-focus country. It seemed so far away still. I still felt so sharp, so defended, so driven. And like so many women I knew, I felt I had plenty of time. I was still only twenty-nine, and I realize when I say that now, what a dramatic change had already been wrought since 1950, the year of my birth, when nearly one-third of all American women had their first child before they reached the age of twenty. Fast-forward to the end of the seventies when more than one-quarter of married women in their late twenties were babyless and studies were predicting that one-fourth of us would remain that way. The fertility of American females had fallen to what is called the replacement level: just enough new babies to keep the population at status quo. In our fear and in our fervor we had actually stalled out the population growth, bent it to our contraceptive wills.

As my friend Julie said, speaking for many of us at that point: "I could have done without sex let alone without babies, hell, I was doing without. The work was all. It was almost sexually satisfying. You know, I don't think men understand that our attitude about work is very much like theirs is. Mine sure was after what happened in my childhood. I was just so determined to survive. And I was always waiting for the phone call from the daughter I gave away. I'd been in and out of therapy and was relatively happy with myself, though part of me was always steeled against old pains, even though I know the world's perception of me at that point was as this big, ballsy successful woman."

There we were in the late 1970s still looking like the media's dream girls, many of us, these postliberation (rather, post-hoopla), softened-up superachievers who might pull it all off, even though many of us didn't feel that way inside. We had had an exhilarating kick into a new world but now came the reality, the personal reckonings, just at the time when the phallic undertow was about to get a big manly pat on the back by that actor-turned-president. Yes, Ronald Reagan was coming and abortion was being challenged and it felt as if the dream of women's liberation was being taken away before it could be realized, leaving us hopeful if occasionally tart-tongued and heart-battered young brides of the 1970s to fight the good fight in private when everything had simmered down in public. After the sweet moment of euphoria, of clarity, when it seemed everything would work out, men would get it, learn to share at home and at work, be happy to share, be happy to be tender and relieved of their hefty bravado, everything turned muddy again and we confronted anew our own impotence. It was, said a friend of mine, like walking upstream on icebergs. At the end of the 1970s, babies were further from my mind than ever.

13

HOME TO MAMA

It is early summer and my embryos are coming home to roost during a stretch of the hottest days in Los Angeles history. I am wearing kids' clothes, short skirts and beach shifts, thigh-high and breezy, like the ones I sported back when I was a much younger woman. But I am, after all, trying to cheat fate here, cheat time, turn the clock back, and these frocks seem the appropriately auspicious garb for my embryo rendezvous.

There hasn't been a day in the intervening months that I have not thought about it, about them hanging there in that frigid tank, not a day, probably not an hour. They have followed me around, hovering, dipping up and around and through my brain no matter how hard I tried to concentrate on other things. Before this infertile siege, work has always been my place to go, my place of joy, of escape, of elemental excitement, sitting day after day staring at a piece of paper, or now, a blank screen, and trying to make words make sense, laying them like bricks, carefully, one after the other. But always now, part of my mind is elsewhere, never more so than this stretch when I am on permanent embryo alert. They're there, waiting for me.

And finally it's time. I have been taking estrogen tablets, which have considerably lightened my mood (I will definitely take them when I hit menopause if my mood drops) while thickening my uterine lining and making my womb ready for the embryo transfer. Now they are adding shots of progesterone, those big, oily, mean shots again, the ones that linger in muscle memory long after they're over, so that if you move wrong in bed there's a twinge of remembered soreness even months later. I have my first sonogram of this go-around on June 22 and everything is coming along fine; the lining of my uterus is appropriately thickened by the hormones, a squishy bed for my embryos. I experience again that momentary elation that good news brings. Great. Maybe this is it, maybe this time it will work. They will take the embryos, or pre-embryos, as they call them, out of the deep freeze tomorrow, baby-sit them for twenty-four hours to see if they divide, and then transfer them back into me on Sunday—the day of the Lord, the day of rest, the day of immaculate conception via technology.

For those hours right after, technically, I suppose, I will be pregnant.

There will be embryos in my uterus for the first time in my knowledge, full-blown embryos. The word itself, "pregnant," makes me wild with hope. It's another one of those hard sensual words like fecund and suckle. Pregnant, fecund, suckle—a trio of hard-edged, soft-meaning words. All so sexually loaded, certainly to someone who is trying to procreate in this decidedly unsexual manner. I miss those body voluptuous feelings and wonder if I'll ever get them back, ever be able to tumble lustily into bed without hoping against hope that a baby will be conjured up out of it. Procreation has been the death knell of sex—as contrary, as weird a thought as that of an immaculate conception made possible by technology. The normal categories have broken down, are broken down in this world, one of the reasons I feel so unhinged, a kind of philosophical unhingement that goes right along with the hormonal unhingement.

More good news. "They thawed great," the nurse says of my family of four when she calls on the morning of June 23. They will put all back in tomorrow, and the minute I put the phone down, the thought suddenly makes me incredibly lonely and I wish I had kept one in reserve, permanently frozen, so that the possibility would always be there, leaving my mind to dance around that tank in homage, way into old age. The doctor would no doubt again laugh at me. For him, embryos are embryos, each one a chance for a baby, and I must, if I am going down this scientific road, toughen up and get with the program. Put them in. Let it rip. Nothing, not one, no one, held back for posterity. I pray for them in the wakeful hours of another long night, imagining them there in their dish, doing their dividing thing with any luck.

Again, the good news, bad news. The nurse calls early the next morning to tell me one of the embryos didn't make it, so we're now down to three. Presumably the one that fell by the wayside would not have made it inside my body either. Now I am down to the three heartiest of the lot. I started with nine, the number of eggs they originally took out of me. Of that nine, seven were "mature." Of that seven, six fertilized and two fragmented before they could be frozen. Four went into the tank, four came back, but there's already been a casualty. Does this arithmetic bode ill? I refuse to think so, refuse to query the doctors in my normal journalistic manner. No, better not to know at this point. The day is luminous, full of promise, hot and summery. I am dressed as if for a date, a date I might have had twenty years ago with the man who sits beside me in the car, so very handsome still, so very gray (when did that happen?), with his ever-resolute jaw. And here I am in a blue-jean mini-skirt, a fuchsia T-shirt from The Gap, a forty-year-old teenager in spirit hoping to get knocked up today.

The process this time is very benign. No shots, no IV, no anesthetic, no surgery. Drugless, I am wheeled into the operating room, tilted up in preparation for the insemination. That's all this will be, the catheter threaded up into the uterus and in they come—that's all, nothing fancy. But at the last minute the doctor asks if I would like to see the embryos first. I follow him down the hall in my gown and slippers, sit down in front of a microscope and peer in. There they are, each one nothing more than four intersecting circles, four overlapping little cells, reminiscent to me somehow of an unfinished Olympic logo. Are they life, a life? What is it I peer at with so full a heart, silently imploring them toward whole-ness? Girls, boys, who are they? It is so amazing to think that it is all done, so much selection already made by nature, and, on this hot summer Sunday, I am in awe, imagining their lives, imagining how later we might laugh over the manner of their beginning. I saw you, I will tell them, when you were two days old—no really, two days old.

The insemination is nothing, the same standard stuff, and I lie for two hours on a slanted bed, head down, legs up, not uncomfortable, but feeling a little off kilter, a little silly. I am advised when I go home to stay relatively quiet for the next thirty-six hours—that's all—and then after that I can resume my normal life, which is, of course, a joke. There is no "normal" left. I am already up and down and sideways. How can my three beautiful embryos simply disappear? How can they not? I know the odds.

I am taking my embryos on holiday, to Santa Cruz no less, my favorite place on earth. I want them to see it, to see the boardwalk and my beloved campus. Guess I'll show them my old dorm room in the redwoods. Anything's better than hanging around the house for the next two weeks. I have a send-off blood test and everything looks fine. I have to have my progesterone daily while we're away, but my husband has turned into an excellent shot-giver. We drive up the coast and as always, these later years, I am struck by a certain emptiness, as if the stage has been struck, the players sent home. There are no hitchhikers with signs, no ragtag army of the young and dirty and blissed-out save those I conjure out of memory, no whiffs of marijuana floating into the car along with the smell of the coastal sage. A new era, cleaned up and presided over by country-club Republicans.

During the time away, for long stretches, I am able to suspend the pregnancy watch, though it's always there. My sister, brother-in-law and niece are with us and a couple of their friends, and we play in the sand and paint our toenails and hang out at the nearby boardwalk, falling asleep at night to the shrieks of the roller-coaster riders. I watch my niece's face, so familially reminiscent, hooded blue eyes, strawberry-blond hair, and wonder why I can't just move on and adopt, throw a new dark-eyed, dark-haired look into our mix. Why do I have to be so tribally beguiled by her face, by what it carries—fragments of all of us? Why must I so love her profile? Why can't I understand that mothering is just an act of love? Wasn't that what it was to be a stepmother? That was no tough leap. My stepsons came into my life and I loved them without reservation. So why not let up on this high-tech nonsense and get on with it, just get a baby in the house? Because I can't yet. Because I can't.

We retrace the miles of the highway and are home all too swiftly. It feels as if we have never been away at all. Tomorrow I will have the pregnancy test. I have not bled yet. At least that's a positive sign, but I also know that the progesterone shots can often delay the onset of menses.

I feel nothing, nothing one way or the other. Can this be pregnancy—this non-feeling? Early the next day I go off and stick out my arm for the last prick of this round. Everyone's sweet in the office, vicariously hopeful, but also taken up with the new people and their quests. It goes on, the high-tech machine, lurching ever forward, conjuring up ever more embryos in ever more willing patients. I see them as I leave, a bright, shiny new crop of hopeful infertiles with their white paper bags. I don't recognize a one of them.

Now it's the wait, the women's wait. That's what we do, wait to hear if we are pregnant or not pregnant—whether we want to be or not. Countless women have held their breath as I now hold mine, hoping indeed that they were not with child because what a wrinkle that would be, what a mess. We are flip sides of the same watch. In fact, I am connected today to the great continuum of waiting women, waiting for everything, not just news of pregnancy, but everything, waiting to be asked on a date, waiting to be asked to marry, waiting to have enough money to leave home, leave an abusive husband, waiting for word of a husband at war, a child at risk. Waiting, waiting, waiting. All of us. I cannot imagine quite what's comparable to this—waiting to hear about the fate or possible death of a child. That must be the worst of all, though this feels a little like that, more than a little. I want to leave the house, get away from the phone, go play, shop, eat, pretend it doesn't matter so much, regain perspective. Only embryos, I say, lighten up here, go off into the day. Life will go on. It will. And maybe, just maybe, you'll be one of the lucky ones. They will not have died or disappeared, but will have taken root—just one of them, that's all I ask for, just one. I will hear after one o'clock.

The call comes: a reprieve, of sorts, a ridiculous, perverse exhilarating reprieve. I got in there a little late this morning so my little vial of blood didn't get out in time. Now I will have to wait until tomorrow, another thousand years, for the result. So be it. Twenty-four more useless hours during which, like someone drowning, I can once more rehash my life, add up all the goods and bads, rummage through the history and begin to prepare myself for the news.

14

THE EIGHTIES:
THE SITCOM DAD
COMES BACK TO HAUNT

I t was a grim joke to spend the decade of your thirties, the years my mother had always told me were a woman's best, with a staunch conservative at the helm of your country, someone absolutely averse to the stirrings of your soul, but that's exactly how I was spending them. For us still young women trying to find our way, it was hard not to take Ronald Reagan personally—the big square-headed, joke-at-the-ready sitcom dad of old come back to run the country, stepping right off the TV screen and into the White House, making the world safe for us, his daughters, his "kittens," by turning the clock back, by restoring the country's manly self-image and by rescinding abortion rights. It was morning in America and men were stroking their nostalgia.

I had known Reagan's daughter, Patti, growing up—she was in the same grammar school—a pretty, big-eyed, self-conscious girl turned frantic aerobicizer who would spend her prime-time years penning poison books about her allegedly abusive mother, Nancy of the adoring gaze. Long after they were gone from the White House, she would be making the talk-show circuit, this perennial First Daughter hawking her latest book and reminding the country that indeed her family was not and had never been the sitcom ideal. In her own wound-baring way, she was skewering the happy-family fifties mythology by which we were all being re-seduced in the 1980s. Poor, brave, embarrassing Patti. Our National Daughter come back to haunt. Our divorced, childless National Daughter, a living rebuttal to the family myth.

Years had passed and here we were and it was only getting harder and lonelier and everybody, feminists included, was talking about family values. Attempting to heal the wounds, to make up for lost ground, to redefine feminism for the new era, the feminist foremothers themselves were back throwing their own pro-family manifestos into the mix. Here was Betty Friedan herself saying that it was time for "The Second Stage" of feminism, time to understand that women wanted husbands and babies—her apologia, it seemed, for all that earlier venom. I read them all as if my very life depended on it, on them, on their words, shaking my head over their new impassioned message. What was going on here in these dark days of Reagan's reign? Had everyone, even my heroines of yore, gone misty-eyed over family values? What was a young and, yes, still struggling and angry young woman to do? I read Friedan and underlined:

> From the totality of our experience as women—and our knowledge of psychology, anthropology, biology—many feminists knew all along that the extremist rhetoric of sexual politics defied and denied the profound, complex human reality of the sexual, social psychological, economic, yes, biological relationship between woman and man. It denied the reality of woman's own sexuality, her childbearing, her roots and life connection in the family.

And then there was Germaine Greer hitting the same note in *Sex and Destiny,* a big, passionate, windy indictment of the politics of fertility or how the white Western, capitalistic male world—of which we hip young American women were now, by virtue of our ambition, a de facto part— had conspired to demean childbirth, turn it into a lonely, commercialized trap. Falling back into my studently ways, pen in hand, I tore through her book as through Friedan's, wide-eyed, disbelieving and yet with grudging admiration for her ideologic chutzpah. Mid-read of the script, someone— no, not someone, everyone, it seemed—was switching the cue cards. Greer was pulling an impassioned 180, as certain of herself this time as the last:

> Because motherhood is virtually meaningless in our society is no ground for supposing that the fact that women are still defined by their mothering function in other societies is simply an index of their oppression. We have at least to consider the possibility that a successful matriarch might well pity Western feminists for having been duped into futile competition with men in exchange for the companionship and love of children and other women.

Was this the same woman who but a decade earlier had so loudly proclaimed: "If marriage and family depend upon the castration of women, then let them disappear"? Was Greer now mourning the child she herself had never had? Was this just the contorted cry of her unused womb? Reading these words, these books, I felt completely torn, irritable, confused. On the one hand, they sounded not unlike what I had subversively posited myself back in the radical heyday, that there were some differences between men and women and that those differences ought to be preserved and celebrated, drawing rebukes at the time from my purer feminist friends. Now, at this juncture, these up-with-motherhood tomes sounded like a consoling pat on the back of the second sex as we began to run into brick walls everywhere, in both our personal and professional lives, and made me, at the beginning of the 1980s, feel slightly stranded. Was I destined always to be a contrarian, to be out of synch, to be swinging one way while the pendulum swung the other, a childless victim of the "feminist mystique" hung out to dry at a time when the phallic undertow was gaining steam along with the economic backlash? Women were not getting to the top spots anywhere near as fast as we had hoped, so was this the time to go into this corrective swoon over motherhood, especially as we were still doing all the homework? It was fairly clear by this juncture that most men were not going to do much around the house, period, they just weren't, though their self-assessments on this score were rosy, much rosier than that of their wives. I literally threw a *Psychology Today* across the room after reading a survey in which men cheerfully said they shared the housekeeping and child care fifty-fifty while the wives said emphatically no, that the women were doing almost all of it, which was certainly my experience. Already here in the early eighties, men's movement guru Robert Bly was putting forth the notion of wounded masculinity, the poetic rendition of Reagan's own message, whose politics Bly allegedly loathed. Bottom line for both: Men are warriors not dusters. And there was a fatigued accession to that on the part of many women I knew, myself included. It wasn't just about actual chores, it was that women were doing the emotional work, too. We were supposed to be the family cheerleaders, bandaging knees and egos with indefatigable tenderness while also advancing our own lives and careers. It was a new tangle: All the old roles and old conditioning added to the new expectations. I had simply begun to lose the thread of resistance, though sometimes I still flared over undone dishes and unmade beds and the inference that that was still my domain—that I was a maid, no matter what else I was— though who, as a grown woman, wanted to bellyache about dishes and dust balls. I didn't want to but I did. It was that or a lapse into the famous maternal sitcom scold, and God knows I didn't want to be that. Or—and how many women had I heard say this?—you could use sex. No, that's not what they said. They said: You just have to give him a good screw, then he's a pussycat. The big bang in reverse. A pacification campaign (wasn't that the euphemism from Vietnam?). I didn't want to do it that way. I wanted to play it straight. I wanted it to be fair, tender, open—my own little family unit. I didn't want to fall back into the coy importunings of old, though I was certainly capable of it.

These were the most depressing years for me and the women I knew, even the ones who were more easily married, because that pro-family lid was back on. That's what it felt like, as if someone had come along and put the fifties lid back on and now we were supposed to be good little girls again, albeit grown-up girls proficient in oral sex who didn't mind going to see *Behind the Green Door* and offspring. The fifties meets the eighties. The whole culture was poised to rout your dreams with a one-two punch, one part family, one part pornography, a reactionary and lascivious chokehold around the idea of female liberation. I just hated it, often shivering with a kind of unarticulated distaste at all the burgeoning ugly erotica. Many of us hated the trend but were reluctant to object lest we seem to court censorship or find ourselves back in the old, lonesome, on-your-back, wham-bam postures. They had us cornered: Object and you'll be the sweet little brides of yore. Else lighten up and act liberated and let the pornography roll.

A friend told me a ruefully amusing story of the pornographically laced denouement of her love affair with a man she had hoped to marry, whose two young daughters from a previous marriage she adored. Nearing the end, he had taken her to some porno films, buoying up their attenuating sexual connection, and she says she remembers being turned on in spite of herself.

"We had great sex afterwards," she said, shaking her thick, dark hair, seemingly on the cusp of both anger and tears. "OK. But what's great sex? Everything and nothing. Wildly proficient and for me at that point completely empty. It was ending. I knew it. We were at different points in our lives. He didn't want to get married and he didn't want any more children. Finally one rainy weekend afternoon—he had the whole thing planned, the house would be empty, the kids weren't there—I just walked out of the theater with tears streaming down my face and left him sitting there watching these two women going at each other."

That night, she moved out of the apartment they shared, leaving behind not only a man, but, as she says, the idea of herself as being part of a family. Family, family, family. It was the word on everyone's lips and everyone's agendas. What did my friend do? She threw herself back into work and signed up at the local gym.

I knew many women like her then and I shook my head a lot those years, watching them throw their all into corporate ladder-climbing and muscle-building in some sort of frenetic compensation for something that had been lost or maybe that we had never found. In the classic marketing marriage of pseudo-feminism and capitalism, Jane Fonda's first book came out in 1981—Jane of the chameleon incarnations, from celluloid sexpot to antiwar activist to exercise entrepreneur. It was a flex-the-pecs world now, for women, too, make that upscale, gym-going women. I would sometimes go to gatherings of women in those days expecting the old camaraderie and be given instead a name tag and the agenda for the evening's inevitably competitive conversation, only to come home feeling complicitous and dirty. I had wanted more, something bigger, better, freer, nobler, more sisterly, less divisive. I didn't want to imitate men, not sexually, not professionally. And on that score, their lousy timing to the contrary, I certainly didn't think Friedan and Greer were wrong. It had always been my long-held hope that it would be different, that we women would be—kinder, gentler, more inclusive, all of it. But just seven years after my first *Newsweek* piece had appeared prophesying the potential demise of what I had called "female ethnicity," I wrote a follow-up essay for *The New York Times Magazine,* a bristly lamentation called "Women and the Spoils of Success."

Whenever I enter a room of people these days, I am conscious that it is the women, not the men, who give me the once-over, a quick, slightly veiled, not entirely ungenerous instant appraisal. I look back at these women across the room as if it were empty of men. Who are you, our eyes say to one another, what joys and sorrows have you known, what do you do, where do you work, where do you buy your clothes, but mostly, mostly, we ask one another, are you successful, do you have what you want, do you have what I want? There then ensues a kind of amiable grilling, a sizing up, a comparing of husbands, children, children's schools, numbers of miles run that day: the underlying question always: is she farther ahead than I?

We were being subsumed into the male world with all its pushes and tugs, competitions and centerfolds. It was the moment of assimilation and I didn't like it and I didn't like myself for being part of it but I didn't know what to do anymore, how to resist, just as I didn't know how to resist over the housework issue. Increasingly money seemed like the answer, the only answer, the great equalizer in our big capitalistic free-for-all (and in that sense, of course, we were Reagan's inadvertent handmaidens), enough money to buy respect and independence from men not to mention someone to do the housework or look after the kids—another woman, of course. Getting in was everything, getting a piece of the action, apparently even the pornographic action. In that *New York Times* essay I went on to decry the recent rash of kiss-and-tell-all books by female movie stars, another perversion, or so it seemed to me, of liberation.

"I just don't find anything liberated or even witty in this table-turning," I wrote. "Kissing and telling and talking about body parts—as women should know better than anyone—is an unpleasant business, as demeaning to the teller as the told-upon."

A bleat in the dark against the onrushing triumph of the consumer-pumped sexual revolution over the women's movement, make that the women's liberation movement. Voyeurism and commercialism had won out over intimacy. Women themselves were now staging raunchy bachelorette parties at male strip joints, and childbirth, like sex, had become the territory of camera-wielding men intent on recording—and in a sense violating—the most intimate of acts. Our ultimate pain like our ultimate pleasure had become fodder for the lens, as packs of nice new-wave daddies, with no doubt the tenderest of motives, poked their long-nosed video cams into the convulsive recesses of the female soul. We were on display. We had put ourselves on display. Yes, there was a backlash; the sexual backlash of the 1970s was now being reenforced by the economic undertow of the 1980s, and yes, it was picking up steam as more and more women got into the work force, there to be demeaned, pinched and denied promotion. It wasn't exactly working out the way our ideologues had planned, and now they too had fallen into rhapsodizing over motherhood while a lot of women I knew and read about were busy turning themselves into muscle-bound material girls, these super-competent muscle-flexing sex-object control freaks. The gender roles hadn't been broadened, just perverted by men and the marketplace. What we had was femininity redux, coated in male affect, in muscles and gabardine.

Catching sight of myself one day in the mirror bouncing up and down in my aerobics class I thought: My God, what is all this, what are we doing here, what are we doing to our bodies, our innards, this is absurd, a new tyranny. It was the same kind of tyranny natural childbirth was now exerting over women who felt they failed somehow if they didn't make it through labor without drugs. The punitive message of these new "postliberation" tyrannies was always the same: You say you're as tough as men—fine, prove it. Gut out childbirth without drugs, take care of the kids, run the house, climb the career ladder and hone those muscles. And no sooner, in fact, did we women attempt to effect muscles than the surveyors of pop culture, notably *Time* magazine, pronounced them sexy: "Women, liberated from the courtesan's need to entice, have become more enticing," said the *Time* issue of August 30, 1982. "To be in condition is not only healthy, it is sexy—and inseparable from a strength of the self and the spirit." We couldn't outfox the phallic brigade. No way. Our muscles would be their turn-on. To showcase them properly, miniskirts were just then making a comeback, which they would do again at the end of the decade, and yes, I was wearing them, not as mini as the teenagers, not as mini as I once did, but certainly well above the knee. To the question, Where is a woman's place? the early-eighties answer was: At work, in the home, in bed and at the gym. All of it. You want in, women, fine, do it all. And we did, many of us, or we certainly tried. The popular magazines were now full of mini-profiles of hard-driving, expensively dressed, well-toned women, as were the ads. These were our new "role models." Success was sexy. Just like muscles. No, we couldn't outfox them. Might as well join them. Helen Gurley Brown was back with one of her syrupy pep talks for the gals of America, a postliberation manual for manipulators called *Having It All,* with chapter titles like "A Husband Comes First," " 'Good in Bed' Is Still Possible," "His Beautiful Penis" and "Never Underestimate C——— Power." How far had we come to get back here?

We were outfoxing ourselves, rushing around, pretending we could do it all, getting more and more estranged from our authentic selves, all right, our authentic female selves and whatever communal vision we might have had of the world we wanted. It certainly felt that way to me and other women I knew, women who were running into mean tenure fights, even in women's studies departments, no less, women feeling unwelcomed by other women in their firms, law firms, architecture firms, political relations firms. In the face of the backlash, this wasn't something that you dared to admit, that sisterhood wasn't exactly shaking out here, just as you couldn't go around being cynical about networking or mourning aloud for an aborted baby or exalting your womb, your innerspace of creation, your link to eternity. But finally, in spite of myself, in spite of my deep reluctance to jump on the family bandwagon, I had indeed begun to hear ever so faintly beneath the tight-fisted little body I had honed, the first tickings of my own so-called biological clock. Ever so faintly. It was not the first twinge of procreative longing so much as the first inkling of mortality. Did I really want to face the grave womb-tight and woebegone, to use my old phrase from that *Newsweek* essay? Did I not want somehow to put a foot in the future by having a baby? Did I not want to try something wholly new, court a different avenue of love—maternal love, now that this other kind, this man-woman kind had proved so thorny? Mine was not a full-hearted embrace of motherhood at this point, not at all, just a tentative step toward it, an awareness of the womb urge deep down inside like the first rumbles of hunger or the first flicker of thirst.

But I still couldn't imagine what sort of life, what sort of family I could make or wanted to make. I didn't like much of what I saw around me—everybody rushing around and women still being pushed around, which is the way I still felt in my own marriage, although now nobody much was talking about it anymore. Here I clung to my husband with a solicitous tenacity that continued to surprise me, abash me at times, clung, too, to his mostly grown boys with a pride in the ongoing love we all continued to share, though as the decade advanced and the internal ticktock grew louder, I increasingly found myself making love through clenched teeth (to refuse? No, never that) and praying for the courage to leave and start over somewhere else, with someone less addicted to the male postures, someone less afflicted by the old notions of father-knows-best masculinity that Reagan et al. were so busily reenforcing. We skirmished some days over every last little thing (oh, I was an ever-vigilant combatant myself): what to have for dinner, where we would go to eat, who would make the bed, the endless combat of sexual warriors. I would awaken many mornings with knotted stomach, ready to do battle, a taut, volatile and furrow-browed aging child bride. What had happened to all of us? I found myself thinking back to what or who I was twenty-five years earlier. Where was the voluptuous sprite who had salami sandwiches for breakfast in a Paris bistro, where the May Queen no-show, the kid who had cantered the neighborhood with the boys, so frisky and hopeful—all layered over now. Were they right, those analysts of adolescence like Carol Gilligan, who told us that something was fatally lost back then when we turned into our teens, some sense of assertion, of gumption, of authentic selfdom, and now we were just papering over the loss with some muscles and mock-maleness as previously we had papered it over with the welcome feminist chutzpah of the early seventies?

As I moved around, the women I talked to or interviewed were feeling the same things, fighting the same fights—or often much tougher ones. I was running into single black working-class mothers with two kids, no alimony or child support—no aerobic classes, either—vibrant women whose sturdiness and humor I admired and beside whom I felt squeamish and privileged. I met struggling stay-at-home moms, pretty blonde thirty-something women with three kids and abusive, alcoholic husbands, women who were saving every penny to afford small houses in cul de sacs in middle America, and lesbian mothers quietly having sperm-bank babies. They were the kinds of women, the pretty blonde stay-at-home mom or the successful black single mother—certainly not the gay mother—who might easily have turned up in one of those spin-doctorish, morning-in-America anecdotes for which Ronald Reagan was so famous. And what was happening, of course, one of the by-products of this gilded-age redux, is that we women were being divided from one another. Incomes of women at the top of the economic heap were rising while the bottom 25 to 35 percent of women were on the way down and would be among the decade's biggest losers. And the popular culture was busy widening this gulf by telegraphing to the less blessed endless pictures of us allegedly liberated hussies abstaining from motherhood and running marathons, women like Ann Rubinstein and me. If they only knew. Never has the female public image, purveyed even by many magazines put out by and for women, seemed more out of whack with reality than it did then. The first half of the 1980s were the loneliest years I had known, the toughest, as they were for a lot of women I knew. Some drank too much, some ate too much, some hurt too much, so that by the late eighties, the 12-step programs and the talk shows of America would ring with their litanies of angst and abuse (more voyeurism, of course), rehashed in nightly TV movies-of-the-week—the teary-eyed denouement of the pro-family decade.

MEANWHILE the women I knew were all beginning to make family noises of their own. In fact, both Ann Rubinstein and Julie Templeton would turn up pregnant in the early eighties. Neither would carry the pregnancy through. At that point, her law degree in hand, Ann had moved across country to join a high-powered political consulting firm in Washington. She had briefly practiced law in San Francisco, found it unexciting, and taken this sideways career move, quite the chic, West Coast newcomer in a tough, still mostly male firm, dilligently stashing away a percentage of her salary every month in her growing baby slush fund. Shortly after she was relocated, her life took a sharp, dark turn when her beloved younger brother was diagnosed with cancer, leaving the eighties to be a blur of love and pain as she set aside her life to look after him, spending every dollar in her baby fund commuting to be with him in Ann Arbor, Michigan, where he was doing a residency in pediatrics. Family values. Mid-siege, she would turn up pregnant in a brief romance and have a difficult, reluctant abortion. It just wasn't the right time, as she saw it; there was no father, there was a sick brother, a full-tilt job in which she was always fighting for her share of the good clients, and in her head and in her heart she could not assimilate all the dissonant elements. "Annie, you've been through so much, fought so hard," her brother told her when they discussed the pregnancy. "Now I'm sick. Don't try to do this now. That soul will wait for you." That's what she did. She postponed the baby. She would see her brother out. She could do no less.

Julie Templeton, another shining star of a woman who had made it in a man's world, exuberant and battle-scarred and nearing forty, recently divorced from her husband and newly in love, also turned up pregnant just after she had moved to Chicago to start her own talk show. But her suitor, recently out of his own marriage and already the father of three, wanted no part of it, wanted no more children, and she, too, ended up terminating the pregnancy.

"I just felt all that old shame like when I was seventeen and alone and pregnant," she told me when we talked. "It went right back to the childhood, no matter how much money I was making or what position I had. I just couldn't imagine doing it on my own. I remember, the doctor called to congratulate me—he assumed I was one of these middle-aged women lucky to turn up pregnant—and I just put down the phone and wept. For all of it. For the daughter I'd given away and for the girl I had been. I knew this was probably my last chance but I just couldn't face doing it alone."

Another female narrative, another story beneath the headlines. On the surface either Ann or Julie could have been read as one of those caricatured, high-achieving babyless baby boomers. So, too, could Jane Allen, a well-dressed businesswoman assertively strolling the avenues of New York in her suede pumps. She had moved there to join an environmental design firm, hip firm, hip clients, on the cutting edge. But if you looked more closely beneath the quietly elegant facade, the ever-appropriate skirt length and light-handed makeup and tousled blond shag, you would see at least a hint of the history, a quizzical wariness left over from an unwanted divorce and a lonesome childhood in that big, chilly house on the Hudson.

I, too, no doubt, would have appeared as a successful sun-streaked yuppie with a decent writing résumé rather than as the bruised but still hopeful renegade I felt like. Long married and nearing the age of thirty-five, I finally stopped using birth control. I knew it was that or move on. I wasn't at all happy about the world I found myself in, a world that in so many ways seemed to be going backward. Nor was I happy about the marriage I found myself in—so many small things contested in a given day. And yet I was finally feeling the press of time and the tethers were still so strong. We shared a family and our work lives continued to wind around each other, and deep down I didn't think it was going to be all that easier somewhere else. By that point, still free-lance, I had begun doing political commentary in a newspaper column and for CBS radio, a new professional joy—to let go, let fly, not just about men and women and the enduring inequities, but the whole political scenario, El Salvador

and Israel. I felt as if I were using a new part of myself, and my complicated, sometimes threatened but equally politically impassioned husband
was visibly proud. He was now the repository of half of my history on
the earth, a kind of vault as I was for him. And, wounds aside, one did
not easily leave that, all that shorthand, all those meals. There is, after a
certain point, so much connective tissue. So I finally stopped using my
diaphragm, my faithful, my trusty diaphragm, which I had inserted with
relentless vigilance for fifteen years, never once forgetting it, never once
being sloppy, always, always getting up and performing that pronouncedly
gooey and counter-erotic act of putting contraceptive jelly in that rubber
disc and then scrunching it up inside me. It was my ticket to freedom, my
ticket out of my female fate, my foreordained biological destiny. Now,
finally, I set it aside and lay my unprotected body down beside my
husband of twelve years, lover of sixteen, as if I were a virgin, as if we
were beginning again somehow.

And indeed there was something virginal in it—the odd thrill of being
unprotected for the first time in my sexual life. In that early stretch of
non-contraception, of not putting in that barrier, I began to have an
inkling of what birth control had wrought in my psyche, of how completely sex and procreation had become separated, of how indeed estranged I had become from my own body. The pill (and attendant
contraception, but really the pill) was the great liberator, unquestionably,
and yet, as these things can, it had also taken something away. It had
exacerbated my estrangement from my body, my fertility (as did the
muscles, in their way, as did the pornography). I could see that only in
hindsight, as I bedded truly naked for the first time in my postpuberty life.
It was a strange feeling. The sex was different, more potent. It had its own
licentiousness born of optimism, the sense that something could be
created. I tried on the optimism, the womby, fill-me-up optimism I had
so long blocked. It felt good amid the daily struggles, a tentative celebration of body, of biology, of destiny, of womanhood, all that I had so
resisted in an effort to dismantle the constraints on my sex.

I have often wondered what would have happened, how different my
life would have been, had I simply turned up pregnant in those giddy,
naked months. But even then something in me—I don't know what: my
mother's history, my own premonitions, my sense that on the most
profound sperm-and-egg level, this husband of mine and I were indeed

incompatible—told me I would not easily conceive. And yet I began to flirt with the possibility, began to relax toward it, toward the idea of creation and procreation and family and the feeling that a baby just might be a balm to my frazzled, divided, angry, Reagan-era female soul. I did not wish, down the road, to give vent to the bitter, infertile eloquence of Germaine Greer. No, that was becoming clearer; I did not want to be womb-tight and woebegone, after all, and on my good days I allowed myself to succumb to the optimism implicit in this new procreative sex. We had come a long way, we women, hadn't we, Reagan and company notwithstanding? After all, hadn't Geraldine Ferraro been nominated that year? I stood in the convention hall in San Francisco when her name was announced as the candidate for vice president of the United States and was unexpectedly jolted with emotion, just as the previous summer I had been in the bleachers at Cape Canaveral and watched Sally Ride, the first female astronaut and an old schoolmate, be blasted into space, my heart launching after her into the sticky Florida morning. And the year before that, 1982, there had been the unveiling of the Vietnam monument in Washington, a monument designed by a woman, a monument that could only have been designed by a woman. There were no heroics, no men with guns or marines hoisting flags, just an elegant headstone for the dead and a wailing wall for their survivors—a monument, if you will, in what writer Ursula LeGuin called "the mother tongue." Standing before that wall, I wept for the dead and the living and the clear eye of the young woman who had conceived it. My pessimism notwithstanding, we were making our mark on the landscape, even though in due course, megabuck entrepreneur turned presidential candidate Ross Perot would lobby hard to see that an old-timey assemblage of bronze soldiers be erected near that wall in an effort to obviate its dirgelike power. Stroke and counter-stroke.

And then, of course, in 1984 Ronald Reagan was resoundingly reelect-ed, by women as well as men (61 percent of the men who voted voted for Reagan and 57 percent of the women), and he shrewdly coopted the mother tongue by finding himself a female political poet, Peggy Noonan, to cloak his programs and his patriotism in liltingly feminized, personal-ized phrases. Noonan, a master image-meister, an anti-choice Irish Cath-olic working-class woman, gave Reagan the kind of folksy eloquence he became known for, as in his Pointe du Hoc speech given in France on the fortieth anniversary of D-Day, words about the air being "soft and full of sunlight," about "the snap of flags and the click of cameras and the gentle murmur of people come to visit a place of great sanctity and meaning," and then the turn back to forty years ago when "the air was dense with smoke and the cries of men. . . ." It was good stuff, goose-bump stuff, female stuff in the service of male stuff, of war. No, we couldn't outfox them. Might as well join them. Some quippy "liberated" women were also playing right into the hands of the retro-chauvinists by decrying the alleged epidemic of wimps. "Suddenly I crave James Cagney to squeeze a grapefruit in my face," wrote one female journalist. "I long for the old days of LBJ and John Wayne when the talk was minimal, the moves were fast and furious, and nobody had time for regrets, let alone a panel discussion on 'Power and Impotency.' " Trendy, malevolent stuff written by angry, lonesome women.

Oh yes, it would be hard work to stay the course, not be taken in by the market-driven male world, turned into their poets and pundits and post-feminist sex objects, even post-feminist procreative sex objects. Feminism, materialism and maternity were now the chic ménage à trois, and we aging boomers were being subsumed into the pro-family myth as our clocks started ticking down in high-decibel concert. We were at that age, no longer the golden girls of the New World Order. We were fifteen years past the hottest flare-up of feminism, now facing mid-life, which for many of us meant motherhood or at least a reckoning with it. We couldn't help it, couldn't help that it was happening on Reagan's watch. The time was nigh. Our protracted and adamant and, yes, revolutionary journey away from maternity—away from our fifties childhoods and out through the venturesome sexual terrain and on into the feminist upheaval of the early 1970s—was coming to an end. The revenge of the wombs. And as I began to heed the call of my own, I became increasingly attuned to my body, learning its ovulatory rhythms, being seduced at long, long last by its life-making potential. But my body, as it turned out, would not do my bidding. That became increasingly clear. And finally after a stretch of months of giddy, unprotected sex without contraception, I succumbed to outpatient diagnostic surgery, in which a gentle-spoken, bespectacled surgeon peered into my reproductive parts through one of those laparo-scopes. The beginning. The diagnosis was not good. I had scar tissue and adhesions around my ovaries and tubes and would need major surgery to remove it were I to have a good chance of pregnancy. I moaned up at him through my post-anesthetic fog, "But it's unfair; I was so good," by which I meant, in my schoolgirlish parlance, that I hadn't fooled around. Wasn't that the problem: all those partners, all that random sex back when? Apparently not. The long-forgotten "minor" infections I had in my earlier years of courtship and marriage were apparently much more serious than anyone knew. He suspected chlamydia, which, as he was the first and certainly not the last to tell me, often had no visible symptoms in women and rendered thousands—possibly hundreds of thousands—of women infertile, back then, even now. I did remember a spate of apparent "minor" vaginal infections and cystitis—inflammation of the bladder— that Karl and I exchanged in our first years of marriage, back when we were riding around the Malibu hills on his Triumph, which he could have, the doctor told me, unknowingly brought with him to our honeymoon bed. What to say, whom to be angry with? The medical profession that didn't catch it at the time? My unknowing husband? Myself for not being more vigilant? Any and all of us, depending on my mood. And as I reckoned with that damage and the surgery that loomed, I recorded another more immediate loss: Sex was now for naught. After such a brief and charmed interlude, an all too brief stretch of months post-contraception and pre-diagnosis when sex seemed larger than itself, when I had thrown myself into it with renewed sauciness, the possibility was taken away, and I realized with anguish that I might not now be able to conceive in the normal manner. And as the sex lost its life-making luster, I increasingly lost interest in it—an ironic turn for someone who, like so many women of my ambitious, eroticized generation, had clung so long to my sexual prerogatives. Now, without the possibility of a baby, sex felt empty, laborious, clumsy, and I cursed myself for having waited so long to test my procreative potential. I cursed the medical establishment for its inevitably lackadaisical attitude toward women's health, ruing the reality that it was from them I would now have to seek surgical redress. But I also cursed again what I saw as the misplaced emphasis on equality—it was I, after all, not my husband, who had been rendered infertile by our shared act—and my own inability to protect myself back when, my uniquely female parts, my uniquely, vulnerably female parts (why didn't somebody tell me?), knowing I was now destined to play out my baby-longing while Ronald Reagan played out his hand against the escalating pro-family/pornographic din of the second half of the 1980s. It was not a happy prospect on either account, though I knew I would proceed. I had no choice. I was beginning to suffer from pronounced procreative longings with the fervor of many of my contemporaries, my psychic and erotic energy now increasingly concentrated on getting a baby.

15

THE CALL

N^{o.}

HITTING BOTTOM

I had surgery in the spring of 1985. It was warm out and I lay for five days in a hospital room nursing a small fever and sneaking peeks at the six-inch slit across my lower abdomen that had been stapled shut. In a procedure called a laparotomy, a couple of hours of major abdominal surgery, the doctor had removed the scar tissue, extensive enough to have bound my left ovary down and under my colon. In short, as he had suspected, I had been a mess inside from some old, untreated STD or PID.

All the internal tugging and accompanying morphine left me feeling raw and emotionally vulnerable but given to wild mood swings of hope as I lay there recovering. Maybe this was it. Maybe my journey was over. Maybe I would get pregnant the next time out. After all, the surgeon was cheery. The prognosis, he told me, was positive, though I had read the strange statistics. I had somewhere between a 10 to 70 percent chance now of conceiving—a variance as large as my moods. At least everything was now where it should be and the tubes themselves did not look damaged inside. That was the key, of course, that those all-important conduits be free of scarring. So ostensibly, it was restored to me—the procreative act—and I vowed to plunge forward with avidity as soon as the thought of something or someone near or in my body did not make me shiver with pain. I toted up, lying there in my post-op pain, my good deeds—political commentary (that was worth a little something); being a loyal and committed friend (that, too); and what about my stepmothering, tenacious and nonjudgmental (ah, yes, certainly the fertility gods would take that into consideration and give me my own baby in return).

It was 1985, and the baby din was reverberating all around me as the children of the fifties were breeding at last. The earlier prognosis that as many as one-quarter of us would never have children was being proven wrong. Ultimately, we older boomers would catch up with most of the preceding generations, in that only 15 percent of us would remain childless. So after all was said and done, after all the protestations—mine included, God knows—motherhood, apparently, was finally too irrefutable, too primal, something not to be left undone. I began to feel as if I had a grain of sand in my womb, agitating to become a life.

Through the millennia women had had babies, when they didn't want them, when they did, but I belonged to this hellfire, change-the-rules, psyche-scratching slice of a generation, arriving at the point of baby-longing at mid-life as my fertility waned. What a crew we were. What a long revolutionary, evolutionary way we had come. And now everywhere I went, everyone I talked to was wrestling with the issue. Some of my friends already had children and were frazzled over the juggling act, even happily married women with warm and decent husbands, men easy in their skin who curled up with their wives and wives' friends for late-night chats and weren't averse to vacuuming, the ones who got the idea of sharing. But even for these couples, the juggling act was prodigious; American parents were spending on average just seventeen hours a week with their children. Not only were fathers gone long hours, but now mothers were too, handing off their babies to high-priced care or low-priced—swooping down on them at day's end. I was now witnessing so many of these scenes—the combustively guilty mothering of deeply tired women—and felt lucky, should I get a baby, that at least I worked at home.

Clearly there had been a revolution, a partial one, anyway. By 1985, 49 percent of mothers with children under six were in the work force, 62 percent of those with children six through seventeen, and they were all finding out the same thing: Sentimental, fair-minded America wore motherhood on her sleeve but provided no day care and no mandated maternity leave, unlike at least 100 other countries in the world. Meanwhile women were still doing almost all the home work, the "second shift," as Berkeley sociologist Arlie Hochschild and Anne Machung would call it in their 1989 book. Adding together jobs outside the home and in, American women worked, she found, an average fifteen hours more a week than men, which over a dozen years stretched to a full extra year worked by women. Bracing stuff.

Playing to female fatigue and guilt, the marketplace was now bombarding boomer parents—translation: mothers—with explicit advice. Magazines and experts proliferated. But in the language of commerce, which was now greedily gobbling up "parenting" as it had previously gobbled up sex, there was no room for poetry, our uniquely female poetry. In the process of assimilation, in which mainstream feminism had become a handmaiden, we had become female eunuchs again, stripped of our womb-songs, our songs of joy and grief over sex and abortion and infertility and mothering. Maternity, like our sexuality, was now being remade in the manly image of the culturally dominant. It became a matter of flowcharts and time management. There were now $35-an-hour lactation specialists teaching women to breast-feed as if through the centuries they had not somehow managed on their own. Talk about the market nursing at the mother's breast. It reminded me of those gorillas in captivity who lost their natural instincts for nursing and manhandled their starving newborns with rough and heartbreaking detachment. My churlishness about the mothering enterprise, however, did not mute my own burgeoning enthusiasm for the idea of nurturing a new life, though I feared it would be another avenue of disconcerting love and no doubt anger.

I was finally hearing it again, that female anger, rather the reborn whisper of it, after a long quiescence. I heard it specifically when I took to the road the next summer after my surgery and traveled around the country interviewing women for a *New York Times Magazine* story on "The American Wife," of which I was indisputably one. We met in their tidy tract-house living rooms and in coffee shops out on lonesome highways, in Holiday Inns and lock-up shelters for battered women, and I was struck by their openness, their buoyancy and their distress, all of them trying, in the absence of any outside hoopla, to rewrite the relations between men and women at home and in the workplace. That was no less true of the coastal career woman trying to do it all than it was of the working wives of the working poor, women running day-care centers for $12,000 a year, one of whom said to me succinctly: "A husband's feeling is that since he out-earns his wife, he is in charge; men just want to dominate you."

There were some happy stories, some couples who had jointly moved toward some new sharing kind of coupledom, and those wives radiated their good fortune, even as many of them observed the old forms. I interviewed a congresswoman whose husband had stayed in their home district. Every Friday night, en route home from the airport, she stopped at the market to pick up food. She saw it as a small price to pay, a nod to the traditions in which she had long ago married. But for most it was tough going, especially as we found ourselves in a world that seemed to be slipping farther and farther backward. Here's what I wrote:

It is clear in 1986 that the notion of being a wife, of a wife's proper place, hasn't changed as much as we blustery young brides thought back then (in the early 70's), and that even then we carried that notion deep within ourselves. We may not have been deferential to marriage, but we were deferential to men. For all their early bravado, the wives I knew kept right on cooking . . . and they kept right on wearing lacy underthings beneath their serious suits, a gesture of covert coquettishness by which they assured themselves that, even as they were trying to make their professional marks, they were still feminine, desirable, wifely. So it's not surprising that women are now in a world that seems in a lot of ways to be going backward, a world in which Rambo and his like are the male cultural icons while the tenderized men of the 70's are now scorned as wimps (even by some women), a world in which the bookracks are full of best sellers with titles like "Too Smart For Her Own Good?", "Women Who Love Too Much," and "Smart Women, Foolish Choices," post-liberation primers on how to please, get, hold and handle a man, a world in which even once-determined career women are celebrating refound domesticity and child-rearing with unblushing enthusiasm while single women, however successful, are portrayed as lonesome rejects. . . . [Most women] are struggling, mostly quietly, since anger is once again considered unfeminine and femininity is once again high on the list of desirable qualities for the American wife, just as a kind of hip insensitivity is now considered desirable again in American men. It's all so strange. I still shake my head; I can't believe so little has changed when so much has. I think of all the wives I talked to—60 or 70 of them. Their faces blur, diverge and blur again, and I wonder how many of them will still be married in a year's time, or 10, and whether they'll be happy. Right now, at a time when there is no discernible women's movement left, so many of them seem caught between the parts of themselves they can't reconcile—the part that wants a hero for a husband and the part that wants a partner; the part that wants to be the perfect, ever-present mother and the part that wants to be the perfect career woman. They're caught and they're uneasy, wondering just how much backsliding is going to go on and just how much of it comes from the irreconcilable differences within their own psyches.

No question, it was tough out there, tougher than I think I even anticipated—so many women being hurt one way or another—and I came off the road angrier than I had ever allowed myself to be, always holding myself in check, the perennial good girl, the girl men would love—feminist or no. But I had finally seen and heard too much. I knew the statistics. I carried them around with me: Every six minutes a woman in the country was raped; every eighteen seconds a woman was beaten. I knew that, but it was still bracing to run into so many of them, survivors of a world that had proved so mean, so male, so rock-hard cock-hard hard. I found them everywhere, these women, without even trying.

What I did not find on my magazine rounds was that media-hyped split among women, the hard-bitten coastal career women like me versus the monogamous midland moms who cherished their families. That alleged split was made much of that year in a book called *A Lesser Life—The Myth of Women's Liberation in America*. Its author, Sylvia Ann Hewlett, insisted that there were two hostile camps of women and that the traditionalists hated us would-be equalists who had denigrated their life-styles, their values, their men. But the women I talked to evidenced none of that. They did not look at me like some smug anti-family intruder. We laughed and commiserated, and they were as tender about my baby-longings as I was about their child-care problems. But Hewlett, along with Lenore J. Weitzman, author of the previous year's *The Divorce Revolution*, was the signal of things to come, the first feminist-tinged anti-feminism. Sheaves of this stuff would fill the late-eighties shelves, as women themselves, looking for someone to blame for their woes (too little child care, too much violence), started to cast a dark eye on the very idea of liberation for women, implying that the women's movement had somehow failed by letting men off the hook rather than putting them on it.

The books only abetted my anger, pushing me at long last from my irreverent middeland into a passionate defense of a movement that had long ago lit up my life, not so much a movement as an idea: the idea of liberation, of being free of the old forms, all the masculine/feminine role-playing that strangled joy, love, intimacy, work, sex, everything. True, all along the way I had quibbled with doctrinaire feminism, wanting

women to hold on to some of their uniqueness, their instinctive or
instilled tenderness—I held out hope, I guess, that men would ape us
instead of us aping them, which had happened in some rare instances. I
had quibbled with its priggishness (I liked to look pretty), its lack of
poetry (about sex), its tacit embrace of materialism as the route to independence, its occasional segue into a McCarthylike rigidity and name-
calling, its misplaced insistence on equality rather than on equal rights, its
inability to reckon with the different contours of our female lives. But
after that reporting trip, I was full-tilt angry for the first time in my life,
angry for women, for their pain, angry with the women who didn't have
that pain and with the men who inflicted it.

Here I was again way out of synch, angry way late. That belonged to
fifteen years ago. In fact, I had not been angry then. I was too young, too
hopeful, too optimistic. I realized that the anger had belonged to women
the age I now was, mid-life women, and maybe that's what it took, some
getting along in life to get really angry. But what was I to do now, wanting
this baby with increasing hunger? Try as I might, I could not revive my
procreative lust. That moment was gone. Between the surgery—which,
deep down, I somehow figured was only a precursor of difficulty to
come—and my burgeoning anger, I could not refind that zest. I would
think back on it, in the years ahead, with fondness, with longing—that
brief, lit-up stretch of joyous bedding, of baby-making sex, unlike any I
had known since or would know again, an altogether different kind of
eroticism. A matter of months really. That's all it had been. All it would
ever be.

MY FRIENDS WERE also being taken up by the baby chase, or certainly the
baby reckoning. Still single, still adamantly successful and bedeviled by
that yet-to-be-disproved Harvard-Yale study about the lousy odds of
marriage for women her age, Jane Allen turned up with breast cancer the
same year I had my surgery. She was, in a way, lucky. She needed only a
lumpectomy and was pretty much able to pick up the pieces of her life,
though it was a discommoding emotional experience and she worried
that, even should she remarry, there were so many other issues: the
cancer, the fear that she wouldn't be around to raise a baby and the

niggling fear underneath all of that that somehow she could pass on the gene for breast cancer to her own child.

"I mourned and I didn't mourn, you know," she told me. "It was late. I was glad to be alive. I had always been active and involved and right through the ordeal, the diagnosis and the treatment, I kept going to the gym and going to work. And a funny thing happened: My father came with me sometimes, sat with me through the treatment or he'd be there at my apartment when I got home. He'd been through a second divorce and had made some lousy business decisions, but there he was. We didn't talk much. He sat there—he still postured a little and was sometimes inaccessible—but his presence was a comfort. And I knew he was proud of me, of what I had accomplished. My mother turned up, too, of course, and after all my confused feelings about her in my childhood, she was really quite heroic and very helpful. She really pulled through for me and I enjoyed being with her, which was a big surprise. Her presence was also a newfound comfort, in a different way. To come up with the gumption and fight to deal with the cancer, it was very important for me to believe that I could go on to create life. And I thought that that was what the future would hold for me. But as time went on and I didn't find an appropriate partner, the other realities kicked back in. I couldn't just take up with someone who would disappear, some dance-away dad who wouldn't be around if something happened to me."

I liked listening to Jane, her modulated voice, her soothing, no-nonsense pragmatism and sense of responsibility, her directness. She was the best of us in many ways, us of the Sacrificial Generation, the best of what had been media-translated into a spoiled, unsexy cliché, the solo superachiever, make that the childless solo superachiever, from the privileged background via the Ivy League. In the wake of her cancer, she left her job to start her own company, a kind of ecological clearinghouse and fund-raiser for a lot of the smaller environmental groups, which she staffed almost entirely with women. She started flying back and forth between Los Angeles and Washington to fund-raise and lobby, trying, as always, in her earnest, dogged, ever-so-slightly-fragile way to matter, taking charge of rooms in an easy, nonauthoritarian way.

Meanwhile Ann Rubinstein was heading into her own darkest days, too—we were all in perfect synch here—for which no amount of previous family reckoning, previous shrinkage could adequately prepare her. Caretaking, a woman's place—it was all there, no matter what you did, no matter how much professional armor you sported. Was it the worst of us or the best of us, a hiding place or a noble achievement? All the women I knew asked themselves that constantly as they juggled competing calls on time and heart, trying to figure out, late in the late eighties, just how much caretaking was appropriate (and conversely why so many men were still doing so little of it) or how much of it we used as a crippling crutch. For Ann Rubinstein there was never a choice. Her brother's end was in sight and every fiber of her bristly-tender being was attuned to his dying. Wrinkled, tear-stained and exhausted, her thick, dark hair an unruly mass, she commuted up and down the East Coast all through the soggy summer of 1986, from Washington to New York—where he'd gone for treatment—and back again. At the very end she moved up to stay with her parents in a borrowed apartment.

"There I was at age thirty-eight, unmarried, no children, back in the malevolent bosom of my family, and we were all just shell-shocked with sadness," she told me. "I promised myself when it was over I would put my head down and find a nice man and get married and try to have a baby before it was too late. And within a month of my brother's death, in fact on my very first night out at some friend's house, I met the man I would marry, a very nice, solid lawyer type—I'd had it with all that high-voltage stuff. Within months we were living together and within a year he consented to us trying to get pregnant. He was very independent, very sturdy. Every morning for a year I woke up crying about my brother and he just held me. He didn't try to talk me out of my tears and he didn't over-identify. He just held me and taught me finally a lot about love. I wanted very much to have a baby with him, though he did drag his feet on that one for a while. There had just been so much loss, the person I had loved best in the world was gone, the person I had helped raise, really. Now it was finally my turn to make a family."

Despite her grief over her brother, a grief that still easily causes her to tear up and turn away, Ann says she was finally feeling cautiously hopeful, more whole than she ever had been. She liked getting older, feeling less need to please and perform, more her own woman finally, farther away from her melodramatic childhood. It had indeed been a long, hard road.

Progress? We baby-boom women were making it, at last, it seemed,
baby step by baby step, even as all around us those years the reactive
pro-family stuff swirled and swirled, joined in around 1987 by a media
blitz of bimboized images. It was the second comeback of the miniskirt
in the decade, but this time the fashions were not only short, but adamantly clingy. Here were the youthful "whores" to counterpoint us
mid-life Madonnas. (Where had time gone?) I took note of a sort of sea
shift in ads; a more overtly lascivious tone had crept in (of course, rap
music was beginning to explode by then with its bitch-laden lyrics, and
male comics were becoming bolder in their anti-femaleisms). Maiden-
form had a new campaign, a variation on that old "I dreamed I charmed
the spots off a leopard" line (actual copy from a 1962 ad). Now a
no-nonsense lawyer with a string of pearls and glasses in her hand was
standing before the defendant's box in, you guessed it, bra and panties.
Message: Even a hard-bitten, success-oriented woman is a sex object
underneath. These were the ads I really resented for their smirky squeam-
ishness. They were like mudwrestling, a spectator sport that had sprouted
up during the seventies and eighties, a lowly upstart, it would seem,
amidst the gilded-age redux with its limousines and unlimited, purchasable pornography. Mudwrestling was a slimy, schoolyard throwback,
pretty girls mucking about, in mock-copulation, trying to yank each
other's bikinis off before a hooting crowd of the presumably aroused. If
you're going to undress us, then put us in bed, not in a mud pit or a court
of law. I also didn't like the ads featuring clear-eyed female execs with
briefcases in one hand, baby in another, in part because they played, as
always, to male definitions of success and in part because they were an
unconscionably successful sales pitch to my own wish fulfillment. Even
television journalist Diane Sawyer fell to centerfold fever, submitting to
a high-class sex-kittenish spread in a 1987 *Vanity Fair*. Same reassuring
message: I might be smart and high-paid but I'm still a babe underneath.
An end-of-the-eighties progress report on women in television program-
ming found that women were still mostly sidekicks for the men, usually
scantily clad and often victims of violence, and at least a third were
pictured as secretaries, waitresses and bank tellers. Only 5 percent were
shown as entrepreneurs. In keeping with the trend, Hanes, the stocking/
pantyhose makers, now had girls with long legs smiling at handsome men

who gave testimony to their ditziness, like, "She's still a little suspicious of microwaves. Always remembers everybody's birthday. Ahh, and her legs . . . Emily's legs."

Like a lot of women I knew, I capitulated, somewhat anyway, to the new fashions: I shortened my skirts and lightened my hair, for the first time, wondering how far down the slippery slope of cosmetic make-overs I was capable of going. By this time some of my friends were already having their eyes done or their breasts augmented, and I felt alternately grateful for the scalpels that buoyed their self-esteem and rageful at the beauty tyranny that my own movieland hometown had in no small part inflicted on all of us. A January 1988 display in *Vogue* shows a female torso in transparent body stocking marked all over with arrows and lines showing how the body could be surgically improved, nipples raised, thighs sucked off, tummy tucked, you name it. Smart women, foolish choices.

There were new manuals aplenty, the *Cosmo* imitators, about femininity redux, about how to keep your mate monogamous, pages of explicit advice, as always, about oral sex (because it reduced male performance anxiety?). The penis was, they co-jointly averred, maleness itself, and had to be kissed, fondled and appreciated as such, especially if you wanted to hold on to him, your man, that is. So there we were in the homestretch of the Reagan reign worrying about our cellulite while being schooled in the art of oral sex. A blow job for monogamy. A blow job for family values. A blow job for America.

In the ultimate oral act in the ultimate eighties postmortem, Bret Easton Ellis' much misunderstood and generally lambasted 1991 novel, *American Psycho,* a designer-name-dropping Manhattan yuppie actually has sex with the severed head of a young woman in an act of ex post facto fellatio that represented the gruesomely logical extreme of the decade's marriage of materialism and misogyny. The perfect paranoic's blow job: no lips, no life, no tongue, no teeth, no flesh, no female, nobody, nothing—at the heart of which is the homicidal fear of women that was given such tacit license to bloom all during the family-inflected decade. As Norman Mailer pointed out in his *Vanity Fair* review of the book, Ellis might not quite have been the Dostoyevsky of the eighties, in the sense that the evil he conjured seemed so banal. But that was the point—that evil itself and certainly evil directed at women had in a way been stripped of its evilness, so banal and pervasive had it become, such a part of our culture and a staple of our entertainment. One out of eight Hollywood movies now featured a rape, and a Rhode Island survey of sixth to ninth-graders showed that one-fourth of the boys and one-sixth of the girls felt that a man had a right to force a woman to have sex if he had spent money on her, which the twelve-year-olds defined as $10 to $15. The phallic undertow was turning into a tidal wave. To the question, Where is a woman's place? the answer now was: in a mud pit or a maternity ward. Or a morgue.

I MYSELF WAS finally about to be pushed into the cushioning arms of psychotherapy. I couldn't get happy anymore. That new self I wanted— or maybe it was the old, preadolescent self, whichever, I couldn't find my way to her without help. That was now clear. My longtime good-girl act was nearing an end. I got pushed over by the protracted visit of my eighty-five-year-old mother-in-law. I came off the road from the American-wife interviews, astir with old angers and ready to start writing, and found her ensconced in the second bedroom of our small house. She had come for a visit, fallen and broken her hip, and here she was, a tall, angular, snuff-dipping character out of another country, the country my husband was from, those lonely flatlands of eastern North Carolina, where both had lived their early years in poverty, in unpainted shacks out in the country. Uneducated and unskilled, she had been married and widowed three times before the age of forty. By turns spunky and defeated, she ended up sending her two small children, my husband and his younger half-sister, to the Methodist Orphanage in Raleigh, where my husband stayed from age seven until he joined the Navy when he was seventeen.

Our first summer together he took me back there, and to my nineteen-year-old California eyes, the sprawling campus of big old brick buildings and overbearing trees seemed the ultimate representation of Dickensian deprivation, and I don't think from the moment I set eyes on the place that I ever quite forgave the woman who put him there even as, in my husband's dark times, I tried to assure him that she had done the very best she could, which, I think, she had. It was just that on many days my love had not seemed a match for his wounds.

And now here she was, the authoress of his pain and, in some ways, of mine, lying propped up in our small house spitting tobacco juice into a Dixie cup and beckoning me often from my writing to get her something or empty her bedpan. I churned inside, a full-tilt gender identity crisis: How could I not go to her, how could I? Sometimes I stubbornly refused to hear her, castigating myself all the while. What life had she had? I knew from her son that she'd never loved any of the three husbands, that her heart belonged to an earlier suitor who had spurned her. So she married and had her children, was widowed, and sent them away and settled down in the small, then segregated town of Wilson, North Carolina—"niggertown" on one side of the tracks, the white on the other—where for the next twenty years, until she retired, she sold popcorn at a stand next to a movie theater and went to visit her kids a couple of times a year. That was her life, day in and day out, and I realized I was a product of her as surely as I was a product of my own mother and grandmothers, of their restlessness and unrealized dreams. We carried them all, we would-be subversives; in their names, we had fought, however ineptly, though God knows I had no words, no way, to share this with my mother-in-law.

We did have our sweet times. In the afternoons after I'd finished writing in my little office at the back of the house, we would sometimes visit, she a gravelly-voiced, Bible-reading, homily-spouting grandmother with a taste for racy jokes and Dubonnet on the rocks, and I, a thirty-six-year-old career woman with no children and a perhaps predictable yen for Chardonnay. We'd sip our drinks and talk about her four grandsons, my four stepsons, all of them grown by that time, but near enough to visit often. My own mother, to whom I had remained very close, drifted in some afternoons after work to chat and attend to my mother-in-law's pills and pillows as if to compensate for my slackened compassion. This, she seemed to say by example, as she plumped and fussed, is what women do, women like us; they take care of people no matter their other work. To do less was simply to be less, less than female, less than a woman. And even as I bristled at the implication, I found her presence as soothing as did my mother-in-law. We'd sit there, the three of us, one born in 1900, one in 1924 and one in 1950, a continuum of women making comforting small talk, colloquial, feminine, lightweight: hair, food, weather. What had changed? We spanned the century but we seemed of a piece. Sometimes my husband's ex-wife would visit, a gritty, determined survivor who, like my own mother, had never remarried. By this time some of the scars had smoothed over. It had been a long time. I had lasted. I was not the young fly-by-night second wife; the second wife indeed I was, but not so young anymore and certainly not fly-by-night. I had now been married to her ex-husband for as long as she had been married to him: fourteen years. She had followed him across the South as he moved from one journalism job to another, from Raleigh through Atlanta and Houston, ending up in Los Angeles, by a fatal fluke of timing, in the mid sixties, just when everything was about to come unglued, including her own marriage, one of those heartland moms who ended up in a development of tract houses with four little blond boys. But here she was, upright and employed as a saleswoman chatting easily with her ex-mother-in-law. They had shared roots, a history that predated mine. I sometimes lingered outside the door listening to them, reflecting that unwitting or not we were somehow tethered as women tend to be, unrelated and deeply related, destined to be gracious and get along and forgive ourselves the pain we had caused each other. With our smoothing small talk, we were the emotional hub of the house, of the family, kibitzing about birthdays and holidays and graduations—the logistical arrangements, the presents to be bought, the sizes everyone wore now—while the man who brought us together went about his life, his work, over there somewhere, apart from us. It was into this maw of femaleness, this comforting, nursing-tending zone that I feared I might somehow disappear forever. That had always been the fear: to be swallowed up no less than all those women before me whose life work it was to look after men and children, which is why my mother-in-law's visit served to nudge me toward some edge. It brought everything to a point, brought me finally to a face-off with my endemic conflict, my love-hate relationship with my gender, my flesh, my femaleness, that had begun so long ago in my childhood family. I had started the baby quest without effecting this healing because indeed I heard the damn clock ticking. Now it was inescapably time. I had become this distorted thing: an angry, ambitious woman sugarcoated in feminine affect, both halves having taken on a comic opera extreme. I was a gabardined career woman with crotchless panties. And I was bereft.

My mother-in-law finally recovered from her broken hip, determinedly hoisting herself around the house with her walker, a tall clanking apparition in tangerine-colored nylon pajamas with curlers in her hair. Those curlers, with their life-affirming vanity in the face of the nearing grave, tugged at me. We had our final dinners together in the kitchen, her son dutifully re-creating the massive fried Southern meals she had taught him to cook: biscuits and gravy, pork chops and fried okra, cakes and cobblers, a greasy benediction on her visit.

And within days of her clattering down our front path en route to the car, the airport and home, her few belongings in an old hard trunk and her perennial Dixie cup in hand, I found myself in a psychologist's office trying to figure out what had gone wrong. The act was up, my act, the good-girl act; I could no longer pull it off, I could no longer pull off the pro forma lovemaking, no matter the baby-lure, and it felt like a death of sorts—or was it the long overdue beginning. For long-married women, long-married, sexually engaged women, I should say, that point at which you can no longer open your legs and take someone inside you is a stunning moment, a juncture of freedom and loss so liberating, so alien, so new. There is no precedent for it, just as there is no precedent for sexual initiation. There is an opening, there is a closing, way deep down somewhere, something we women, despite our perennial intimate chatter, don't talk about, much more easily confiding adulterous encounters (because adultery still keeps us in the acceptable and accustomed female role as the available sex). Cutting off sex, on the other hand, feels too scary, too bold, too untethering. It is the marital analog of hitting bottom, and can, of course, be the end of a marriage, or, at the very least, the often unaddressed harbinger of a flattened-out conjugal arrangement or a tacit license to extramarital passion. In rarer instances, that closure can also be a beginning.

That's what I hoped for, as I sat in that man's office week after week, talking to him and to my phantom family. That was his technique: I had to sit there, squirmingly, talking out loud to my imaginary foes. No, I said, to the husbandly ghost sitting there, no, I cannot do that, no, you cannot say that to me, you cannot ask me that or tell me that. No, I said to the paternal ghost, you cannot say that to me, you cannot ask me that or tell me that. No, I said to all the female ghosts sitting there, you cannot tell me what to do or how to behave, you cannot chastise me if I fail your notions of appropriate femaleness because I will. And you must not any of you anymore quiet me down. No more. No more hushes coming down through the years, hanging over my exuberance. I won't be quiet, I won't be a good sport, a good girl any longer. It will be done, it will be over, if I have to sit here for months, which, in fact, I did, rehearsing over and over and over and over again, talking to those imaginary people so that I could then go out and face my nemeses up close and personal, which I did, going to the mat over anything, any little remark or sharp look aimed in my direction, any quip I deemed offensive, making a real pain of myself, no doubt. Why did you say that? What are you looking at? You can't talk to me like that. On and on, I challenged, fortified by my weekly visits to the good doctor who told me if I didn't do it that way, I would never get it right.

And thousands of others, I knew, were out there doing the same or some variation on it, trying to heal, to assert themselves, make good on the old long-forgotten chutzpah, trying to make good on the revolution, if you will, on the imagined and longed-for improvement in the way men and women related and how they shared their lives. The battleground had shifted for a moment, that's all, turned inward. The reactionary brigade could smirk at our touchy-feely, heel-the-inner-housewife narcissism if they wanted to. They could fling their retrogressive rebimboized images around all over the place. They could talk about the new traditionalism or any other such thing, while we struggled to get out from under those we loved or worked for, all those women I'd talked to out there on the road, across the country, doctors and lawyers, secretaries and supermarket checkers, it didn't matter which, so many of us still tiptoeing around men, seeking to please, seeking not to be hurt on some level. Not physically hurt. For many of us that wasn't an issue. It was something else, their assumption of superiority that made everything so lonesome and harkened back to our childhood homes. I remembered what Sally Kempton said about men in that long-ago piece: "What I couldn't figure out was whether I hated them because I was afraid they would leave me or whether I was afraid they would leave me because I hated them."

Shere Hite hit the same note of woe in her 1987 best-seller, *Women and Love—A Cultural Revolution in Progress,* a mesmerizingly lugubrious tome of woe, a tapestry of female soliloquies bemoaning the behavior of men. My father called me when he saw the *Time* magazine story on Hite's book. "Are women really fed up?" he said, repeating the *Time* cover title. "Yes," I said. And we talked and I told him what I knew or what I thought and he listened. I didn't back off and he didn't come out swinging, this heartland American man-come-to-Hollywood with his big booming voice and his hunger for fame and his family values. He had held on to us post-divorce, my sister and me, with absolute determination—all those trips and weekends—and was audibly proud of us, even as he sometimes cuffed us about with rough humor and edged compliments. I don't know if my father remembers our conversation about the Hite book. I can't imagine that he would. But I do and later, during the worst of the infertility, he would be very tender, close by, just as Jane's father had sat beside her recovery bed. Reconciliations. It was a long arc out of those formative, deformative fifties which the eighties had only reinvented, albeit with a frantic sexual edge. But we were getting there, however slowly, which also involved, certainly in my case as I was now aware, letting go of my own sharp edges accumulated over the years, my own sharp-tongued defensiveness, thirty-odd years in the honing. I was finally ready to stop identifying with the aggressor. I was ready to reconcile myself to my own sex. I was ready to have a baby. Indeed, what a long road; what a long road back. I had been distorted by my culture, my country. In an odd and necessary twist, the women's movement had only magnified the distortion while trying to correct it, or more accurately, had intensified my sense of alienation from my sex and certainly from its biological givens, especially the possibility of motherhood. I began to look at women with children with new and covetous eyes, seeing something I had not seen before, the specific courage they had, one that came with motherhood, the courage of bringing someone on the earth with the intent to shepherd. I wanted now to know that kind of courage, to be the author of a new life that would in turn write new chapters in mine. After so long trying to control everything, get everything nailed down, my work, my marriage, the very shape of my small, slender body, I wanted to let go, swell up, take on flesh, to be fully female, fully fleshed female. I looked back at the picture that accompanied my decade-old baby-making manifesto, I should say, my non–baby-making manifesto: a long-haired, still baby-faced young woman—and shuddered with compassion for her long-ago certitudes. I did understand it—that time, that resolution. Abstaining from motherhood had been a revolutionary act, much more profound than abstaining from marriage. It was the boldest way to step out of the prescribed and proscribed sex role, and that, at the time, had felt like the essence of being fully alive, the only chance of being fully alive, not being trapped. And as I faced forward into the discomfort of my continuing infertility, I tried to hold on to the memory of the exhilaration of that sometimes forgotten step out now that I so desperately wanted back in.

With increasingly heavy heart I watched the months go by with no pregnancy. I became increasingly dogged about monitoring my cycles, taking my temperature to see when I ovulated, initiating sex only then with less-than-seductive adamancy. Now. Here. Go. Start. We were able to laugh some still at the turn our lives had taken, at this on-demand sex, after all the years of high-decibel and hotly contested passion. But finally in 1988, submitting to the obvious, realizing that my post-op hopes were not coming true and that I had irrefutably entered the sisterhood of the infertile, I ended up in the office of Dr. Richard Marrs.

17

GETTING ANOTHER FIX

I am losing heart here and they are too, the clinic staff, the normally fluttering-around, supportive staff who now seem as dispirited as I over my repeated failures. There is this polite, professional, compassionate interest, but it's clear I am no longer a contender, no longer someone who anyone thinks is going to turn up pregnant. Fair enough, I suppose. Clearly I am not at all good for the statistics—repeated attempts with no success. I am dragging down the average. It's time to let go, move on. But why not one more quick GIFT—just one more? It is still showing by far the best statistics, and as I reason out loud to my impatiently patient husband, I only did one, after all. Some women do three, four, six, so why not one more? I promise myself it will be the end. I promise my husband it will be the end. I tell nobody I am going down this road one more time because at least I have the good sense finally to feel slightly embarrassed about my obsession, as if I have fallen in love with entirely the wrong man and bored everybody to death with tales of his perfidiousness. Mum, this time, I will be, stoically shooting up and adamantly keeping my mood under control. I can do that. I am bigger than these drugs. There is no reason for me to succumb to their influence. Surely this time, knowing what to expect, I can rise above their hormone-altering, mood-altering powers. Of course I can. I can work through them this time, put my head down and write, carry on, function. Enough is enough. I'm an adult here, and in a perverse sense this process is getting easier because now I don't expect it to work, not really. I anticipate failure, and that's easier, even as a scintilla of hope still forces me onward.

As to medical science leading me astray, dangling a baby in front of my ever-empty arms, as high-tech critics accuse these doctors of doing, I have to say that Dr. Marrs is only reluctantly amenable to my going down this road again. I think he has his own suspicions that something unknowable is at work here, something even he cannot defeat or surmount despite all his intentions and expertise. My bad tube or tubes, my hyperactive ovaries, my age. I see a slackening interest on his part, too, which makes me feel foolish, invisible, passé. He has a whole new crew of potential successes out there in the waiting room. But, of course, he will proceed. He is certainly not going to throw me out of here, though he is appropriately subdued now when we talk.

I ask the question I have asked before. Why don't I try a straight IVF, one with fresh instead of frozen embryos? After all, that's just about the only thing I haven't tried yet, and with my gambler's instinct rising up, I put that to him, hoping he'll get on my bandwagon. I am still nurturing the suspicion that the supposedly good right tube is somehow dysfunctional. Plus, he has a new IVF trick, so-called assisted hatching. Before the embryos are put back into the uterus, their outer membranes are ever-so-delicately nicked. The idea is to make it easier for the embryos to hatch out of their skins, their zonas, and attach to the uterine wall—something that happens roughly on day five post-fertilization. Since implantation is the big hitch in IVF—a lot of us have made a lot of embryos over time, only to see them float off into never-never land—this is a promising new step and Dr. Marrs is increasingly using it on his IVF patients. In a variation, the embryos are bathed in a chemical bath to soften those outer skins—the aim being the same: to make it easier for them to escape their zonas and take root in the womb. Jaded as I am, I am re-dazzled listening to this explanation and clamor to try in vitro myself.

But no. The GIFT odds are still better, the doctor insists, and if I am insistent on trying something, I should try that once more. Obedient still, try as I might not to be, I sign up for another GIFT. At least there are two cheery new twists this time. One is that Dr. Marrs' wife (now ex-wife) and partner, Dr. Joyce Vargyas, is my hands-on physician. She has opened a branch office nearer my home and it is a strange relief to be going through this with a woman. I never really thought about it, wasn't one of those women who actively went looking for female doctors, but the difference is immediately apparent. Our chatter, Dr. Vargyas' and mine, is easy and intimate, and my flesh seems almost to exhale under her hands. When I tell her I can't bear to take Lupron, that I think my body—not to mention my psyche—is too old for the up-and-down, one-two punch of the Lupron/Pergonal cocktail, she smiles. "Listen to your body then. I think you may be right. We'll go with straight Pergonal." The office in general has a different tenor, lower-decibel, easier, more informal.

The second bonus is that one of my closest friends is doing a GIFT at the same time, not at the same clinic, but we're smack on the same menstrual cycle, one of the cheery things that often happens to women in close proximity, as we are, living a block apart, walking together every afternoon at the end of our work days, dining many a night at each other's house. There is something tender and hopeful to me about us cycling together, plunging in here together. Unlike me, she has a long history of getting pregnant but not holding on to the pregnancies and is now a high-tech victim along with me. We will shoot up together, keep walking and talking and make it through, hoping to compound each other's luck. She has a bracing straightforwardness that is very appealing and brooks no mood swings of her own. That I welcome, hoping it's contagious.

After all, I say to myself as my hips begin to ache again under the daily needles, this is only my second GIFT. My friend has already done two. She got a positive pregnancy read the last time, but within days her hormones dropped and she was back among the infertile, a cruel, cruel seesaw. At least I had missed that. The drugs quite often give a false positive and then you have to wait it out, one more mean wrinkle in this misbegotten world. Luckily, this time, with her at my side, I neither hurt the same way nor hope the same way. I get through it, that's all, and on the appointed day, hormones high, follicles full, I am knocked out again and they retrieve seven eggs and put four back in my one good tube and I am home recovering before I know it, before the whole process even registers. I am on automatic now. The next morning the nurse calls for a rush order of more sperm as the three remaining eggs, the ones that were not put back in my body, have yet to fertilize. Off he goes, my weary but still willing donor, to masturbate in some pornographically laced room at the clinic as neither of us is in the mood to do it together at home, as we have long done, in an effort to keep some semblance of connection, silly and sentimental as that might sound. I bid him goodbye, thinking of all the women out there in the world, sending their husbands out into the morning world. Surely his is one of the stranger missions, and I am even able to laugh, imagining all the other men out there suiting up to take on the world, driving by him oblivious of the weird nature of his outing. But alas, it is for naught. None of the eggs fertilizes, not one, no one.

My friend is a little slower than I and ends up under the laparoscope two days after I to have six eggs placed back into her two good tubes and we begin the long, mean two-week stare-down, taking our progesterone and maintaining our humor. I am true to my word; I work and function in a way I was unable to do during the earlier countdowns. I am ever-mindful of the internal drama, and yet able to carry on reasonably well, taking my shots, having my blood tests, the same old rigmarole, everything looking propitious as always. As I turn the corner into the second week, I start to cramp already, and am despairing. Surely I can't start bleeding a whole week early. That would be a new twist, but, of course, there always is one. The cramps come and go through the week, and finally are sufficiently discommoding, even for someone fairly well used to lower abdominal discomfiture, and stoic about it, that I take to bed and watch endless hours of mindless TV, endless talk shows of women—men, too, but usually women—bleating out their life stories, all the requisite psychobabble about healing their wounded children within, and it strikes me we can no longer talk about ourselves except as clichés. We have even commercialized our wounds and now can find true intimacy only in public.

Again I make it to the pregnancy test without bleeding, but nothing in me says the cramps are anything but a bad indication. Of course, the doctor is ever-hopefully mum, and yet when once again the call comes, I am not surprised. "Sorry, Anne," the nurse says, and need say no more. No elaborations necessary. My heart lurches up the road to where my friend waits. She has two more days to get through before her test. I anticipate good news and am not wrong. She turns up pregnant. We circle around each other for a minute and then embrace. I shed my tears away from her, because her news is joyous and I have no wish to dampen it. Her good luck has no bearing on mine. I believe that with everything in me, though I know I will have a twinge down the road as she swells. And yet at least a pregnancy gives me hope, at least someone I know and love is getting a baby out of all this high-tech marathon. For me, surely it is time to call it quits, to leave Marrs and get on with it. I must begin to detach, cut the cord to the clinic, which will not be easy. I have been coming here forever it seems, so completely has this place been the locus of my attention and my dreams—and my losses. I tally those losses: three eggs put back in me on the first GIFT, three embryos on the ZIFT, three frozen embryos on the FET, and this time, four more eggs and still nothing. I mourn them all, the eggs only slightly less than the embryos. And will. They are as close as I have come. I have a last rash thought of taking umpteen drugs, masses of them, and pumping out dozens of eggs to turn into embryos to put in the deep freeze, just anything to keep from extinction, from being out of the game. But I know it's late for that, too late, and that I have to start the process of detaching. I have to. I find myself steering clear of the streets I used to take to the clinic. I find a new coffee place to stop for my morning pickup rather than go back to the one I used coming and going on those mornings with my sperm in hand, either high on hope or morose with anticipatory failure depending on how things were going. I am weaning myself away, a baby leaving its mother or, in this case, a mother leaving her unconceivable baby. It is from the dream I must be weaned. I have spent the better part of this decade trying to have a baby, and I want it over. I want the decade itself to end, the endless decade, the endless 1980s, taking with them the sitcom dads, the slippery-smooth father figures who have been running the country all the while I have been trying to get pregnant. The whole thing begins to seem like a bad dream and I long for it to be over without having the idea how long that will take and whether I truly am ready to let go. During the process the hunger has only grown in response to the failure. I am an addict, a junkie in need of a detox program. The doctor kindly suggests a postmortem on my long haul. We will sit down and together reconstruct my long and futile quest as a way of laying it to rest. But I am not ready and put it off for a few months, hoping the time away will do me good, and before we sit to rake through the ashes of my procreative folly, I will be well on the mend. One day at a time.

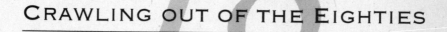

18

CRAWLING OUT OF THE EIGHTIES

It was all I could do to crawl out of the eighties, toting my fractured but ever-so-slowly-healing sixteen-year marriage, my jars of sperm and my heady contempt for the pornographic/pro-family world in which I found myself. As I felt increasingly healed, more whole, my own rent psyche finally on the mend, the society at large only seemed to be getting more split, more dichotomous, more surreal—part fundamentalism, part MTV. In 1988, Ronald Reagan's heir, George Bush, wrapped in the flag and armed with the sound-bite poetry of Peggy Noonan, was elected president. The contest had seen the first woman presidential candidate in Democratic Colorado congresswoman Pat Schroeder, whose run was noted mostly for her teary-eyed 1987 abdication from the race. Those tears became a cause célèbre, women digging at their souls and psyches again—Should we cry in public? Shouldn't we cry?—and down the road one of the leading national women's political groups would encourage would-be women leaders to learn to quell their tears by talking about some painful subject ad nauseam until it was bereft of its emotional punch. Grown-up mutant ninja women.

Meanwhile almost every movie I saw—the ones that didn't feature a rape—seemed to be about babies, almost every woman I knew seemed to be talking about breast-feeding, with me yearning to crawl into their lactating sisterhood and out of the culture in which I found myself, certainly out of the 1980s with their somnambulistic, nostalgic pull toward those fifties families, now personified by Bush and his radiantly grandmotherly spouse, the very families that had long ago set me and my peers on our lurching road toward liberation.

Everywhere I turned, everything was about babies. My two friends Ann and Julie were in the same place—that is, taken up with motherhood, for Julie with sorrow, for Ann, in joy. In 1989 Julie Templeton finally heard from her daughter. Forty-six, happily divorced and firmly established in her new city and her new job, saucy as ever and outspoken and full of optimism, actually learning to play the drums—a childhood desire—she was always, way deep down, girded for the telephone call she was sure was coming. She wasn't wrong.

"It sounds crazy, but I just knew who I gave birth to," she told me staring out the window of her elegant Chicago apartment, "and if she was anything like me, anything at all, she would find me someday. I was sitting in the broadcast booth, the show was just over and they put a call through and the minute I heard her voice, I knew. I just knew. 'Is this Julie?' she said, and I just knew. 'I think I'm your daughter,' she said."

When they hung up, Julie picked up the phone and called her mother and finally, twenty-eight years later, unburdened herself of her secret to the one person above all she had dreaded finding it out. And she wept as she told me about it. The relief after holding on so long. Her mother was wonderful. She said she would do whatever Julie wanted her to do, see the girl, not see her. Another reconciliation. They flew the young woman to Chicago, and as a complicated surprise, she herself turned out to be pregnant. The three generations—make that three and a half, given the impending baby—spent a couple of strained days together right after Christmas, but for Julie and her mother it was like being with a stranger. She talked to her "daughter" when the baby was born and went on exchanging cards and pictures, but it was not a family that could be reconstituted, and listening to Julie talk about it, her characteristic buoyancy flecked with sorrow, I compared our lots: me craving a baby, her having given one up years earlier. We were exemplars of our time, bookends of the Sacrificial Generation, she just that much ahead of me, a product of a still-repressed age when an unwed mother was a shame. And now the zeitgeist had changed and many single women were having and keeping their babies. Perverse progress.

The days we spent together, I watched her go about her work, all confident and informed and irreverent, fast on her feet and full of juice. Like Jane Allen, she was the best of us, too, a woman desperate to make her own way, to matter, not just to work but to do good work, advance the dialogue. Like Jane, she became a determined mentor to younger women, something I also was trying to be, out of some admixture of political passion and compensation for not having had a daughter of my own. Julie and I never again spoke of what had happened, but it lived in her, with her, just as my phantom baby lived with me, and I was capable, on many a day, of fervent rage at the country in which we now found ourselves, a country full of girls in garter belts and push-up bras and foul-mouthed male comics talking about bitches and sluts, but a country in which birth control pills still couldn't be advertised and the antiabortionists were threatening to take us back to a time when women like Julie Templeton had to give birth against their hearts and deal with the rupture for the rest of their lives, and a country that continued to punish us other would-be mothers by refusing to spend money on hardcore infertility (IVF and the like) in part because the pro-lifers were averse to high-tech baby-making, in short, an infuriating world. Against that, I could only throw the progress individual women I knew seemed to be making.

That same year Ann Rubinstein finally got pregnant at age forty-one, after eleven months of self-monitoring, temperature-taking and "increasingly tedious sex," as she described it. Did I not know? With a baby imminent, her earnest young Washington lawyer lover asked her to be his wife, and on a soggy summer afternoon in 1989, surrounded by his "uptight Wasp family" and her still-unhinged-by-sorrow parents, they were married in the backyard of the house they were sharing.

"I wanted it all, the corny trappings, the wedding, the ring, the baby, a life and family of my own," she said, laughing at herself, "though there were times I was still very distrustful of my happiness, days I'd wake up and be sure the baby was gone. Then I'd feel a kick and tears would just well up. I was my father's daughter and some of his darkness, for better or worse, was lodged deep down in my soul. And why not, there was some proof he was right; I had lost my brother, really the light of my life in many ways, my child, but now he was finally sending me a replacement. That's the way it felt.

"My husband had a crisis at work right after we got married: He lost a big case and came home feeling fragile and defeated and saying things like he thought he might be in the wrong job, that he wanted out of the whole profession. There was something comforting about it almost. He had never needed any caretaking; he wasn't one of those narcissistic, needy men I'd always fallen for. But now he did need something and I was glad to be able to give it. It felt like appropriate caretaking, not the obsessional kind we'd all done. I said to him, 'Look, it's OK if you want to quit, I can take care of us if I have to.' I remember him looking at me as if for the first time, seeing me in a new light, that I was sturdy underneath some of my craziness, real sturdy and that I'd be there for him, and I remember thinking that after all, we were lucky to be who we were, who we are: women who were able to look after ourselves and somebody else, children, even a man, if need be."

What a funny mixed bag she had turned out to be, Ann Rubinstein, her own mixed bag of tough and fragile, sentimental and stoic. I thought about her ministering to her brother, her parents' clear favorite, and not caring at that point, and earlier, trying to hold on to her self, her female self, in her melodramatic, male-centered household. And here she had cheated fate, as she saw it, survived, and was putting down her own roots with an eminently decent man. Late, oh yes, we were late, we of the Sacrificial Generation, we Girls of the Chasm, acting out through all the revolutions, trying to heal, be whole, trying to get the caretaking and the ambitions in proper balance while the phallic tidal wave slopped through the culture and we reckoned with the joys—if we were lucky like Ann and turned up pregnant—or the wages of delayed motherhood.

Finally, finally, my husband and I, after two decades together, were ready at last to be parents, in my eyes. The terms of our union had been fairly successfully redrawn. I spoke up, a lot, we tussled less, he did more dishes, I was less inauthentically assertive—those sideways Edward Albee jabs in the middle of a dinner party, dazzling the onlookers with my ever-quick tongue at his expense—and there was about us the cheery sense of survivorship. A year earlier he had stopped drinking, a problem neither of us had really identified as such. And yet in the absence of alcohol, his volatility, precisely the passionate volatility that had charmed me as an eighteen-year-old and then unsettled me in the years after, calmed. Add to that a leap out of corporate journalism into a business of his own, a media-consulting business, which allowed us to work at home together, meeting for midday lunches and even sneaking off to an after-noon movie (we still in all our years of marriage had not disagreed over a film or book or even a magazine lead). Whole days it seemed we saw the sun and not the clouds that had hung over us for the better part of fifteen years. In his business Karl was now helping smart, working women who ran their own companies, women like Jane Allen and Ann Rubinstein, and he liked it, liked them, liked what he saw as their generally less abrasive, more inclusive style of running things that allowed him at last to let down his armor and be softer in his own professional life.

I had carried my own armor into this marriage, and into the working world as well, and it had thickened along the way, further masking that free, whole, giddy preadolescent self I so desperately wanted back. Now that I had her in hand again, at least in part, I was finally ready to be a mother. The happier I felt, the more intense became the desire for a baby. Karl was less thrilled at the idea, having crossed the threshold of sixty, having just started his own business and having finally achieved a modicum of marital peace, marital reconnection, and now here we were throwing petri-dish procreation into the mix, wildly expensive petri-dish procreation, I might add.

I had to make more money. That was the final hurtle for me, the final acceptance of responsibility. It was high time for me to surrender the last vestige of my childlikeness and kick up my income so I could go on pursuing this expensive high-tech breeding. The truth was that even with the constant failure, the infertility business had a maddening momentum. When you were in it, riding back and forth to the clinic, toting around needles and drugs like a junkie, having your ovaries prodded and peered at on the sonogram screen, day after day, you felt perversely alive, part of the baby-conjuring process. The problem was that as I disappeared further and further into infertility, it started feeling less like a life-affirming process and more like an obsessional search for that embryo, that baby, that thing. Going through all this, it struck me again that we women are, by virtue of our normal bodily cycles and of the nature of child-rearing itself, nature's true existentialists, tethered to the moment-by-moment ongoingness of life, not the end result. One of the things that had happened to us in the assimilation process was a shift in emphasis from process to product—the job, the pay raise, the marriage, the divorce, the baby, the baby-sitter, the right school, the right orgasm—which had set up for numbers of us a troubling shift in emphasis, a troubling spiritual shift in emphasis if one can use that word. I was hearing women use it again, the word "spiritual," not in a hard-core way or a New Age way or a goddess way, just in a connected-to-the-flow sort of way. And that often and inevitably led back to femaleness, motherhood, or at least nurturing, to use that much-overused word, to what it was and what it wasn't and how big a piece, how big a spiritual piece of a woman's life it was.

On the outside looking in, face pressed to the delivery room window, I now thought of it as a huge piece; to me it loomed as salvation, redemption, fulfillment after the years of work, not a substitute for it, not that, never that, but an extension, another piece, a way to buy a little mortality, to fold oneself into the genetic time line. En route to the clinic I often saw my mother or father driving in the other direction—my so-long-ago sundered parents who had remained friends through the intervening years and who, like my husband, had both quit drinking in recent years. There was in our multitiered gatherings now a calm, warm sense of familial survival and support as there was between my husband and myself, and catching sight of one or the other poised behind the wheel of a car, I saw them not as they were but as they used to be back when, young, glamorous, hopeful, and wished now, after we had all come so far, that I could have their grandchild, child of our survival, of our line.

The eighties were ending, thank God. What a decade, lonesome and glitzy, and indeed numbers of us had become material girls in the bargain. You had to, you had to have your own money. You had to be big enough and strong enough, like Ann said, to look after people, even a man, if need be. There was a thrill in that. I knew single women who were having babies on their own, adopting and making families and they were delirious—feeling not only fulfilled on some level, but also out front, bold, liberated from old expectations. In fact, the number of unmarried American women with at least one child had gone up 60 percent in fifteen years—from 15 percent to 24 percent. And the most pronounced increase was among women like me, white, educated, professional women who couldn't find or couldn't wait to find or didn't want to find men.

I also knew women who, like Jane, had given up on having families of their own and spliced them together out of friendships and other people's children, making of themselves wise aunts/surrogate mothers, the role, in fact, I often took as I journeyed around and bunked in with old friends, nuzzling their babies or sprouting preadolescents with vicarious maternity. In short, we weren't talking *Ozzie and Harriet* anymore, not for many people I knew. No, the mom-and-pop operations of the fifties were gone, re-mystified in the eighties. Yet there was brewing hope that things could be different if we kept at it, brewing anger—which, of course, feeds on hope—that would be easily ignited again after a long dry spell by a few chosen episodes in the early nineties. It felt at least as if the lid was ajar again, after being so firmly in place, as if everyone, certainly my fortysomething crew, were stirring in their skins, getting ready for the next act.

For me there was one last ending: In the early summer of 1989, Nana died at age ninety-one. For the last twenty years of her life she had lived in a small stucco apartment in a funky courtyard complex a few blocks from the ocean. I saw her or talked to her two or three times a week. I took her to lunch and to the hairdresser and to the doctor, and when she was too old to be taken to a facialist or a dermatologist but still vain, I cleaned her face of blackheads, squeezing her wrinkled skin with emphatic tenderness, as she had tended to mine thirty-five years earlier. We were tethered. I had never really broken away. She was a piece of my family and had been a formidable presence in my life, more than that, a formidable moral presence, someone who believed in right and wrong, someone with no tolerance of prejudice, someone who moved into our spiffy Hollywood household when it was whole and the stuff of fan magazines and went the distance with us after everything had fallen apart. She had left her own family in Sweden when she was sixteen, heading off for a new life in America. She had worked in gift shops and coffee shops and cafeterias, marrying once, having a son, a hard, abusive trail that ended at our front door, and though she and I never talked about women's lib per se or women's rights, we never needed to. It would have been redundant. She wanted for my sister and me everything and was therefore very tough on us, and indeed she was one of the ghosts I had to deal with in that psychologist's office. But over time she and I had learned to laugh a lot at our own quirks and foibles and those of the world, and when she finally got sick, way at the end, and didn't know me anymore, I simply could not bring myself to visit her in the convalescent home. I could not handle her not-knowingness; it made me feel lightheaded, bereft and unmoored. Her dying then was a relief. And in my silly heart of hearts, I believed—oh yes I did, just as Ann Rubinstein had said of her brother, Stephen—that she would find a way, some way, to send me a baby.

19

SCRAMBLED EGGS AND
POSTHUMOUS SPERM

Dr. Marrs and I are having our procreative postmortem. Although it has been only a matter of months, it seems a thousand years ago that I was here, so hopeful, so eagerly leaping into the stirrups and stretching out my arm to be pricked for blood. I feel very calm and uninvolved, not disinterested certainly, but detached. Maybe it's a protective covering or maybe I am actually on the mend. The doctor tells me, in his ever-enthusiastic, soft-spoken but authoritative way that the only thing left to offer women like me is . . . and I almost want to cover my ears because I know full well what's coming. Those damn donor eggs. That's the real panacea now for us older women who aren't getting pregnant even through all this high-tech intervention. Donor eggs—a phrase that I keep trying to tiptoe around. But there it is again, there they are, big as life, bursting with life, and I am going to have to reckon with it, with them, with whether I am able to buy eggs from another woman and carry them as my own—if I can carry them. To me, after all this high-tech business, this is still a daunting new edge to dance on somehow, this scrambling of eggs, of genetic lines. I don't know how I feel about it, confused I think, hurt somehow. Watching the doctor's face watching my face, I wonder if he sees the confusion, the sadness, so effervescently cheerful am I, the dutiful girl of old doing her antic, impish dance in her heavyhearted childhood home. I don't want him to feel he has failed. Oh no, I'll shoulder that burden. But now he wants me to have the eggs of a younger, fertile woman, make embryos out of those with my husband's sperm and then carry them myself—or at least try to carry them. He tells me the odds with donor eggs on an IVF or GIFT procedure go up to as high as 25 to 33 percent success rate per cycle, no matter the age of the recipient. Big, fat, juicy odds from where I'm sitting, from the procedures I've been trying. Since 1984, when egg donation was first reported, there have been a couple of hundred babies born this way, and the doctors themselves are very enthused over the procedure. They advertise it as the least invasive, the least medically and legally encumbering way for older couples to get babies, far less entangling, they maintain, than surrogacy or adoption. Just eggs, that's all. So, are eggs and sperm totally analogous

finally, equally purchasable? Is this the logical reduction of liberation—
this absolute biological equality?

For my part, I am still of faint heart. This somehow strikes me a little
as conceptual hanky-panky—my husband's sperm and another woman's
egg. I imagine a stranger floating in my amniotic fluid. And what do I
tell this child, and when? Anything? This is all too new still for there to
be enough couples out there who have done this. Ninety percent choose to
do it anonymously, I am told—in fact, most clinics won't do it otherwise—the same way couples have been buying sperm for lo these many
years. They simply pretend to all concerned that the baby is 100 percent
genetically theirs.

Can I do that, be matched up with a woman whose physical character-
istics approximate mine and then just carry the conceit on to the grave?
In a word, no. That's not me. I would have to tell, have to do it
non-anonymously, have to know that down the road my child could see
and meet his or her biological mother. I could not keep a secret like this
from someone I brought on the earth. I simply couldn't do it, though I
don't like imagining the psychic tear should my child take me up on the
offer and go looking for that long-lost egg donor down the road. I get
dizzy with the moral and emotional ramifications of this donating business, but I don't absolutely shut the door of my womb on it. I am not
ready to do that, especially since there's no time urgency here, especially
since they can work their donating magic even on postmenopausal
women. The age of the uterus is apparently not a problem, just the age of
the eggs, so a no-longer-menstruating woman, with a heaping dose of
hormones, can be primed to carry a youthful egg.

In a pilot program at the University of Southern California, run by Dr.
Mark Sauer, eight of fourteen women between the ages of fifty and
fifty-five conceived with bought eggs. But do I really want to be a
fiftysomething first-time mother? Isn't that finally beyond the limit, procreating in the final trimester of life? The thought is both ridiculous and
seductive, though I am not game to jump in yet. I am moving out for a
while, maybe moving on, but certainly out, out of this clinic, away from
my hopeful sisters with their little white bags. For me, for now, it's over,
even as I know there is still something out there I can try down the road,
some bedeviling possibility still of becoming pregnant. That's what I'm
left with now, the pregnancy part, as the baby would not be of my genetic

stuff. Do I want it so badly—to have someone, anyone, doing somersaults in my gut? I can't answer. I leave it up in the air, tossing it around in the days and weeks and months after I have officially declared my independence from Dr. Marrs and his seductive magic. But I don't begrudge anyone else's choice to do so. One of the by-products of this quest is that I have learned to have great tolerance for other women's choices. I was always prone that way by instinct and disposition, but going through this, with all the disapproval from various quarters, feminist and counter-feminist, friend and foe, I am aware of how lonely certain decisions can be and how large a thing tolerance really is and how one must act in accord with one's own moral and emotional judgments.

As yet, I am not ready to get into the egg-buying business and as I peruse my charts, my telephone book–sized medical records, again and again, looking for some clue, I begin to hatch the notion that my procedures were all done perhaps a day early, given the size of my follicles and the levels of my hormones. Timing is all, and I begin to think that my last GIFT in particular was—judging from the numbers—done prematurely in order to make sure I did not have the premature LH surge, my old bugaboo. What am I doing here: preparing the case for another go-around? Please no. In the meantime there is one other alternative that will still allow me my own embryo. Gestational surrogacy, as they call it. Rent-a-womb. A friend of proven fertility has, in fact, offered to try to carry my embryos for me, one of those offers that transcends love. And I think about it. Why not? I could make them—that we knew—and she can certainly carry them, or at least has carried her own. We laugh at the possibility, but then, in an offhand moment, she says ebulliently, "I'll breast-feed them too for a few days, just to get them started," and something in me tenses despite the overweening generosity of her offer. My babies? You will breast-feed my babies? And in that instant I have a sharp inkling of how fine the lines are in all this talk of scrambled eggs and borrowed wombs. The doctor is not enthusiastic anyway about this plan, saying that if my embryos are indeed good I should be able to carry them myself, and if not, then the only answer is to buy some eggs. But hell, what's the rush? I can wait until I'm fifty, by which time, of course, my husband will be seventy-five. Now that is ludicrous.

In the meantime I mourn. Karl doesn't really. We have survived. He feels no stubborn need for our baby, as I do, as the younger husbands of my friends do. His detachment is faintly annoying but mostly restful. Who needs to carry two hearts through this process? There are days I feel as if someone I loved died. I have been blessed, losing only two old people, Nana and Hattie, three grandparents. My friend with the frozen sperm has buried her husband, having tended him all during the time I have been baby-crazed, and she appears one day at my house, irritable in mourning, stricken still, with a packet of unopened bills from the clinic where vials of his sperm are stored. She cannot bear to look at them and is worried they might simply, for lack of payment, have thawed the sperm and put them down the sink. No way, I assure her, ripping the envelopes open, and indeed it is still there—a piece of him on the earth—and we laughingly wonder aloud about when you get rid of the stuff. At what point do you pick up the phone and say, "OK, toss it"? When you fall in love again, if ever, or remarry, or get sick yourself? Do you just call at that point and have it over with? "Thanks, I won't be needing it anymore." Is that what you say? The truth is she doesn't need it now. It's not about need. She is forty-four already and, like me, has never been pregnant and cannot imagine starting down that road now. "It's a bus that passed me by," she says of motherhood, without a trace of self-pity. A widow with a history of good show-business jobs, she is currently unemployed and facing the prospect of selling her house. Our narratives. That's what happened. But what to do with the sperm, all that was left of the man she had so loved, frozen stuff with the tantalizing intimation of life? Keep it, at least for a while longer. That's what we decided. One bill at a time. One day at a time. That was the best we could do, and with tumblers of wine we toasted the reprieve of the posthumous sperm and all the embryos I had made and lost.

20

THE JOURNEYS END

It was in 1991, October to be exact, that my journeys came together in a surreal fashion. But of course I was used to surreal. That's the world I had more or less been living in, or so it felt. Anita Hill was about to testify before the Senate Judiciary Committee when the doctor called to tell me I was pregnant. Not Dr. Marrs. Much as I liked him personally, I had moved on from his by-now-very-full practice, which left the waiting room stacked with eager women, some of whom could end up waiting close to an hour of a morning to get in for their sonograms. It was taking six months now just to get in for a consultation. Infertility was chic, at least where I lived, and he was still at the forefront, one of the half dozen internationally known high-profilers working the ranks of LA's infertile population, all of them doing pretty much the same procedures, all of them with pretty much the same success rates: low.

Yet I was not quite done, not ready to surrender, and decided I would try one last procedure, this one with an oddly appealing and autocratic Eastern European doctor by the name of Jaroslav Marik, who worked in a small and decidedly unflashy office in Westwood near UCLA. I had interviewed him some years earlier for a magazine story. It was he who had gotten my closest friend from up the street pregnant; his lab tech—the person who actually handles the sperm and eggs—was hot, his numbers good. The clinic GIFT statistics were up near 50 percent. I was beguiled anew, even as I was aware that Dr. Marik had been the doctor in the much-ballyhooed Frustaci case back in 1985. After taking fertility drugs and having an insemination, Mrs. Frustaci was found to be carrying septuplets. Catholic, she refused to have an abortion, leaving the hospital finally with only three, quite damaged infants, and subsequently winning a major lawsuit against Dr. Marik's clinic. I remembered the pictures of her in the last stages of pregnancy, lying in a hospital bed, facedown, her huge belly protruding through a hole they had cut for it. Disturbing, animal stuff. My rather brisk attitude at the time, which was only re-enforced when I got into the high-tech racket myself, is that you had to be prepared for the aberrant likelihood of a "litter," be prepared to have a selective abortion rather than jeopardize the lives of all the babies. To do that, to try to carry seven to term, was to be a ghoulish high-tech martyr, and I hated to see women do that.

I arrived at Dr. Marik's office with my prodigiously heavy medical file and one last shred of hope. After all, my friend had done three GIFTs to get her little boy and I figured perhaps three was the lucky number. I was game for one last GIFT, he taking it on faith and on my voluminous records that that right tube was working. Once again I was doing just straight Pergonal, and the routine was the same as I was used to, though it felt different being somewhere new. The office was scruffy, comparatively, the clientele much more middle class and mixed, and I liked it, even the tall, graying doctor who seemed to belong in some old pre–high-tech movie. Down the stretch I had blood tests every day and even at three-hour interludes, right through the nighttime hours, had to wake up and prick my finger with a shard of glass to collect blood so they could monitor the LH rise. No chances that I would shoot off and ovulate on my own.

There was a new hospital, too, also scruffy and a little deserted down on Pico Boulevard in an old commercial section of the city near our home, and I arrived there one still-darkened morning in late September 1991, toting a belly-full of thirteen follicles. Once again I was wheeled away, knocked into never-never land, awakening in a warm, dark room, my husband beside me. I was spending the night this time and wasn't even allowed to move from the operating room gurney onto a bed. On some level it seemed silly. Normal women got pregnant after having sex. They jumped up post lovemaking and played tennis or went jogging. What was all this bed rest nonsense? But I was not normal and I was willing to play by the new rules. Dr. Marik appeared in his leisure wear sometime in the afternoon to tell me he had put five eggs in one tube and three in the other one and put the rest in a dish with my husband's sperm, the embryos to be frozen for later. "Wait a minute, what other tube?" I said, in my grogginess. "Where did you find it?" He told me he had dug my left tube up out of the mess of my abdomen, freeing it up and using it. I must say, the thought made me nervous—how could it possibly be undamaged inside and therefore passable—but also hopeful. I had new odds, I figured.

The countdown was the same, though for some reason—maybe just the new place, the slightly different methodology—I was more optimistic than I had been in a long time. I had booster shots of the hCG to keep my ovaries cranking out hormones and up they went: up, up, up. I could tell the nurses were themselves optimistic, though in this business everyone's careful not to betray hope. I seemed to swell visibly and grow queasy and a week passed quickly. Of course, that first week postprocedure is always the good week, you're always optimistic. Turning the corner into the second week is the tough part, and indeed on day eight, a hot Sunday, I felt my hormones drop out from underneath me, as if I were a balloon that had been pricked with a long pin. Pfft, my body went as in those tormenting dreams, and the next day I was in there for a blood test. Dr. Marik was puzzled; he said he had never seen hormones fall so far so fast. I was sure it was all over, but he insisted on giving me more progesterone and hCG to rev everything back up. Now I was inescapably in the grip again. The clinic staff was obdurately optimistic now, but by the day of the pregnancy test I was sure I was right, that the hormonal drop-off was a sign of another failure, and indeed they called that afternoon to say, stop everything, it's over.

I didn't even weep this time. Nor did I make plans for the next assault. I determinedly set about mourning to see if I could get it done, throwing dry-eyed resolve into the process. As if it could be done that way: grief. But a strange thing happened. Within about five days of stopping the pregnancy-support shots, I started to bleed and I did not stop. I bled hard and long, all that lining, all that uterine nesting lining came out in clumps and gobs and then the flow tapered off but did not stop. I didn't think anything of it. We went away to visit friends and I was jagged with what I assumed to be sorrow, but finally when we returned I went and had another blood test and a sonogram. There was nothing apparent in the uterus, but that afternoon the doctor himself called. "Are you sitting down?" he said in his pronouncedly accented English. "You're pregnant."

What could I do with that word now? How could I embrace it, the phrase I had longed to hear all those many years—"you're pregnant"— knowing that history-long, women had heard it with varying degrees of angst and exultation and that I was now in their number. I had finally heard it, but it was not a blessing and I knew it. I knew without him telling me what was up. Clearly the pregnancy was in one of the tubes—an ectopic pregnancy—otherwise we would have seen something on the sonogram of the uterus. "Now what?" I said, trying to draw cheer from the very thought that at the moment, come hell or high water, come the inevitable surgery that would remove that pregnancy, I was with embryo—at least that. Indeed surgery was indicated, he said, a full-scale, tummy-slicing laparotomy. I knew from my friends who had had tubal pregnancies that other doctors would have dealt with the problem in a far less invasive laparoscopic procedure, but I was used to Marik now and I simply went along, amused at myself, as always, in the aftermath, at my courageous docility in the face of medicine.

"When do I have to do this?" I asked him, when he had finished his explanations, wondering if I would have a day or two to revel in my weird, distorted luck, wondering if I might have a grace period to practice saying "I'm pregnant." He punctured my perverse revery. "As soon as possible," he said, in answer to my question, and within twenty-four hours I was back in that dark, strangely deserted hospital, checking in at the emergency room, where a few stray victims huddled in the wee hours of the morning, bloodied here and there. Before I knew it I was in a gown and on a gurney being wheeled through the dark halls, the light so bright for a minute in the operating room the way it blares down, and then I was out and it was over: my one, my only pregnancy. My trophy pregnancy, after so much sex and so much longing and so much money and so much invasion. That was it and it was over.

And as I lay in my recovery bed, knowing the quest was at an end, an IV of morphine dripping in my arm, there before me on the television set was the match-up of the century, or so it felt to me in my woozy, blissed-out state. Anita Hill and Clarence Thomas, in the epitome of the *mano a mano* sexual combat, stand-ins for their respective genders duking it out in prime-time live. It was a great distraction, theater of the absurd and theater of the explicitly real. Pubic hairs on Coke cans, porno flicks and two immaculate, up-by-their-bootstraps blacks facing off over the issue of sexual harassment and race and class and gender and every other thing you can name. There were plots and subplots, feckless Democrats and fierce Republicans, swaggering Romeos and angry working-class white women, all railing and defending their protagonist of choice.

Once again much was made of the old devil split between the salt-of-the-earth secretary types who allegedly backed Thomas, because they knew sexual harassment just came with the territory, and the prissy women farther up the economic ladder who went for Hill. Mind you,

MOTHERHOOD DEFERRED   243

there were no polls on this, just informal surveys. Peggy Noonan once again got in the act, saying the Thomas-Hill imbroglio highlighted the split "between clever people who talk loudly in restaurants and those who seat them." The working-class Irish Catholic political poetess once more allied herself with the Realfolk—the secretaries and waitresses, etc., who were the honest feminine backbone of America—and the Realfolk knew, or such was the intimation, that boys will be boys and bosses will be bosses; they'll push you up against the watercooler and brush against your body and ask you out on dates or back to their Palm Beach mansions or frat houses where who knows what would happen. That was just the flip side of life in the America Noonan had so elegantly conjured for Reagan, an America of mini-malls and Sunday dinners and teary-eyed patriots, an America where men were men and women were women and *Roe v. Wade* would, in the future, be a thing of the past. At least it was all out in the open again, that's the way it felt from my hospital bed—as if the battle lines were drawn and visible again, thank God, and the lid off. I did not think the story of Anita Hill was a perfect feminist parable, or that she was the perfect heroine, coming forward so late, hanging on under Thomas' allegedly offensive tutelage, staying in contact when he moved on to another job. One had to wonder what byplay had gone on between the two, what looks, what flirtations. Nonetheless, like Thelma and Louise, the windblown, cinematic duo who a few months earlier had blasted their way into the national dialogue with their acts of female vigilantism, she was to become a rallying point in a world in which the long-smoldering tensions between the sexes had erupted again all over the place and it was a relief. At least, at last, the phallic undertow was being forced out into the open.

On the very same Sunday that *The New York Times* ran a front-page story on workplace harassment (courtesy, of course, of the Anita Hill affair) stating that almost all of the reported cases in American companies turned out, upon investigation, to be true, there was dead center of the front section the quintessentially hip, perversely "liberated" ad for Barneys, New York: an alluring full-page femme fatale in a long dress slit up to the top of her thigh, her shapely leg poking out into your face. "A Freudian Slit?" the ad asked, brazenly using one of those slang words like "gash" that refer to the female genitals.

The previous fall, in my continuing cultural stock-taking, I had seen two of the high priests of the undertow up close and personal. I saw men's movement guru Robert Bly in Denver, Rocky Mountain High Country, one night, and male comic Andrew Dice Clay in Blue Collar Country Detroit the next. In both arenas, one full of the sensitive turtleneck-and-hiking-boot set, the other full of assembly-line guys in zip-up jackets—white guys in both places—there was an assertive, intense frat-pack bereavement. In his charmingly autocratic manner, his voice full of a singsongy nasal assertiveness, Bly delivered his standard message about men having lost their way. Decidedly over-mothered and under-fathered, they did not know how to be male, he told the receptive audience, precisely the message of his book *Iron John,* then on the *New York Times* best-seller list. Underneath all the talk of male sorrow, the wily Bly was playing the phallic card (was there not in the very title of his book a clear phallic implication—*Iron John*?), the fear-of-women card, as surely as Andrew Dice Clay played it the next night with his rowdy working-class claque in embossed jackets. The audience—including many of the girls—seemed to be on some perverse aphrodisiacal high as they chanted together some of Dice Clay's signature nursery rhymes, like:

Georgy Porgy, Pudding and Pie,
Jerked off in his girlfriend's eye;
When her eye was dry and shut,
Georgy fucked the one-eyed slut.

Full-tilt audio harassment. That's what it felt like some days as a woman in America, as if you were the subject of constant cultural harassment, a stream of vile lyrics and violent images of your sex, your luminous, your lovely sex being verbally or visually dissected. "Girl, let's get butt naked and fuck," intoned rap "artist" Ice-T, "I mean real stupid and nasty / My crew got to have it / And after they dog it, I autograph it." Then, of course, there was the additional blast from those two radio ranters turned best-selling authors: Rush Limbaugh and Howard Stern. One represented himself as a real meat-and-potatoes common-man commentator, while the other postured as a joyous vulgarian. But you could hear in both their shticks exactly what you could hear in Dice Clay's nursery rhymes or Robert Bly's poetic phrases: the frantic fear of women.

Limbaugh's line on feminism was that it was the refuge of the ugly, while Stern was obsessed with lesbians. "When you girls don't get any penis, you fall apart," he wrote in his 1993 book, *Private Parts*. There, in its brute simplicity, was the essence of the phallic undertow: men's fear that liberated women wouldn't need them anymore—not for sex or money or even procreation. Not for anything.

No question, that fear was selling big in 1990s America. Even a once-esteemed magazine like *Esquire* was in a pouty, sophomoric spin many months, offering up covers like "The Secret Life of THE AMERICAN WIFE" (June 1990), which included a quasi-undressed woman and quippy subheads like: "Her bra: What really keeps it up?" and "Her plumbing: How much should you know?" Where were the nice men and why didn't they object to this diminishment not just of our sex, but of this trivializing, drooling reduction of their own? In private, the men I knew, to a man, even those who had voted for Ronald Reagan and George Bush, did say it, did admit—when they didn't give in to the pervasive reflexive pro-family frat-pack phallic fear—that the women's movement had been a good thing, and abortion, too, else many of them would have had unwanted children along the way, and that women who had full lives and families and made money and were alive to their own pleasures were a far happier, sexier, nicer, more vital, more supportive, and yes, challenging, breed than those who had been circumscribed by the old roles. I kept waiting for some of them to say it, big time, in print, the new Mailers or Roths having at the great adventure story of their time, the confoundingly complex but exhilarating redefinition of the sexes, their wives, their daughters, themselves, but it was not forthcoming. The new literary guard tended to offer up half-formed men who drank too much and couldn't commit, and the old literary guard kept looking backward. Reviewing a book of essays by Camille Paglia, author of the 1990 anti-liberation tract *Sexual Personae*, John Updike wrote in *The New Yorker* that "the roots of sexual attraction and excitement go deeper than our codes of civilized behavior. There is a tragic grandeur to the gulf between the sexes." These were the words of a man nostalgic for the old world, the world of male-female misunderstandings and shivery suburban adulteries, the world out of which we young subversives had crawled so long ago, hoping, in our ensuing rage, not to alienate men but to befriend them, hoping to earn enough money and stature to be able to square off with the ghosts of our fathers and the men who had controlled our lives. It was that act of befriending, not the rage or messiness with which it was sometimes carried out, that so threatened Rabbit's WASP creator, for whom the idea of sex between consenting friends simply carried no guilty or erotic sting. Updike, who was admittedly discomfited by the sixties in part because of their self-righteous licentiousness (what fun was adultery if there was license to commit it?), had inadvertently joined with the rappers in their insistence on keeping the sexual war as alive as possible.

Of course, women were playing the phallic game now too, flexing their muscles and flashing their crotches in some sort of hustling parody of liberation. What we had now was a uniquely perverted American form of highly commercial machisma masquerading as liberation, for which feminism was both the perfect excuse and the perfect scapegoat, Madonna the perfect icon, Camille Paglia the perfect academic apologist, and Helen Gurley Brown the perfect everyday practitioner. And it was a lonesome, coy, greedy and perverted form of freedom, if that's what you could even call it, a narcissistic blend of sex (we got that from the seventies) and materialism (and that from the eighties) and the old masculine/feminine roles (from forever). "Learn how to use a vibrator—maybe even buy a pair of velvet-lined handcuffs," instructs the *Cosmopolitan* of December 1991. "Choose positions that emphasize your best features or angles. Pop his favorite X-rated cassette into the VCR—and keep the remote control at the bedside. Men love erotic visual surprises."

There you were suddenly in the hippest, postliberation threesome: you, he and some luscious on-screen fellatrix. Even ubiquitous columnist and commentator Dr. Joyce Brothers endorsed these video threesomes in my morning newspaper, there amidst the world news and weather report. In response to a reader who was bothered by her lover's habit of coming home at lunchtime and making love to her "while watching steamy scenes on TV soaps," the doctor replied:

> It sounds to me as if this guy is unusually creative, imaginative and romantic. I see nothing wrong with it. No one is being injured or hurt, and as long as you're both having fun, enjoying each other, what could be wrong? Often, because of our backgrounds, we develop inhibitions regarding sex that limit our enjoyment and make us feel guilty when we do have pleasure.

I winced for the woman reading this cheery, let-it-rip reply, this lunch-time coupler getting it on in the mushy glare of the soaps, her lover looking over her shoulder at the TV screen. This was not liberation, not the tender, lusty, partnering liberation envisioned back when and toward which some among us had successfully groped or at least were trying to. This was the world of dehumanized, voyeuristic sex, of pubic hairs on Coke cans, of video threesomes. It was the perfect solution: If you couldn't be the "whore" he needed, he could always watch one on the screen and she could provide the stimulating pyrotechnics and heavy breathing. And it was women who were now offering this stuff up right along with men. After all, who gave us Glenn Close as the homicidal heavy of the so-called erotic thriller *Fatal Attraction* (and earlier, Meryl Streep as the unsympathetic runaway mom in the 1979 *Kramer vs. Kramer*)? A woman, that's who: producer Sherry Lansing, held up to young women as a Hollywood success story, the first woman to run a major studio. And who turned motherhood into radiantly tawdry cheesecake—in a hip convergence of the whore-madonna images—by slapping a flagrantly nude and pregnant Demi Moore on the cover of her magazine but a mom herself: celebrated *Vanity Fair* (now *New Yorker*) editor Tina Brown. And who gave us battery-powered sexual fantasy books but a woman, author Nancy Friday, not to mention the full-tilt sadomasochism of novelist Anne Rice's "erotic" fairy tales? And who gave us a lot of elegant women in peekaboo, pin-striped suits—male garb slit to the crotch—but clothier Donna Karan? In one of her ads, an apparent political candidate rides through a ticker-tape parade with her shirt open, her black lace bra clearly apparent. The reassuring message to men was: We are still available to you, men of America, take heart, available though pregnant, though presidential, though anything. Don't worry; we have our videos and our handcuffs to welcome you back from your masculine retreats and gender identity crises.

With rare exception, we had not found the poetry of our own eroti-cism, our own swimmy sensuality, did not speak its language yet, but were stuck in an indefensible posture, brandishing our dildos—as women were doing now in books and movies—our mock-cocks, and proclaiming our equalness in a vulgar, precarious world that had turned liberation on its head, rather fixated on the sexual part of liberation, separated it out from the whole at that crucial juncture back in the early 1970s. The once juicily irreverent heroine of Erica Jong's *Fear of Flying* was back in the 1990 book *Any Woman's Blues*, but she had degenerated into nothing more than a whiny pornographer enamored of sadomasochistic sex while the author of the 1992 book *The Erotic Silence of the American Wife* offers an unlusty, feminist rationale for adultery—to wit: Women in cold marriages appropriately seek warmth elsewhere. This was nothing but the aeons-old male rationale for infidelity in drag, as if women still could not own their own impulses but had to blame them on someone else. Adultery was one thing, and a lot of women were engaging in it (somewhere around 30-odd percent apparently, though surveys varied widely), but to blame it on men and give it a feminist rationale was quite another. It was all distorted, a transmogrification of liberation, and it could break your heart if you let it. It did break mine often in those days, even as I was trying to take hope in the timely appearance of Anita Hill and in the love of my ever-earnest and tender if sometimes still maddening suitor, my husband, who sat by my recovery bed, decrying the Senate treatment of Ms. Hill with more vehemence than I and trying to help me find a way to heal. What: Was my memoir turning into a love story? Maybe it was, in part, always that.

I took hope, too, in all the books documenting the backlash against liberation, a culture-probing spill of them arriving weekly, it seemed, notably the high-profile, best-selling troika: *The Beauty Myth* by Naomi Wolf, Susan Faludi's *Backlash: The Undeclared War Against American Women*, and Gloria Steinem's strangely impersonal if occasionally moving memoir, *Revolution from Within*. One wanted more from Steinem, the big looking-back-over-the-shoulder take on the women's movement, on work and pornography and sexuality, on the phallic undertow and the uneasy alliance between feminism and materialism and her own life without marriage and children, but got instead, befitting the times perhaps, a kind of mushy feminist self-help book from an attractive and indefatigable leader/icon. Faludi and Wolf, on the other hand, were full-fledged fighter pilots dropping their statistical bombs all over the landscape, both decrying the male media cabal that had circumvented liberation. In that, they were a welcome corroboration of what so many of us had felt, certainly during the 1980s.

But in their zeal to ferret out any and all reactionaries, some of the new young ideologues, certainly Faludi, hit any of us who celebrated motherhood, fingering us as part of the backlash, including the old icons Friedan and Greer. But there had been a baby boom—or certainly a baby boomlet; we were never going to get back to the 1950s—right in tandem with the backlash—and didn't I know it?—as the aging baby boomers had their babies and swooned over them. In a 1985 Roper Organization survey, 51 percent of the women said they'd rather work than stay home with the family; in 1991, that number fell to 43 percent, and 53 percent said they would rather stay at home. A 1992 Yankelovich Skelly survey of working women similarly found that 56 percent, especially those with small children, would quit if they did not need the money, up from 33 percent in 1988.

And what all this was, what the sharp-eyed authors missed in that swoon was the non-coercive joy of it, the celebration of maternity, of femaleness, of fecundity, of family, in opposition to the aggressive and ugly male-defined sexuality that the culture, in its upending of liberation, was hell-bent on selling and into which we had inadvertently played. For us then, for us girls of the 1940s and 1950s, last-ditch maternity was a reconciliation with ourselves, with our memories of our own mothers. Not to get that was to miss the revolutionary loop of the last forty years, not get it in its totality (just to explicate the reaction to it), the desperate determination of young girls in Mary Janes to be something other than their mothers, not to duplicate those lives, but to be more, to want more, to try to step out of the confines of our sex, the second sex, and then, down the road, after fighting to adjust marriages and get jobs and hold them, to reembrace our femaleness, not in a corny, doctrinaire, reactionary way, but hopefully, joyfully, expectantly, fleshily, protectively (as I, for one, had not protected my own fertility). That notion of our taking responsibility was something that got left out of all our cultural railing sometimes, our railing at men. "Responsibility" was the buzzword of the nineties, used—beginning to be overused—by everyone from the president to impassioned young women writers like Katie Roiphe, whose book on date rape was a diatribe against feminists who were strangulating the sexuality of the young. Young women had to look out for themselves, was her message, one echoed in Naomi Wolf's *Fire with Fire,* her cheery new, "You can have it all, women" second book. It was a spunky and unapologetic 180 from her first book, this one positing a new kind of "power feminism" as opposed to the old "victim feminism" she herself had helped promulgate. There were fashions in feminism as in everything else—and the new fashion was a brassy "Give me mine" take from the sexually hip daughters of the Reagan era who were determined to get theirs, meaning both money and sex. The Census Bureau was predicting, in fact, that as many as 20 percent of women in their thirties would never have children. In some ways, then, they were our younger sisters; in some ways, a whole new breed.

THE LAST TIME I saw Ann Rubinstein she was cuddling her two-year-old on the floor of her Washington house, learning, as she put it, to be silly again. It was, she admitted, a long way back.

"The baby has given us a sense of energy and youth again," she told me, crawling around on all fours. "I felt so old during that whole vigil with my brother, running up and down the coast and trying to keep everything afloat. I just lost my thirties really. I am actually thinking of quitting my job or at least taking time off and staying home for a while, not forever, just for two or three years, which is fine with my husband. He's very supportive. I've been working since I was fifteen. That's a long time, and it was all so hard for so long, fighting to do work I cared about, fighting to survive my family, fighting, fighting. I'm trying to learn how not to do that. We women do a lot of caretaking, I think, reflexively, but I'm not sure with all the abuse and anger we've been exposed to and all the fighting we've had to do along the way, that we don't also finally have to relearn kindness even as men do. I realize, as I slow down at work, that we women were pitted against each other at that place. It was as if I were somehow competing only with the other women, you know. And believe me, I could be plenty tough. The result is that I ended up with only one fairly close female friend from there, but she isn't a mommy type and doesn't visit much. So I have to find new kinds of friends. That's what I want to do, that and maybe try to have one more baby before the clock really ticks down."

For Jane Allen there would be no babies, and I realized over the time I spent with her that she had about her a kind of elegant but not off-putting solitariness, and beneath her calm and refined demeanor I could always see and hear the small, shy, emphatic ten-year-old she was in her big old childhood house on the Hudson surveying the wreckage of the nights before. She had finally passed her danger-zone, five-year post-op cancer scan, holding her breath as the years ticked down, and said she felt great, if a little restless, ready to try something new. She was still running her environmental PR company, very successfully, and was involved in a couple of interesting romances, one of which segued into a nice, sustained friendship, and she became more involved with her own family.

"It's funny," she said. "I always know when change is coming, when I'm going into a transition, into a new period, because I have these fervent dreams. I realize I'm probably in a growth period. I want to get more involved in cancer awareness. Breast cancer now hits one in nine women, and I'm thinking about putting together some big concerts to raise money. I have the luxury of doing that because I don't have a husband or a family. You ask me if I regret it. For the first couple of years after the cancer, the doctors advised me to wait awhile before trying to get pregnant. And after that I felt that if I did have them, I didn't know if I'd be around long enough to be a mother. That thought made me feel awful. And now? I guess I've found substitutes, made a different kind of life. If I thought I would never laugh again or have that sort of exultant moment when none of the petty cares of the world matter, like being really caught up in work or making love on a mountaintop with the sun coming up, that would upset me. But marriage—I don't think I need that anymore. I mean, after all, when you count up how many weeks of passion you've had in your life. I don't think anybody ends up with dozens of years' worth. That's not the way it goes. You don't get it all."

No, you don't. We were all learning that, you just didn't, though we did have a sense, I think, many of us transition women, that we were part of some revolutionary phalanx, and that sweet if corny sense helped to offset the sense of loss. After all was said and done, battle wounds accounted for, we had had an amazing journey, coming from that other world into the new one, the bridge generation trying to make good on female values while taking on traditionally male roles. I could, in fact, always spot transition women because of that mix, that male-female, tender-tough mix I loved, which on our good days, as we got older and more healed, we kept in arresting balance, and on bad days, we let widen again into a baleful split, of which First Lady Hillary Rodham Clinton was a classic example, her assertively competent edges often poking up through her intentionally softened veneer. Like Anita

Hill and Clarence Thomas, the Clintons became symbols in the war over the war of the sexes, an ambitious sixties-era couple who had their gender identities constantly called into account. Was she too tough? Was he too weasely, too ready to compromise? Nevertheless, her accomplishments and assertions to the contrary, Hillary Clinton was indeed a woman who had stood by her man, despite his wanderings, and she beamed to the wary electorate a kind of reassuring and gritty satisfaction with her choice to do so. In some ways she was the first of something, a full-fledged professional partner as First Lady, a woman as educationally endowed and politically passionate as her husband, and in some ways the last, already an anachronism of sorts in that women like her were running for political office and winning on their own. She would suffer the slings and arrows from both sides of the divide, the feminists and counter-feminists, as she tried to carve out a new niche in the tradition-bound role in which she found herself, and many of us contemporaries of hers watched her with empathetic hope. We had all made our compromises and it was always the test to see how far you could go without selling your soul.

THE LAST TIME I talked to big, ebullient Julie Templeton, she was playing drums in an all-girls' band, lamenting the dismissal of a number of her female colleagues from on-air jobs and living with her mother in a bigger apartment.

"You know," she said, "my life really turned out far superior to what it could have been. And if children had been part of it, I would have had the whole picture in my view. The child business was a problem for us. Nobody said, 'Wait a second, this is primal.' Nobody stopped to think that our group would be in jeopardy. I was in the change of the change of the change. I see that the ads are starting to hit about being gray and gray is beautiful and all the stuff on menopause, all the books, and I'm thinking seriously about having a facelift. We managed to change some things but certainly not all. When I look back, I was at the start of it all and I do take pride in my small part in it. I have to tell you, I thought I was the prototype of the new woman and how I was seen was going to be very important in that I represented a woman who was strong but could also be feminine at the same time. You know, I'm in this all-girl band now and it's quite hilarious. I feel like I'm learning how to have fun again. And I'm close to my mom now after all of it. Here we are back together again like we were all those years ago in that apartment in Brooklyn."

The arcs of our lives. We were halfway home. What an odd, redefining fight it had been, exhilarating, yes, infuriating as well. Other generations of women had been part of the same thing, surely, battling to renegotiate their lives and marriages and raise kids and not be hurt. But we were in the quirky middle of it all, in the thick of things, and it had seemed absolutely essential for so long to break down barriers and, yes, get bylines, in an effort to have a place, a voice in the dialogue of your time, a dialogue so long dominated by men. Collectively and individually, at home and at the workplace, we had often felt, so many of us, like Sisyphus pushing the rock up the hill, over and over, up and up, advancing and backsliding, and there were still so many battles to fight. As Julie said, women were being fired again from on-air jobs—I knew them, too—and, of course, any decent, affordable, cut-across-the-class-lines day care was nowhere in sight.

But in spite of all that was undone, getting older for most of us was a blessing, because we were able to let go of a lot of things, to live with men on our terms or without them if need be, to be accomplished without apology and raucous without restraint in a country deeply ambivalent about women. I vaguely remembered something Alexis de Tocqueville had written in *Democracy in America*, something I had stuck in my college thesis about the then just rising women's movement, and wandering into my office, where I had begun my journey into the past, found him there on the shelf. Thumbing through the book I found the passage, of course, marked and starred as was my wont:

The Americans are, at the same time, a puritanical people and a commercial nation; their religious opinions and their trading habits, consequently lead them to require much abnegation on the part of woman, a constant sacrifice of her pleasures to her duties, which is seldom demanded of her in Europe. Thus, in the United States, the inexorable opinion of the public carefully circumscribes woman within the narrow circle of domestic interests and duties, and forbids her to step beyond it.

In the intervening 160 years since he wrote that, we had stepped out and been pushed down and stepped out and been pushed down. It would go on, no doubt. For me and women like me, we postwar daughters, the stepping out had involved a long, hard flirtation with childlessness as we tried to find our way and make good on the exhortations of the movement mamas. I bid them a last fond farewell there on the shelves, my now quiescent chorus of feminist provocateurs. I was reconciled to my faith, though I knew I would go on armwrestling with it, just as I knew I would never be reconciled to my culture, my country, my own, in no small part because of what de Tocqueville had so aptly noted way back when.

As to my other journey, it, too, was done, but I did not heal as fast as I had hoped. As the months went by and became years, I began to understand that I would not ever completely heal, that I would carry with me always the child I had never had—in times of sorrow, in times of exuberance, in new and foreign places when I wanted that specific someone to show things to. That daughter. Some days I let go of it. But some days I saw her everywhere, not as a baby, a newborn, not as a toddler or a ten-year-old even. I saw her always on the cusp of adolescence, a nymphet on the brink of everything, ready to have at life, right at that moment when things, for girls, became so fraught. That's when I wanted her the most, wanted to mother her, not when it was easy and she was tiny and sweet-smelling, but then at that awkward moment as she teetered out into adolescence on her coltish legs, decked out, no doubt—could I stop her?—in something ever-so-short and ever-so-provocative. Would I have words enough and strength enough and insight enough to shepherd her out there without filling her with fear and destroying the sweet, nubile joy to which she was entitled and which, I thought, was at the bedrock of so much female exuberance and even achievement? We women made a mistake, I thought now, of not emphasizing the gift of being female and specifically of menstruation, what it signaled or allowed, not biological destiny, but biological possibility, and in so doing robbed girls of an element of much-needed pride and security at a crucial juncture. I didn't want my thirteen-year-old robbed of a shred of her irreverence and audacity, even as I wanted her watchful and self-protective. I studied young girls as they cavorted through malls, giggly and bumptious, and I saw her among them, mouthy and hopeful and yet still strangely shy, as I had been. And I wondered then whether I could leave it alone, let her exist as my figment, while I mothered or at least mentored other young women who came my way, or whether I would still have to assuage this longing. Could I buy eggs from another woman? The thought nagged at me, as did the knowledge that in and among all my high-tech trials, I never had done a straight in vitro attempt—embryos made in a dish, inseminated back into the uterus—everything but. Had I not been vigilant enough again? It was always so hard seemingly to do that, something we women had to learn and relearn, how to look out for ourselves. My recriminations on that score, though, were comparatively mild. I had done it. I had hung it, as planned. I had taken the journey. It was the way I had to do it, perhaps foolhardy given the odds, certainly time-consuming and hardly cost-effective as it was. But I had to do it. I had to take both journeys. Backward and forward; forward and backward.

The desire to be pregnant was still in there, and perhaps would be until menopause, maybe beyond, now that these wizards promised they could fill me with child even then. I was still having clinic dreams, two years later, dreams of being poked and prodded and manhandled, dreams from which I would awaken in a panic and be sure I was due there for a sonogram or blood test, be sure I was still on the treadmill, be sure my longing was about to be requited. The days after such dreams were heavier than others and I allowed them to be that, with no apology to myself or anyone else, no effort to be the indefatigable cheerleader. At least the infertility had helped cure me of that, not altogether, but mostly.

I did think of adoption, of course, but was not of a mind to do it through a high-priced lawyer, not of a mind to go through a lengthy bonding experience with a birth mom who would then gift me with her child. We did think of adopting an orphan somewhere, my husband having been raised as one himself, and that was an ongoing possibility that we held out to ourselves, handling it, looking at it, wondering if it felt right. We were not a young couple—hardly that—trying to make a family. We had a family; I had stepchildren to whom I was deeply attached and of whom I was immensely proud. Through them we had three adorable grandchildren, all girls. Maybe it really was too late and I had to face forward and be done, realize that indeed, as I had unwittingly prophesied back when, I had gotten my two out of three.

Such a perhaps bracingly realistic but dark prophecy. Did I really mean it to come true? Clearly not as these last half dozen years had proven. It was a bit of bravado as I tried to make my way. I had been lucky in my two out of three, though, lucky in work, and I began to think that all this talk of careers and career women was demeaning, trivializing. It wasn't a career I had, but work to do, work I loved, work that was my ballast and no doubt would continue to be. I didn't, in my unrequited baby-longing, mean in any way to diminish what work had been for me and for many of the women I knew. A thrill, a recompense, a redress, a chance for full-fledged participation in our time on the planet—and a chance to advance the argument for women's liberation. Nothing more, nothing less. A byline for a baby? Would I actually make that trade, holding the pages of this manuscript in my hands, wishing them to metamorphose somehow into an infant I could put to my breast? No. I had made my choices, sometimes with fierce deliberation, sometimes inadvertently, and I would live with them. No trades, no bargains in the dark of night. That was over.

Lucky in love, too, I had been, perversely, maddeningly, enragingly lucky in love, to still be beside the large, tender, still-so-full-of-appetite-for-life man I had fallen in love with as a virginal teenager all those years ago. We had survived it all, my growing up, his calming down, children of his, no children of ours, though indeed we did still have one leftover frozen embryo. I prayed to have the courage to leave it be, not have it thawed and sent whooshing into my "incompetent" uterus. I would no longer wear their punishing labels. I would stop being "infertile." It was not to be, that's all, and might never have been, even had I tried getting pregnant in those first years of marriage. There was no way to know. I might already have been scarred beyond repair at that early point. No one could tell me. There were certain things about my inability to have a baby that were still a mystery and I was content to let them alone. Enough had been done. I would face forward and rejoin the joyously angry female chorus that was ringing through the land again, taking on one subject or another, knowing that as I did, as I healed and got full-heartedly back in the fray, my mind, on a given day, in a given idle moment, as my hands came to rest over the keys of my word processor, the only instrument I had ever learned to play, would, like a butterfly, alight for a moment on that frigid tank where my lone embryo hung suspended between heaven and earth.